The Yijing Ritual

René Goris

Ordering Information:

Prime Seven Media
518 Landmann St.
Tomah City, WI 54660

Printed in the United States of America

DAOIST MEDICINE AND GONGFU HEALTHCARE EDUCATION

This publication is offered by the IOC Daoland program to help shape the materials received as a student of Daoism. It is not about the yijing alone, it is about cultural exchange and the Wudang Daoland healthcare research and franchise project. It serves to promote the importance of cultural difference as a source for cultural enrichtment and improvement of the general human condition. The program is as independent as possible. We call it studies in transcultural healthcare.

Table of Contents

Introduction

This part of the project serves to make you familiar with the iOC program and its purpose is to get you involved in taking the historical culture of Chinese medicine and exercises systems serious and not use them as an app to your own culture, but as a culture in itself. Chinese medicine is recognized as world heritage and should therefore be studied and restored as a pre-modern topic. This is bound to certain rules, for instance:

1) the exclusion of western styles of thinking,
2) modernist interpretations based on current cultural views etc.
3) traditional learning systems etc.

From these perspective we see that modern TCM usually is western medicine/biology with a sauce of Chinese-sims as dress-up. Even in China itself that is so. Proof is nowadays commonly set or mirrored through western biology, physics, fringe science and spirituality so no space is left for what Chinese culture itself had to propose as a view on reality. That is even so in China and Taiwan, Korea and Japan.

Besides practical courses in about every aspect of Chinese health related culture, we also offer a multitude of online courses to supplement the often limited knowledgebase present in Chinese medicine, taiji, qigong and culture studies. We hope this book tickels your curiosity with some supprises and look forward to develop our program further with you.

Deze uitgave is oorspronkelijk bedoeld voor cursisten van het Oriental College en ten behoeve van hun studies in Yijing, Qigong, Taijiquan, neidan, yangsheng, anqiao/tuina/anmo-massage, acupuncture and food practice en andere expressie vormen van de Chinese klassieke cultuur. Het is ook voorzien van opdrachten onderdeel van hun online leermateriaal.

IOC Daoland

For general support of the program and future publications:
https://www.patreon.com/Daoland_healthcare
Amsterdam Metropole
31 (0)650677883

for the Yijing Coubsellor course with in depth translation and study through online clasroiom, video and text learning, go to:

https://daoland.samcart.com/products/the-yijing-ritual-course

For other studies in Daoism, Neidan, Gongfu and Medicine, please contact us at the obove whatsapp number.

When the cultivated learns dao, he follows it with diligence;
When the commonner learns dao, he follows it on occasion;
When the litigater learns dao, he laughs out loud,
Those who do not laugh, do not learn at all.

Hence it is said:
Who understands dao seems abstruse;
Who progress' in dao seems to fail;
Who follows dao seems to wander.

Dao can be neither sensed nor known;
It illumines sensation and transcends knowledge/wisdom.

Laozi, Daodejing, zheng 41

Part I

Forward

I think the ultimate in Chinese culture studies is the study of yijing. The yijing incorporates studies in ritualisation of life, the need to comply with the will of heaven and fulfill ones designated role in society and family, and as such is sort of antidote against the oracular feel western interpreters usually give to it. It provides tools to understand the world, the past, the future, our selves. It is a means to comprehend health, the therapeutic and martial process, and the chemistry of internalized alchemy (neidan shu). I consider it the ultimate authority in pre-modern and classical Chinese cultures to do things right. The study of the yijing is a big thing. And it can easily go wrong and become a fallacy. After all it is a document revealing principles of inherent logic in a cultural worldview, it is not a text.

My perspective is mixed. The yijing is about 3000 years old it is speculated, but most of our understandings on it originate in the Ming dynasty, neo-Confucianism, and neo-Daoism. Yijing was ofcourse applied much earlier in many things, neidan immortality practice ranks first in that. It is a matter of cosmology.

Something about its creation:

The myth is that the yijing was a gift from the high God Fuxi, one of the three founding fathers of Chinese culture: Fuxi, Shennong, Huangdi. Fuxi was mate of Nühua, the creator of people from mud.

According to the canonical Great Commentary, Fu Xi observed the patterns of the world and created the eight trigrams (Chinese: 八卦; bāguà), "in order to become thoroughly conversant with the numinous and bright and to classify the myriad things." The Zhou yi itself does not contain this legend and indeed says nothing about its own origins. The Zhouyi only shows relationships through stories, not about its origins. Its commentaries from Confucius or of later date add these details. They also added technical suggestions due to new innovative uses developed

in their own times. Commentaries, even the line texts and the diagram texts are post hoc additions. We can learn from the nature of the yi that all written texts are only commentaries. That is so in any culture. Post modernists conceded to the point that there is no original thought.

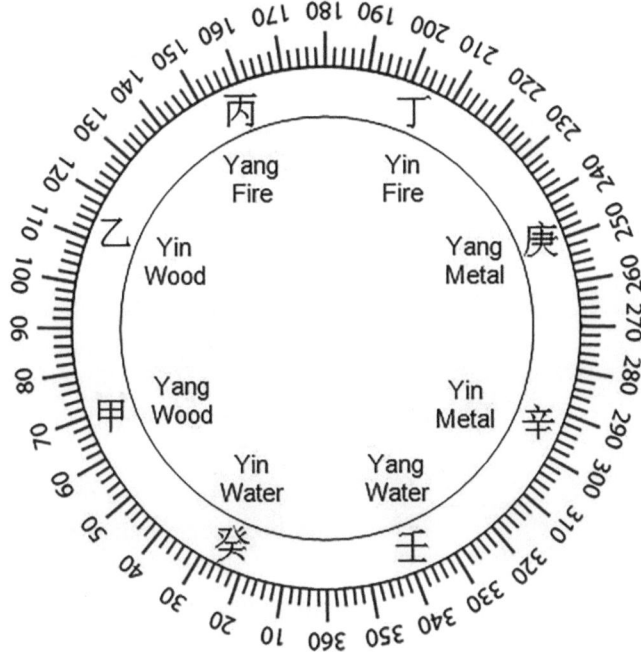

Post modernists allude to the fact that all original thoughts have already been said, but I conclude here that original thoughts are never said. They are the result of joint developments between people. Original thoughts are community affairs, and cultural results. It is just that some write things for the first time. King Wen wrote the the first commentaries by adding text to each diagram of fuxi's work after he calculated all the combinations, being 64.

As far as fuxi was concenrned the 8 diagrams were all people needed to understand the universe. He wrote them as dots, based on scapulamancy, the burning of holes in turtle shells and buffalo shoulderbones and later they were reworked as lines and broken lines.

The poking of burning hot rods in shells was a common practice during the Shang dynasty lasting from 1600-1046 BC. Some research seems to show that the Shan g dynasty was an offshoot from a culture in the north Korean area, maybe a leftover from the culture that spread out earlier from korea-china to Japan when the water levels of the seas were still lower. Finding settlements under water is a new branch in archeology

that promises to add thousands of years of civilization to our history books.

The poking of turtle shells and other kinds of bones used for prediction was used to read the natural omens taking place in the minds of people that in that time mattered, like the emperor and his family. They used a caste of soothsayers from which eventually a variety of schools of thought developed. Diviners would submit questions to deities regarding future weather, crop planting, the fortunes of members of the royal family, military endeavors, and other similar topics. These questions were carved onto the bone or shell in oracle bone script using a sharp tool. Intense heat was then applied with a metal rod until the bone or shell cracked due to thermal expansion. The diviner would then interpret the pattern of cracks and write the prognostication upon the piece as well. Pyromancy with bones continued in China into the Zhou dynasty, but the questions and prognostications were increasingly written with brushes and cinnabar ink, which degraded over time.

The skills were forgotten. Even though aspects of it found their way in the formation of script, of writing, of decoration on bronze vases and eventually the writing of books. The image here shows mostly only script. It has not been cracked by a hot rod, so it served only a ceremonial or decorative function. The existence of the practice was almost accidental. The Shang-dynasty oracle bones are thought to have been unearthed periodically by local farmers since as early as the Sui and Tang dynasties and perhaps starting as early as the Han dynasty, but local inhabitants did not realize what the bones were and generally reburied them. During the 19th century, villagers in the area digging in the fields discovered a number of bones and used them as "dragon bones" 龍骨 (long gu), a reference to the traditional Chinese medicine practice of grinding up Pleistocene fossils into tonics or poultices. The turtle shell fragments were prescribed for malaria, while the other animal bones were used in powdered form to treat knife wounds. But one day someone found out the bones have writing on them, starting a whole trend in discovery, allowing much insight in the early history of China.

At the core of the yijing though, we find the hetu and luoshu as depicted below:

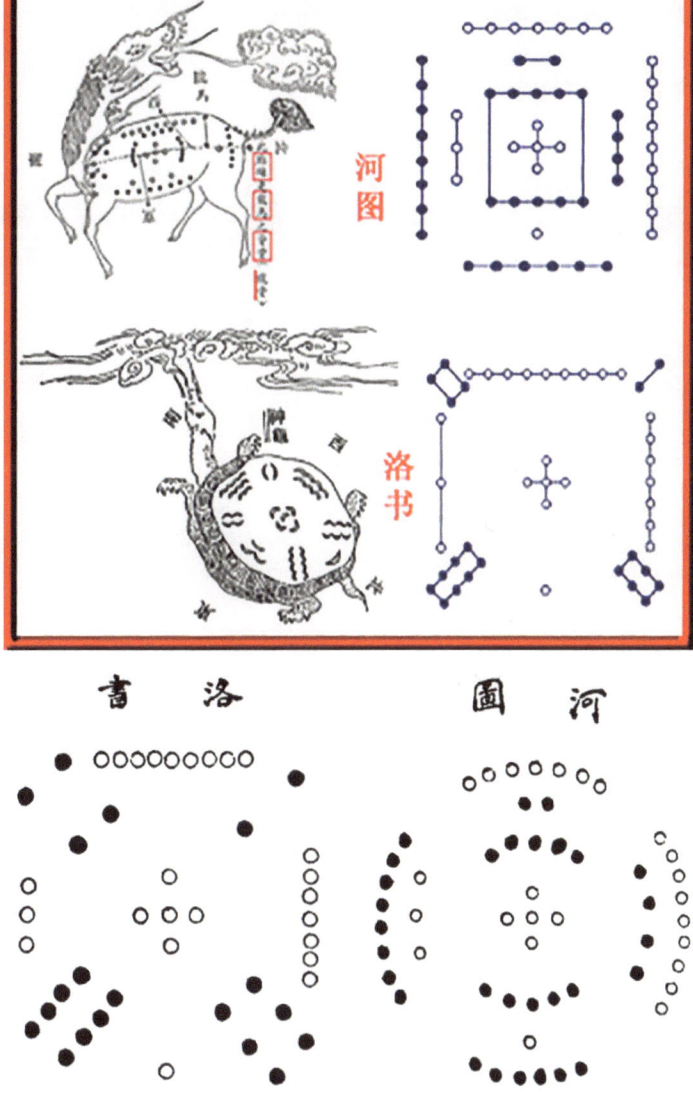

Hetu (left) and Luoshu (right)

The Hetu, or river diagram became later associated with the posterior reality, or later haven. The world ruled by the oppositions of fire and water, the wuxing movement from water to metal to earth and further to wood and fire. It was in the markings of a dearskin. The dear is -by the way- metaphorical symbol for bedroom alchemy too.

Later people found the diagram of before heaven which was an estimated superior diagram, an innovation, that allowed for new ways of thinking already developed. So it was a commentary on its own time, and an addition to previous ideas. They were numerical systems based on starmaps.

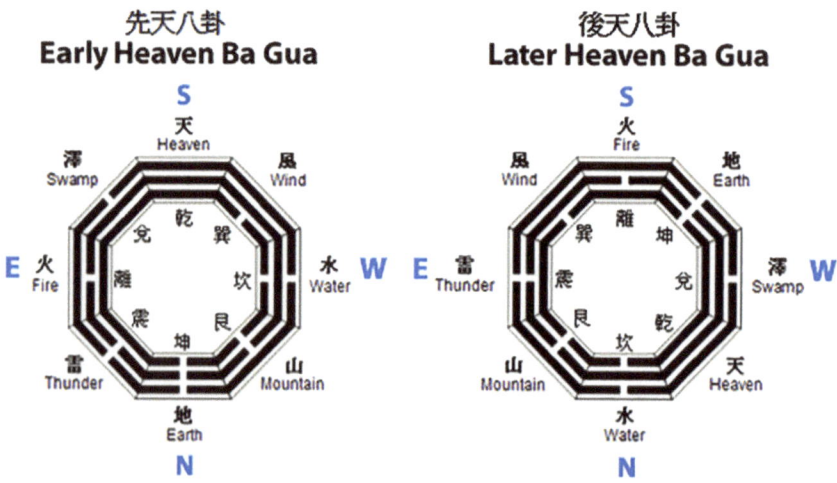

The Luo Shu or Luo script took heaven and earth as its center, rooted in a vertical east-west thinking while Hetu was rooted in a cold heat thinking relating to the north and the south.

Though the south north directions are often given for both maps, the early heaven diagram is a top-down diagram. The water and fire diagram are in fact the north-south axis, formally associated with the heat and cold of these directions. In the later heaven diagram the west east diagrams are symbols for spring and autumn, where the sun risesbeing budding yang (the day)- and sinks, being budding yin (the night). Later these are called the dragon and the tiger in neidan alchemy.

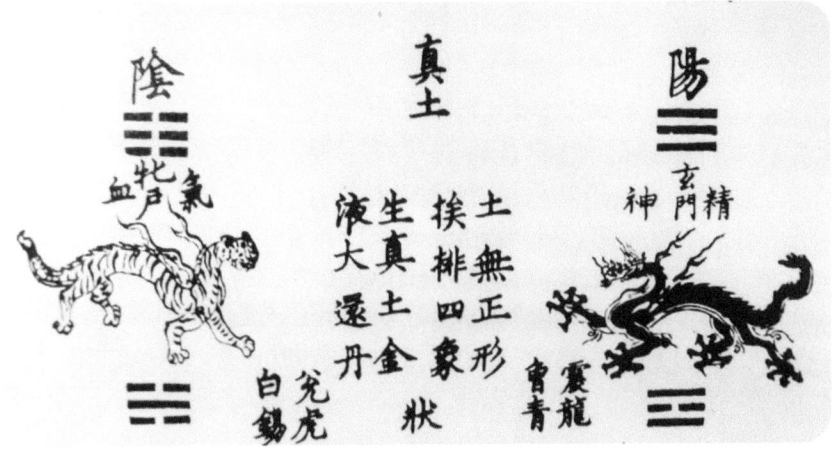

The tiger is associated with the coolness of the dark earth and the coolness of a healthy breath, and the dragon with the generalissimo of the controller of qi, the liver which can soar though the body and can manifest as heat. The lungs are yin metal, and the liver is yin wood. But the dragon compared to the lung is yang. In the yijing, you see, everything is relative. It is the context that provides meaning. In your life your story is the context, the diagram is the explanation and the text is the commentary.

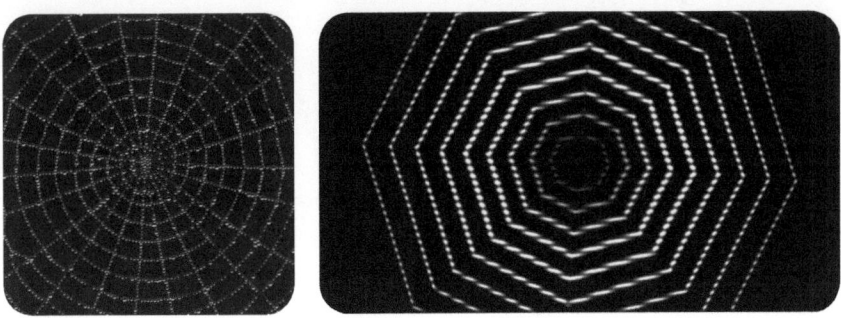

Fuxi's 8 diagrams were based on the shape of a spiderweb and represented 8 natural phenomena and they were placed in such a way -the octahedron- as to represent the world, providing the foundations of language. Yes, Chinese Characters are supposedly based on the 8 diagrams. The oldest characters are supposed to fit in the same format:

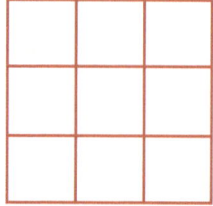

This grid of nine returns in many aspects of reality. For instance, in Chinese writing this format is very helpful to write the complex construction of some characters. In modern photography we find it as a raster to help develop harmonious composition.

For the Yijing we use it to determine the flow of dragon qi in the world, shaped as 9 continents, and each continent with 9 regions. The nine continents being East Asia, Europe, North America, South America, India, Australia, Antarctica, Sealandia (discovered 2017) + 1 we did not discover yet, but which might be the sunken lands of the archipellago from Japan to malasya. China saw itself as a center, not as one of nine. China gives itself the number 5, which is in nine star calculations the center:

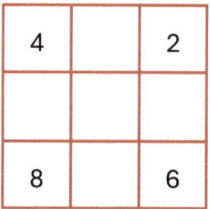

The even numbers are yin, mountains, and the uneven numbers are yang, gateways. These are also the foundations of the idea of the construction of the Chinese world:

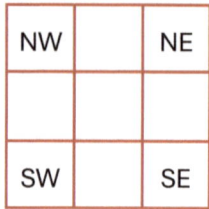

The mythology surrounding the Yijing is mostly from after the formation of the yijing. Historically the compilation of the yijing text is complicated. But the myth goes that the text was written by King Wen, before he became king and while he was in prison, using his prison time to do deep meditation, as ameans -I guess- to survive the probably gruesome conditions of Chinese prisons. Wen was first emperor of Zhou. His son, Duke of Zhou wrote the line texts. What is important to not from this is that the texts are commentary, and not the yijing itself. Analysis of the texts and the diagrams are adding to our understanding, but the gonostic and hermetic wisdom of the yijing is in the diagrams. As a result, all knowledge we have on the yijing is opinion, personal ideas. Even the commentaries of the king and duke of Zhou are opinion, but because they were first in line we consider them canon.

The core of the historical Yijing is a Western Zhou divination text called 'Exchanges of Zhou' (周易 Zhōu yì). Various modern scholars suggest dates ranging between the 10th and 4th centuries BC for the assembly of the text in approximately its current form. Based on a comparison of the language of the Zhou yi with dated bronze inscriptions, the American sinologist Edward Shaughnessy dated its compilation in its current form to the early decades of the reign of King Xuan of Zhou, in the last quarter of the 9th century BC. A copy of the text in the Shanghai Museum corpus of bamboo and wooden slips (recovered in 1994) shows that the Zhou yi was used throughout all levels of Chinese society in its current form by 300 BC, but still contained small variations as late as the Warring States period. It is possible that other divination systems existed at this time. The Rites of Zhou name two other such systems, the Lianshan and the Guizang. During the Eastern Han, Yijing interpretation divided into two schools, originating in a dispute over minor differences between different editions of the received text.

1) The first school, known as 'New Text Criticism', was more egalitarian and eclectic, and sought to find symbolic and numerological parallels between the natural world and the hexagrams. Their commentaries provided the basis of the School of Images and Numbers.
2) The other school, Old Text Criticism, was more scholarly and hierarchical, and focused on the moral content of the text, providing the basis for the School of Meanings and Principles.

The New Text scholars distributed alternate versions of the text and freely integrated non-canonical commentaries into their work, as well as propagating alternate systems of divination such as the Taixuanjing (weft of greater mystery by Yang Xiong, attempting to make the Yi more comprehensive and symmetrical). That is not unsimilar to how modern yijing commentators work with the Yi. In the end original materials and commentaries become a 'Master Ni', my metaphor for a mash-up of truth and opinions that is more confucing than helping. It is good practice to not mix up your opinions with the past. It is also best practice to discern between periods and give proper descriptions for each period. But in the end the study of Yijing is the study of our selves, which in the last millennium of Chinese culture is identified with our form, comprised of the cheng-coherence of our behavior and our Jing-coherence of the body.

From all the commentaries on the yijing we see that the genesis of the world took place in five stages, the distance between heaven and earth (calculated as 84,000 li), as commented on by the neidan alchemists of the Zhong-Lü tradition, which is named after Zhongli Quan and Lü Dongbin, two illustrious Daoist immortals associated with neidan-alchemy. The interaction of yin and yang, the sequence of seasons, the annual and diurnal cycles of increase and decay, the trigrams and hexagrams of the Yijing, and so forth, are correlated with patterns in the human body. Malfunctioning of the five viscera (wuzang - 5 dirtbags) is explained in terms drawn from medical texts, while psycho-physiological techniques are couched in alchemical language and imagery from the yijing. The texts are also strongly imbued with Neo-Confucian speculations on qi. All accept the division of the practice into three main stages (sancheng). The Zhong-Lü methods include massage and gymnastics in the early stages of practice, as well as breathing exercises that vary according to the adept's level of advancement. Other techniques involve the opening of the three passes (sanguan), refining and returning the essence (jing), inner observation (neiguan), and the egress of the Spirit (chushen). Many aspects we also find back in the IOC Daoland program. The reason is simple. Lü Dongbin was one of the teachers of Zhang Sanfeng, the founder of Wudang Xuanwupai. He developed a healthcare proposal to let all people practice by imperial decree in neidan, or a simplified version in yangsheng (life cultivation), which in the deeper levels is similar to the Daoland Healthcare proposal. Daoland roots in these teachings and methods.

Although I am a big fan of the Quanzhen branch of Daoism, their interest in Yijing has been mild. The so called Northern lineage (Neidan Beizong) is equivalent to the earlier stages of the Quanzhen (Complete Perfection) school Daoism, founded by Wang Chongyang (Wang Zhe, 1113–70). While Quanzhen allows for different forms of individual practice, especially apophatic meditation, and also includes forms of Daoist communal ritual, its methods incorporate a brand of neidan that emphasizes the cultivation of one's nature (that xing-form over ming-clarity). Quanzhen advocated also a renunciant orientation, with corresponding ascetic practices such as seclusion, celibacy, sleep deprivation, and voluntary poverty. A branch of neo-Confucianism is rooted deeply in Quanzhen ideology too! Seven of Wang's disciples were selected by the later hagiography as the first generation of Quanzhen masters. Originally an ascetic and alchemical movement, Quanzhen eventually became a major monastic order, which endures to the present day, and which is mostly dominated by dragon gate society (longmenpai), who on the other hand played a major role in the compilation of the daoist Yijing translated by Thomas Cleary in the 1990's and in the formation of Bagua martial arts that takes aspects of Yijing graphics as its foundation. Longmen is more educational than mystical in its approach. As such it aklso plays a role in the development of Chinese medicine. Daoist monasticists sometimes practiced medicine and yijing to comprehend their neidan process better.

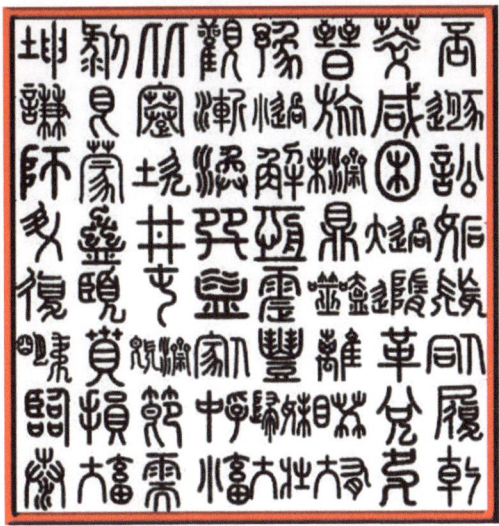

The ancient writing of the yijing hexagram names

Longmen pai absorbed the northern branch of neidan, that rooted in Yin Yang study. Two main branches developed from the original lineage that gave form to northern and southern school. The first is Pure/Azure Cultivation (Qingxiu) branch. The form of cultivation employed by this branch entailed individual practices to join the complementary principles within the human being and transmute them into the internalized pill (neidan). The second line of transmission within Nanzong is the so-called Joint Cultivation (Shuangxiu) or Yin-Yang branch. It is linked to a tantric interpretation of the practice of joint cultivation of nature and clarity (xing ming), yin and yang. While the goal is the same as that of the Pure Cultivation branch, the initial stage of the practice—the union of yin and yang—requires a partner. It roots in the idea of one yang-two yin, which sometimes is explained as one man with two women, or sometimes as the penis flanked by two legs of a woman. It sounds paradoxical that sexual alchemy and its yijing studies is absorbed in s monastic organization, but the thruth is, some daoist rituals require the sexual act to be completed. It is the merging of Qi and blood that is relevant, also called the merging of dragon and tiger.

The dragon is the return to the origin of clarity to heaven and the tiger is the return of fluids to earth. Because the man represents yang heaven,

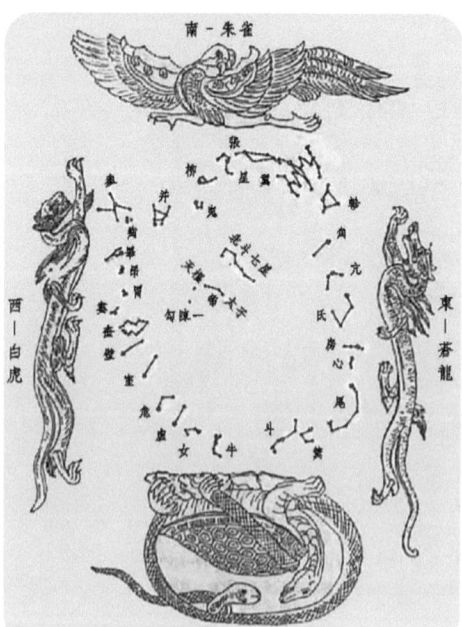

and the woman represents yin earth, the associations of course are clear.

Heaven itself is devided in 4 quadrants. These contain the 60 star palaces. Dragon and tiger are 2 of the quadrants designations, showing their heavenly direction.

The yijing is a compendium of ideas about the nature of reality. It is a meditation tool and it is a study in the inner workings of dao through its qi (yin qi, yang qi, the activities represented by wuxing). There is a variety of names under which the yijing is known which depend on the way the heaxagrams are ordered. Each ordering was trying to prove a point about reality.

The following names are common names for the Kingly Wen ordering we use here in this version:

- Wen Wang Gua (文王卦) is a method of interpreting the results of yijing in divination that was first described in writing by Jing Fang (78–37 BC) in Han dynasty China. It is based on correlating trigrams to the celestial stems and earthly branches of the Chinese calendar, and then using the stem and branch aspects to interpret the lines of the trigrams and hexagrams of the Yijing.
- Liu Yao (six lines) refers to the fact that it interprets the meaning of six symbols;
- Najia method, indicates its internal logic of elemental values derived from the Chinese calendar;
- Wuxing Yi (the five processes of change);
- Wen Wang Ke (lessons of King Wen), which can refer to an actual King Wen (the presumed author of the yijing) or since 'Wen' can mean 'man' the meaning can be "lessons of the kingly man", referring to the way of ritualization of life in resopect to the will of heaven.

As a investigator of health, culture, policy, personal development etc I find the yijing is more than remarkable. It is a lot of things western culture never developed, nor understands easily. In some ways it abhors principles western cultures lived by, or even modern society. It aims to provoke the best possible society for the world, not for politics ort economics. As such it is a very ancient computing device allowing people to do deep thoughts about life and society, not a calculating machine and not a fragmentary collection like for instance tarot. It is a tool for social, political and philosophical activism, it is both conserveative and innovative. It doesn't makle a moral judgement but it shows that non-mopral things have no functional; place in reality. It keeps on putting things in their widest context. Its word content is immaterial, but its meaningfulness is in all the ideas it imples. It is in short a measurement for enculturation.

The history of yijing studies in the west is not that long, a few hundred years at most. But the emphasisi is on the last thirty or so years. Most authors are not involved in chinese language study, or they only know chinese language from writing, do not understand the culture of literary shorthand reference in the Chinese languageit, timed language change, influence of different dynasties, Chinese source materials on Yijing. They know what others wrote or a few of the diagrams. Most of the authors do not have access to Daoists, actual yijing experts etc. it bases itself on apparently similar phenomena in western culture. A collegue writer from the Netherlands who already copied a lot from other people's work also once at a party proudly declared that much of his understanding came from what some Chinese man in a restaurant him once told. But that is not the worst of the field of yijing studies, because everyone involved does so with integrity. The main problem is that investigators usually take themselves as a measure or at best they take western phenomena they declare analogues as a measure, such as Yijin g as a source for shamanic thought, Yijin g and genetics, Yijing and a bunch of other things. Its result is always a secular yijing interpretations and as I often discussed with my friend Harmen Mesker (see also his successful extensive secular and a-cultural blog on yijing) that Chinese culture never developed a secular issue and thus its cultural produce cannot be analyzed from a secular perspective without loosing accuracy. I stumbled over this again when doing research to complete my yijing presentation on this site soon as a first publication from IOC Daoland (a work in progress). people I have heard speaking on conferences, whose books I have met, read and studied great scholars (to name-drop a few like Ruth, Shaugnessy, others) but they all fall in that secular pit and exclude the actual purpose of the yijing in Chinese culture, they isolate it as a textual object. But is is a historical and cultural object, much as people themselves are. In healthcare studies that is specific interesting because it shows a typical alternative to western biological isolationism in regard to medical problems.

The three teachers all working at self cultivation: Kongzi, Laozi, Omidofa

I received my first Yijing when I was about 17 but I have studied the yijing since I was about 23. I have become fascinated and have used it on advice of my teacher Liu An-Dong for anything coming up into my mind. I have published two shorthands on yijing in the Dutch language with Becht publishers and psychology magazine. I have talked about the yijing with fellow students of the yi in the west, collected about a hundred different translations, discussed the yi with teachers from a variety of Chinese religious sects from Buddhist and daoist background. I have received yijing teachings from daoist yijing masters in the purple palace monastery and at golden peak of wudang mountains and have collected ancient collections of yijing uses and diagrams. The yijing is an amazing piece of text, an amazing simple piece of graphic logic and it is no wonder that Confucius exclaimed that if he had another 50 years to study the yi he might get a lot wiser from it.

I have worked about 6 years on my translation, had it ripen for another 2, afte that I recombined the hexagrams and the lines in the current format. I have it now shelved for a few years and decided to open out with it as a give-away of the IOC Daoland to patreon members. I shelved it for a while after having lecturtes on daodejing at Qingchen mountain Daoist community. After hearing the scope of daodejing studies I realized there is much more about these texts that I do not know than that I do know so that every translation is faulty to start with. I was offered several glimpses and practices to learn more and now I feel confident not that my ttranslation is suitable, but that it reflects actual daoist and yijing thoughts and practices. I am also confident it shows something not present in common translations and interpretations because common academic interpretation too often excludes the experiental history of yijing applications in its archiving work. This is understandable due to the high complexity of that material, but unfortunately interpretation then too easily gets europacentric in its expressed understanding, undermining original intent and meaning in many ways. Truthfully, it is hard to bridge knowledge systems from one culture to the next. But by now we have enough experience with Chinese culture that correct understanding should be possible. It is only a lot of work and adaptation.

The purpose of the way how I present the yijing is to prove its internal logic. To make this Yijing functional it had to defy the incoherence that comes forward from translations. Translators in their interpretation and attempt to make it understandable for their non-ancient non-Chinese readership too often focus on the ad hoc textual content and appaerant similarities in western culture. But these similarities often are only superficially similar. When thought through they often do not even closely relate or the trend of their menaing is into another direction. For instance, Chinese directions are inward and western directions are outward. The Chinese concept shen 神 can mean "spirit", but mostly it means "awareness", especially becauser spirit is such a specific anglisaxon-Christian concept where the direction of its purpose is so opposite of that of shen. We should exclude such meanings as to avoid confucion. Translating yin as matter and yang as space is another one like this, and dao as 'the way' is a double confusion because 'dharma'= the way, a Buddhist concept from Indian sanskrt. Dao is similar like the way, but dao is fragile and almost invisible, or difficult to discern, so 'track' is more suitable. We often can only describe meanings, there are no shorthands. A concept of qi is most likely all its translation options, not one of them. So a translation of qi in energy is always wrong, while it might in narrowing exceptions be correct.

The yijing is a way of thinking and it proposes a way of acting out in the world. Due to its nature there should not be error in its texts. All texts should express the goal or function of the text. You do not write a poem and then have a few junk sentences in there. You do not write a novel with a chapter that is about something completely different, and you do not write a science or philosophical treatise without making sure people cannot dismiss your argument due to internal inconsistencies. To achieve appreciation things made need coherence. If the yi is not born from heaven or miraculously came in to existence people must have composed it. They must have had a plan with composing it because its internal reasoning reveals it to be a sort of computing extension for our minds and behaviors. We may expect that there are minor transcription errors but meanings should be consistent. For this argument I also include all the recent findings in yijing research, such as the different time related stratas in which the Yijing and line texts were composed, how the ten wings found their final form, commentaries of politicians who used the yijing over time. The power of the yijing is due to its internal consistency, irrespective of its history of following editors.

It is to understand that the internal logic of Chinese cosmology has to be experienced, and cannot be measured or calculated as in western logic. One has to develop a natural feel for it to make the outcome harmonize. The East Asian logic always points to a hanrmonization with as many factors' satirfaction included. Western logic logic is formulatic: if A than B.

I was told in all the translations that the Yijing is an oracular device. But although the Yijing is often used as such, I do not believe anymore it to be true. Over time I came to understand that the yi is more a ritual manual than anything else. It represents the gradual shifting from heaven-directedness to getting lost in our ways of living, and it maps out possible routes back to the fold of heaven-directedness. The yijing is a book to direct judgment, to generate images to make understandable what happens to us, to point out consequences and thus also rewards. It represents the cyclical passing and overcoming of decay.

The yijing is the representation of a cosmological worldview that is usually excluded when people interpret the yijing. At the center in the current historical placement stands the first hexagram of heaven and all the hexagrams have turned to it. That brings a natural enfoldment of the whole of the yi. On the basis of that we can also criticize commentators from past and present. Many commentators maybe commented on it in their attempt to understand it, not in their understanding.

The nearest heaven standing hexagrams in the following order are close to heaven and follow it from their inner heart, but already in the 3rd and 4th hexagram you see that the asymmetry of the graphics represents the loosing of understanding of the will of heaven and thus represent the first signs of losing the way. The further away you move in numerical order the vaguer the connection with heaven becomes. But at all times you can alter your choices to end up in understanding of the will of heaven, as long as you follow the lines of the diagram to get you there.

So that is the purpose of the yijing. It is a mapping system to show you your placement in respect to the will of heaven. It allows you to make amends, correct yourself, and understand where your current unhappiness or misfortune comes from. It is a beacon to bring you back home into correct behavior.

So the questiona in this context are:
- what is the will of heaven?
- what is correct behavior?

Chinese people, which always calledtheir country "Divine Land", and 'core of everything" has long been aware of the relationship between the human world and the divine. Historically, mixed tribes from China shared the believe that there exist higher beings of greater purity than people; that man should follow these higher beings; and through cultivation practice, that man can reach the level of the divine, become divine oneself. There was no real separation recognized between the realm of ghosts and divine beings. If there was a change it was due to the self-concnetration of the divine beings. They were divine because they willed themselves to be so. For the Chinese that trajectory of development from the common to the ghost-realm / the divine were the options people have as a choosen or accident tal destiny. It is the foundation for a common shared ethics, steering behavior and cultural sciences. The Romans were more like the Chinese than we modern Europeans are. Our culture dictates us to be focused on singular origin of al things due to our traditional believe in the one true god that is the source of all existence. In Chinese culture creation was not seen as that important compared to existence. Existence is "yang", warm, clear and sunny. Origin is "yin", dark, shadowy and vague.

Yin Yang theory suggests that the yang always needs intention to keep motivated and grow. Under normal circumstances things gradually go into decline and decay. It is therefore natural and moral to cultivate oneself and reach for the divine, become part of heaven. So we see that the divine was therefore interconnected with the underworld where the ghosts go to, and the common and men's behavior. From there comes the idea of tripartition of reality in three realms, heaven, men and arth.

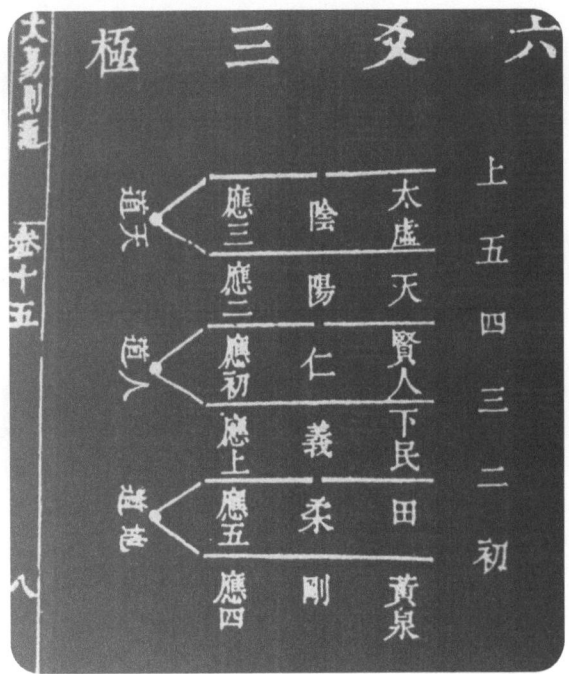

In talking about traditional Chinese culture, people tend to think of the three main schools of teaching: Daoism, Buddhism, and Confucianism. However, even before that, Chinese legends were filled with elements of the divine. The strains of anecdote a bojut the divine was more fragmented, like in the west. These three strains of thought stringed knowledge into systematic wholes and showed how to acces the information.

For example, Nü Wa, a goddess in ancient Chinese mythology, created mankind from clay.

Later on, the water god, Gonggong, smashed his head against Buzhou Mountain, the pillar that supported the sky, and knocked it down. The sky collapsed, and the sky's waters poured into the human world. Nü Wa, being compassionate to mankind, repaired the sky and set up a new pillar. The flood dissipated. When there were ten suns in the sky, creating unbearable heat for mankind, Houyi, the god of archery, was sent to earth to make them stop. He used his arrows to shoot down the nine suns, and thus lost his immortality. Houyi did not want to die and was eventually given two elixirs that would have made him and his wife immortal. Not knowing what they were, Houyi's wife drank them both herself and flew to the moon. Many cultural themes we meet here. But the theories of Confucianism, Daoism and Buddhism make the story through their theories accessible as an example of what we too can do and achieve.

Also, in many tales from ancient Chinese civilization gods came down from the heavens to teach man. Suirenshi taught people to create fire by rubbing two sticks together. *Fuxi* taught people how to make clothes, how to knit a net to fish, and how to throw a spear to hunt.

He also invented the eight trigrams. *Shennong* taught people agriculture and food as a means to health, to understand the concepts of jing (constructive), qi(perfection/purpose) and shen (awareness). He tasted hundreds of herbs to find what could is their jing qi property and understand how every foodstuff alters/shapes us. These are the roots of civilization on which the three religions did build.

As the development of civilization proceeded, Chinese people not only fully embraced the concept of the oneness of man and heaven (man is here; heaven is in another realm; man should follow heaven), but they also explored how man becomes one with heaven and how man finds his true self. In the Chinese language, the way to do that is called "cultivation practice" or "seeking enlightenment." It is a generic term for the practice of mind and body transcendence. There are different approaches such as neidan, waidan, yangsheng, xiushen etc.

Tian is one of the oldest Chinese terms for the cosmos and a key concept in Chinese mythology, philosophy, and religion. During the Shang Dynasty (17–11th centuries BCE), the Chinese called their supreme god Shangdi (上帝, "Lord on High") or Di ("Lord"); during the Zhou Dynasty, Tian seemed to be used at a certain time as synonymous with this figure. But it is not sure they are the same. Heaven was also the place where gods and immortals gathered and from their courts and offices issued decrees to regulate affairs on earth. The Jade emperor was the chief judge in that heaven when things concerned people. And offices were to his right or to his left. The office on th left was attributed to jade emperor's son: Xuanwu, who's humanized incarnation is called Zhenwu. The office on the right is beset by Wenchang, often named to be the god of scholars. This is meaningful because primarily Chinese statehood traditionally is maintained by scholarship, and not military leadership.

Zhenwu's office of the left is dedicated to healing though neidan and exorcism. So it is in fact the priestly office. Zhenwu (true warrior) before was Xuan Wu (dark warrior), the god of the north. Because he is golden he belongs to the western altar. As Xuanwu he belonged to the northern altar. Wenchang belongs to the east, wood, the rising sun of intellectual development. The jade emperor is the southern position. The supplicant faces south.

Heaven then never was one thing or person, like with shangdi or God/allah. Heaven worship was, before the 20th century, an orthodox state religion of China. In this worship heaven and its courts was part of the empire and its government. Heaven was the source of that government. The emperor was its interpretator; the ministers had to help interpret reception by the people. At least, that was the ideal of what it ought to be. So the supplicant, who's palace faces south, is the emperor himself.

The modern Chinese character for heaven, "天", and early seal script both combine da 大 "great; large" and yi 一 "one", but some of the original characters in Shang oracle bone script and Zhou bronzeware script anthropomorphically portray a large head on a great person. So heaven means both "great/large one" as the one wearing the head of rulership. Past emperors in China were asked to carry sort of a scales on their head. The emperors in heaven were expected to wear even bigger ones. The ancient oracle and bronze ideograms for da 大 depict a stick figure person with arms stretched out denoting "great; large". The oracle and bronze characters for tian 天 emphasize the cranium of this "great (person)", either with a square or round head, or head marked with one or two lines. Axel Schuessler (2007:495) notes the bronze graphs for tian, showing a person with a round head, resemble those for ding 丁 "4th Celestial stem", and suggests "The anthropomorphic graph may or may not indicate that the original meaning was 'deity', rather than 'sky'." It might also have been indicator of the divine in general since heaven was seen as model for people on earth to follow, heaven therefore being of a higher order.

Two variant Chinese characters for tian 天 "heaven" are 兲 (written with 王 "king" and 八 "8") and the Daoist coinage 靝 (with 青 "azure" and 氣 "qi", i.e., "azure sky").

First, Herrlee G. Creel (1905-1994) analyzed all the tian and di occurrences meaning "god; gods" in Western Zhou era Chinese classic texts and bronze inscriptions. The Yi Jing "Classic of Changes" has 2 tian and 1 di; the Shi Jing "Classic of Poetry" has 140 tian and 43 di or shangdi; and the authentic portions of the Shu Jing "Classic of Documents" have 116 tian and 25 di or shangdi. His corpus of authenticated Western Zhou bronzes (1970:464–75) mention tian 91 times and di or shangdi only 4 times. Second, Creel contrasts the disparity between 175 occurrences of di or shangdi on Shang era oracle inscriptions with "at least" 26 occurrences of tian. Upon examining these 26 oracle scripts that scholars (like Guo Moruo) have identified as tian 天 "heaven; god" (1970:494–5), he rules out 8 cases in fragments where the contextual meaning is unclear. Of the remaining 18, Creel interprets 11 cases as graphic variants for da "great; large; big" (e.g., tian i shang 天邑商 for da i shang 大邑商 "great settlement Shang"), 3 as a place name, and 4 cases of oracles recording sacrifices yu tian 于天 "to/at Tian" (which could mean "to Heaven/God" or "at a place called Tian".)

The Shu Jing chapter "Tang Shi" (湯誓 "Tang's Speech") illustrates how early Zhou texts used tian "heaven; god" in contexts with shangdi "god". According to tradition, Tang of Shang assembled his subjects to overthrow King Jie of Xia, the infamous last ruler of the Xia Dynasty, but they were reluctant to attack.

The king said, "Listen, multitudes of people, listen all to my words. It is not I, the little child [a humblin kingly title], who dares to undertake what may seem to be a rebellious enterprise; but for the many crimes of the sovereign of Xia Heaven has made clear it decrees [tianming] to destroy him. Now, multitudes, you are saying, 'Our prince does not have compassion for us, but keeps away from our husbandry to attack and punish the ruler of Xia.'

I have heard these words of you all; but the sovereign of Xia is an offender, and, in fear of Shangdi, I dare not not punish him.

Now you are saying, 'What are the crimes of Xia to us?' The king of Xia does no less than exhaust the strength of his people, and exercise oppression in the cities of Xia. His people have become idle in his service, and will not assist him. They are saying, 'When will this sun expire? We will all perish with it.' Such is the course of the sovereign of Xia, and now I must go and punish him. Assist me, I pray you, the one man, to carry out the punishment appointed by Heaven [tian]. I will greatly reward you. On no account disbelieve me; — I will not eat my own word. If you do not follow the words which I have spoken to you, I will put your children with you to death; — you shall find no forgiveness." (retranslation after James Legge 1865:173–5)

Having established that Tian was not a deity of the Shang people, Creel (1970) proposes a hypothesis for how it originated. Both the Shang and Zhou peoples pictographically represented da 大 as "a large or great man". The Zhou subsequently added a head on him to denote tian 天 meaning "king, kings" (cf. wang 王 "king; ruler", which had oracle graphs picturing a line under a "great person" and bronze graphs that added the top line). From "kings", tian was semantically extended to mean "dead kings; ancestral kings", who controlled "fate; providence", and ultimately a single omnipotent deity Tian "Heaven". In addition, tian named both "the heavens" (where ancestral kings and gods supposedly lived) and the visible "sky". (source in wikipedia)

Confucius was a fervent believer in heaven. His dedication to heaven and feeling himself to be sort of channel for heaven through his work brought him the title of "teacher", like Laozi received his title "grandfather" and Xiwangmu "grandmother". He said:

"At fifteen, I had my mind bent on learning. At thirty, I stood firm. At forty, I had no doubts. At fifty, I knew the decrees of Heaven. At sixty, my ear was an obedient organ for the reception of truth. At seventy, I can follow what my heart desires, without transgressing what is right."

Confucius also consulted Laozi on Dao. He said

"If a person hears Dao in the morning, he has nothing, not even death in the evening, to be afraid of."

Confucius' teachings included Dao as a subject, but it was too profound for his disciples to understand. Ranqiu: one of Confucius' disciples straightforward concluded:

"It is not that I don't like Teacher's Dao teaching, it is that I am unable to live them."

Another disciple, Zigong similarly stated:

*"Teacher's explanation of books, we can hear and understand;
Teacher's talk on human nature and the heaven's Dao, we cannot understand."*

This is not exaclty how Laozi perceived it. Laozi said that Dao is easy to understand but it is difficult for people to cultivate it or keep their focus on it. Most of Confucius' teaching, as recorded by his disciples, was about developing one's character, or virtual ethics, in the mundane world. Laozi's Dao tried to bring people into the totality of existence.

These ancient moral teachings both from Confucius and Laozi emphasized self-cultivation, emulation of moral exemplars, and the attainment of skilled judgment rather than knowledge of rules. Some core values that Confucius stressed were:

- Ren (benevolence or humaneness),
- Li (actions committed by a person to build the ideal society),
- Yi (righteousness)
- Zhongyong (maintaining balance and harmony by directing the mind to maintain a state of constant equilibrium).

Confucius' teaching emphasized cultivating one's own virtues. Confucius said:

"If the people be led by laws, and uniformity sought to be given them by punishments, they will try to avoid the punishment, but have no sense of shame. If they be led by virtue, and uniformity sought to be given them by the rules of propriety, they will have the sense of the shame, and moreover will become good."

"If you are upright, things will go well without your giving orders. But if you are not upright, even if you give orders, no one will follow them."

Daoism never really went astray on these inclinations. But Daoism did build on the basic Confucian subjects. In Daoism for instance Zhang Daoling interpreted heaven into a tangible people-like environment to address communication for common people to heaven and to bring heaven to common people. He did not invent heaven as such since the courts were already well known, but he systemized their addressing. But daois holds itself far from a unified view of what haven is about. There are three major schools in Chinese traditional cosmology:

- *Gatian shuo (蓋天說) "Canopy-Heavens hypothesis" originated from the text Zhou Bi Suan Jing. The earth is covered by a material tian.*
- *Huntian shuo (渾天說) "Egg yolk-like hypothesis". The earth surrounded by a tian sphere rotating over it. The celestial bodies are attached to the tian sphere. A summary is in Zhang Heng's article Armillary sphere.*
- *Xuanye shuo (宣夜說) "Firmament hypothesis". The tian is an infinite space. The celestial bodies were light matters floating on it moved by Qi. A summary by Ji Meng (郗萌) is in the astronomical chapters of the Book of Jin.*

Sometimes the sky is divided into Jiutian (九天) "the nine sky divisions", the middle sky and the eight directions. In Daoism usually 36 heavens are counted. Tian has become integral part of Mahayana Buddhism.

In Daoism and Confucianism, Tian as "Heaven" is mentioned in relationship to its complementary aspect of Dì (地), which is most often translated as "Earth". These two aspects of daoist cosmology are representative of the dualistic nature of Daoism. They are thought to maintain the two poles of the Three Realms (三界) of reality, with the middle realm occupied by Humanity (人, Ren).

Daoists teach that 49 (7 x 7) of the Yijing hexagrams describe a moving Dao, (you wei zhi Dao 有为之道, have acting in the dao), Each of the 49 hexagrams of "exchange," yi-wei Dao, begin with one, two, three, or four of mantic code words.

- o   yuan 元, origin, beginning
- o   heng 亨 treat with favor, smooth
- o   li 利 beneficial, utilize
- o   zhen 贞 loyalty, predictable

These words direct preference to the will of heaven. Take for instanced hexagram 32:

32 Heng: permanent, lasting
Smooth, no misfortune
Favourable determination
Favourable to have roots in the past

The text indicates that following this dao will lead to understanding the will of heaven trough understanding how you connect to your/the past.

15 (8 + 7) statements relate to the "Wu wei, or 'Dao of non-moving', (wu-wei zhi dao 无为之道 non-doing's dao or dao's self-so-ness). They teach us about the natural patterning of the seasons as the foundation of the will of heaven. One of them is heaven itself. One of them is earth, the most loyal follower of heaven. If you just observe yourself in the context of your whole life (from birth to either death or immortality), as you ought to, then your inner heart becomes like a mirror for the delicate nature of reality and the not quickly seen, recognized and obvious all of a sudden appears to be the backbone of reality.

This way of looking is part of Daoist and Confucian forms of meditation. Buddhist meditations from East-Asian Mahayana Buddhism are in no way different from this. The now is your whole existence, not the moment before the future and after the past. The now is like a kingdom and thus all inclusive.

In all cases yijing wants to outline the territory between hundun, patterned chaos and the symmetry of yinyang.

The yijing follows about 13 different approaches to the will of heaven. The following are the main ones that are easily identifyable:

1) *yin yang constellation.*
2) *wuxing categories of placement and consummation*
3) *yinyang-wuxing interaction*
4) *tripartition into heaven earth and the human pivot*
5) *transformation/change and exchange as essential to conditioned existence*
6) *dao sets rules on how things come about. Its qi* 炁 *is fragile*
7) *people belong to the people, the divine beings or move between them (daodejing is its confirmation)*
8) *heaven is closest in representing dao, earth is best in following heaven, people are of the dirt of earth*
9) *there is the way to heaven or the way of confusion*
10) *events root in the past or the now, but the root determines the outcome and the method*
11) *change comes gradual or abrupt*

The yin yang symmetry shows itself as follows:

1) *wuji/hundun*
2) *yuan*
3) *dao*
4) *yin*
5) *yang*
6) *yinyang*
7) *taiji*
8) *not taiji*

For explanation of these concepts I have to refer to the MOOC online course on basic theories that you can enter for a single fee of €250,-. To summarize, here anything not taiji shows the disruption of the natural ordering or patterning of things. The yijing says that *if you resist the ordering or patterning of things --within 7 days you will start seeing the results*. It takes that as a warning and punishment. In an alternative description we see the division from hundun to its end also worked out as the following:

1) *yin yang*
2) *wuxing*
3) *bagua*
4) *example*
5) *reality*

What the yijing wants to indicate is set out in the four emblems:

- greater yang
- younger yang
- younger yin
- greater yin.

These four emblems are ofcourse returning in the three partitions of the 6 hexagram lines:

The upper two are the lines of heaven
The middle lines represent the human pivot
The lower two lines represent the following earth.

Each of these emblems represents a trend. The trend is following from the enlarged hexagram. There are only 4 symmetrical hexagrams that represent the principles of the will of heaven:

- *Hexagram 1 heaven (double father diagram, origin)*
- *Hexagram 2 earth (double mother diagram, loyal))*
- *Hexagram 63 helpful (fire nourishes water and water controls fire, predictable)*
- *Hexagram 64 not helpful (fire and water do not communicate, apply the correct)*

From this we can determine in all three partitions the trend of development on that level can be determined, but the human pivot is the most relevant. So the text of the heaxagrams is mostly a specific commentary on the middle lines:

24 Fu: turn around, answer, recover/resume, revenge, again

Going out, coming in; behave accordingly (and there'll be) no illness
Friend comes, no misfortune
Oppose resuming of the Dao and after seven suns comes the answer
Favourable to have roots in the past

Thunder under earth

6 branches comparison:

	Zhoulinetext	Wen'guatext
Line 6		
Line 5		
Line 4	Turn around on your own to the middle path (middle line, could mean yellow brick road)	**51 Zhen: shake, shock, quake, vibrate, greatly exited, deeply astonished** Smooth, Shock comes 'crackcrack!!!' Laughing, talking 'yakyak' Shock frigthens an area 100 li around Do not drop the ladle (spoon) with aromatic spirits (aromatic spirits pictographicly refering to the container of the Po souls)
Line 3	Turn around to the riverbank. Threatening, but no misfortune	**36 Ming yi: safe/darkening of brightness/brilliance** Favourable in a hardship determination

Line 2		
Line 1		
All lines change in opposition		44 Gou: to meet, to encounter, female ruler, intercourse Strong woman Has no use to marry a woman

Line 3 and 4 both indicate returning to emulating earth, the way of listening to the will of heaven. Line 4 relates to heaven and the upper emblem and it shows optimism on following the coagulating aspects in greater yin of heaven. Line three directs to earth and it advices to return to a safer approach of rising yang of earth. Line 4 and the upper emblem are all yin, and thus have resonance of the big leading the small. Line 3 is moved by the rising yang of the lower emblem. It is the rising yang that causes the insecurity factor. The earth emblem represents the alternating dilemma of the helpful and the not helpful of hexagram 63 and 64 due to their harmonious mingling of the yin and yang. The nature of hexagram 24 is then determined by its bottom line that indicates alternation of the helpful and not so helpful as the forming situation. It also shows why the hexagram is structured from the hearth to heaven, and not around the king as is so often suggested by modern interpreters.

The hexagram is constructed from sich lines which are individually yin or yang which are stable or trending towards their extreme and thus change (see about this also the text on casting a hexagram.) The hexagram again reflects the natural order, starting from the soil line, nr 1 and then gradually rising in rank to the king or emperor line who serves a s a lens or pivot between society and heaven. The sixth line is not an advice line as some suggest, but represents the will of heaven in the situation described in the whole of the hexagram. It is therefore a special line to note in making decisions. To give an example:

	Zhou line text	
Line 6	There is no urge to enter the cave. There will be guests: three persons come Respect them and it ends auspicious	*Will of heaven. In the body representing the body form*
Line 5	Wanting in drinks and food Auspicious determination.	*Imperial pivot, interpreting heaven and serving by example, in the body representing the heart*
Line 4	Wanting in blood Come out from the hole/cave.	*Ministerial line, advising the king, executing orders of the emperor, servants of the empire, in the body representing the lungs*
Line 3	Wanting in mud This brings on the arrival of bandits	*Aristocracy line from which generals and ministers are drawn to serve the empire. In the body representing the stomach and sanjiao*
Line 2	Wanting at small grit Have a talk It ends auspicious.	*General line, or war king, the line of teaching and strategy. In the body representing the liver*
Line 1	Wanting at the suburban altar. The use is for a long time favourable. No misfortune	*Soil line, or producing line, the first reaching to heaven. In the body representing the sea of water and grains*

When consulting the Yijing, and one of the statements without a code word (16, 20, 23, 35, 43, 44, 48, 54) or negating them (12, 29, 33, 38, 52, 61, 63) occur, then the writers knew that Wu-wei Dao was present through their language trick. It was time to do nothing but observe from the edge of a state of oblivious wonderment the totality of a situation and stumble over the innate patternings taking place. This method was mentioned both by Laozi as well as Zhuangzi, called cleaning of the heart mirror or a heart-fasting meditation. The Yijing is a manual leading to a four step, contemplative form of prayer and ritual meditation, in accord with the brief readings at the head of each hexagram.5 Images of the Yijing trigrams are found everywhere in Daoist Jiao 醮 festival and Zhai 齋 burial liturgy.

How Daoist ritual uses the Yijing (I-ching)

For healthcare purposes both on the level of the individual and the social Chinese culture traditionally emphasized the ritualization of life. That is, one would submit oneself to the obvious good solutions in cases of where problems or conflicts might come about. The aim of life was therefore not only self-gratification, but also to contribute to a harmonious society. One's own personal self-justification, being right or having success has therefore minor reasons to take the lead. The Yijing as a manual for ritualizing life shows therefore paths to follow to gradually come to understanding. The outcomes of the yijing as an aracular device are therefore not to believe or understand, they are for behavioral corrections.

Daoists are masters of correct behavior. They follow the local mores and adjust themselves in their behavior until they blend in perfectly with the behaviours that are considered best for the common good. They do this to develop inner freedom. They do not do this to develop the freedom to do as they like. Daoists are supposed to cultivate their commitment to society and heaven, but to forget about their own selfish needs. In that sense Daoists are quite puritan. They are considered the ultra consevatives of Chinese society. They serve in modern times as the mirror through which we can understand the use of the yi. The yi is like a calendar, but your passing through its time is not linear. It is corrective to set you back on a trajectory to harmonize you with society and heaven. It is not there to grand you wishes. The yi follows the great adagium of the daodejing, written by Laozi (grandfather):

the Dao that daos is amazing dao.

A couple of things spring out:

1) the purpose of life is to experience it with amazement about its wondrous workings
2) the purpose of life is to adjust to what you are suitable for
3) Life is a ritual calendar with marked moments that need celebration and recognition

We will discuss here briefly the daoist ritual calendar for the purpose of describing how life works according to that vision. The Daoist festival calendar represents an amalgamation of various sources, and varies according to sect, region, and temple, therefore it is not uniform or strictly standardized. Major festivals last for days, from two or three up to seven or more. A two-day service may involve fifteen different rites corresponding to distinct texts, each rite lasting from one to several hours. Typically, each of these rites consists of these stages:

- *purification,*
- *invocation of the deities,*
- *prayers,*
- *consecration*
- *offerings,*
- *hymns*
- *dances*
- *perambulations.*

There are two main types of ritual:

1) *Funeral rites or periodic rites on behalf of ancestors, which are performed only by some sects, sometimes in tandem with Buddhist priests; and*
2) *Rites on behalf of local communities.*

Both types include rites to:

- *install the ritual space in which the event takes place,*
- *rites of fasting the body and the sense organs through food fast and fast of the sense organs, to clean the self and awareness so that nothing gets missed in the event,*
- *rites of communion or offering,*
- *rites to disperse the ritual space after the ritual is completed.*

Rituals on behalf of the community may involve tens or even hundreds of villages, and occur every three, five, or twelve years. They can be extraordinarily expensive, and are paid for by household donations and community leaders. Aside from the rituals themselves, there will also be plays, processions, military parades, and communal meals.

As for the performance of the rituals themselves, no mistakes can be made; no step or recitation must falter. One's performance of affairs should be completed attentive and flawless. Existence is in essence an artistic expression in which you continuoulsly present your innate quality (the 德 de of 道德经 daodejing). A good ritualist is a person of substance, because of the way he or she holds his/her concentration. Much of the Daoist's personal life consists of preparation for these events. There is a clear hierarchy in learning ritual service:

- Apprenticed Daoshi serve as musicians;
- more advanced trainees assist by lighting incense and reciting certain passages.
- The heart of the ritual is conducted by five Daoshi: a Great Master and his four assistants.
- One of these assistants heads the intricate and complex processions and dances, and is responsible for knowing the entire sequence of rites that make up the full ritual.
- Another prepares in advance every communication with the celestial bureaucracy that is used during the course of the entire ritual, and recites all of the invocations and consecrations, the texts of purification, elevation, and confession.

Part of the preparation is learning how to sit in oblivion. This daoist practice is well known but often little understood by non-daoist practitionersa.

Sitting in oblivion is the result of forgetting the body. Forgetting the body is rhe result of holding on to the one, which we will explain later in the text.

On average in the self cultivation of a Daoist seven tasks are recognized:

- *developing respect for all existence*
- *developing faith,*
- *interception of karma and dealing with its retributions,*
- *taming the mind,*
- *developing detachment from affairs,*
- *develop true observation,*
- *develop intense all including concentration,*
- *realising unification wit Dao and the will of heaven*

These seven tasks from societal perspective can be seen as steps of positive alienation because you reconstruct yourself gradually from the common to be an integral part of the functioning of Daoist cosmology. As a daoist at initiation you untie yourself of the knots of common life and dependencies.

Through the practice of the seven stages, a process of double forgetting is carried out sequentially - the forgetting of social affairs and relationships and that of the very method of meditation and forgetting or sitting in oblivion to help develop one's all inclusiveness and sitting in oblivion. Daoist practice is part born out of the need for social activism, to consciously interfere with the ways of the world as to engender positive change. But the rebelliousness here is socialized and internalized. The practices originate from the Tang and Sui dynasties. We can see in the recent 100 hyears that the Chinese interest in qi gong, or tuna breathing exercise influenced by Daoism originate in similar needs. The western interest in qigong, Daoism, yijing and other elements of Chinese cosmological sciences serves a similar goal. The Oriental College Daoland project follows this trend by using knowledge development and internalization of social activism though qigong and health practice to the foreground. Health practice is the ritual enactment of existence. Hence understanding the ritualization and the different levels of ritual enactment of Daoism is very interesting to study. When studying the yijing that is even more so, since the workings or the yijing are also representing how the working of the body go.

- During the activities of the ritual we were describing, the Grand Master is preparing for his role, quietly chanting secret formulas and doing mudras with his hands inside his sleeves. They are secretive sealings of connections he makes with departments of heaven and earth. At times he picks up the incense burner and holds it as he breathes in and out, facing different directions, or he burns talismanic symbols or initials documents. He connects the inner and the outer, the tangible and the hidden. Primarily, he enacts internally the actions spoken by the texts that are being recited by his assistant. We see that the ritual is not something performed by one, but by the social divine group as a whole.

- At a certain point, he rises and performs the "dance of the stars," the step of Yu or Taiyi. Then he falls prostrate, in a fetal position with arms and legs under his body, his face in his hands, as he internally journeys to the Heavenly Assembly, locus of the Heavenly Worthies, accompanied by divine escorts (all described in the recitation that accompanies these acts). In this sense, the master is the mountain, just as the incense burner and the altar are also the mountain. In ancient times, the altar was built upon a series of graduated steps, so that the master actually ascended the steps at this point in the ritual, but these days the ascent is entirely internal.

- Here he presents the memorial that is the heart of the ritual texts. The memorial is a petition to the gods, written in literary language, stating the name and purpose of the ritual, its date and location, the names and addresses of the participants, and a vow —that is a request and a pledge on behalf of all the participants.

- Standing again, the master burns the memorial and scatters the ashes, gathers his escorts, and returns. Afterward, there is more chanting and more music, but the main portion of the ritual has occurred. In breaking down the ritual space, all talismans, writs, and other markers of the ritual space are burned. Afterward there is a communal banquet, with plenty of food available for the orphan souls who cannot become ancestors.

Daoist rituals are colorful, filled with music, incense, and stylized movements. In contrast with Indian ritual, they are not amplifying the experience of bliss. The extatic states that are being looked for have to amplify the immersion into reality as an aesthetical experience of appropriateness. The extacy of Daoism is inwardly directed and cooled to the point where serenity and experience of harmony and everlasting numinousity can be experienced. The experience of bliss and extacy by themselves are recognized as being attributes belonging to fire, and therefore consume a person, like in sexual peaking. They need to be controlled as not to consume the ritualist. It is called dimming of the light.

Much of Chinese and east Asian drama is influenced by Daoist ritual. Puppet theatre especially has roots in Daoist ritual. Daoist ritual itself is based on the Han dynasty court rituals, which share similarities with Korean court rituals up to recent days.

Some forms of ritual involve mediumship, trance, and the exorcism of demons. These usually occur during festivals, and are regarded as being of a lower order than the rituals of the Daoshi, the daoist masters. Tibetan Buddhism, as an offshoot of Tiantai Buddhism (that worships Taiyi as well) has been deeply influenced by Daoist practices. Its role for oracles, such as that of Dorje Shugden, emulates the Daoist oracle directly. The "barefoot masters" in southern Daoist ceremonies walk beds of hot coals, climb ladders of swords, or pierce themselves with sharp objects. In ritual spaces far less defined than those of the Daoshi, they will call on the powers of local spirit generals and spirit armies and, in the course of dramatic performances, invoke their power for aid and protection on behalf of the community. We see these practices to be more popular in the south of China, Vietnam and Taiwan, not so in the north, which is the core of Daoism and has always been more inwardly directed.

To communicate with the dead in a ritual, a miniature sedan chair carried by two people may become the seat of a deity who will, through the movement of the chair, dictate a response to settle a conflict between dead and living family members. Mediums can also undertake expeditions against demons who have caused problems for a person or community. The barefoot masters, like the Daoshi, have their ritual texts, long epics that describe voyages to spirit realms. They often paint their faces in elaborate masks, like those of Chinese opera characters. They might enact a battle against the demons, with swords and military music, and strike themselves with their weapons, even drawing blood. The blood is regarded as protection against evil, and the act, a form of expiation for the sins of all. Tissues are applied to the wounds to soak up a bit of blood, and then taken home and stuck on doorframes to ward off evil. The image of the 'barefoot doctors', an army of grasroot medicine students sent out by the Chinese cultural revolution comitties in the 20th century was based partly on the representation of barefoot masters as champions for social communities.

Of course the yijing doesn't ask such intense self-sacrifice. It only serves to show that correction of a situation will take some effort. Corrections are something that one can execute without actually agreeing. It is following a particular order of events and one should stay attentive. In riotualizing one consciously goes in one direction and closes off another. Rityualisation is therefore a form of consciously deciding. This is often confused with doing affirmations. They purpose is to confirm in both directions. Not only in the wished for direction. The yijing symbols itself serve as tools for contemplation. The contemplation can help you deepen your understanding.

Yijing symbols (not the book itself) are used everywhere in Daoist ritual, as well as in meditation. When performing rites of renewal (Jiao 醮), or burial (Zhai 斋), daoists ritually "close" the trigram Gen 艮 , the northeast "Demon Gate" (Guei Men 鬼门) to the underworld. This prevents pollution by the hungry ghosts and demons spilling over from the underworld during rituals that cross the boundaries between the three realms. After that the "Heaven Gate" (Tian Men 开天门, 乾, 三) is opened on the northwest, to allow awareness of the will of heaven by means of Wu-wei 无为之道 Dao. It serves to heal, bless, and renew, during the entire cycle of life's change. Daoists must first be "one with Wu Wei Dao," by inner cultivation. Only then, can they serve as king under heaven, provide Rites of Passage, to renew and heal the communities in which they live.

Daoists are by nature of their studies not allowed to use the yi for prediction. The yi is used as tool to learn thinking and reasoning. It serves to understand the principles of wuxing and yin yang. In that sense I can here with comfort refer to the online studies in China's basic cultural theories in addition to this yijing. In that study cycle some 1000 collected materials are available combined with exercises to leanr the daoist way of reasoning based on yijing intimately. This course is also prerequisite to make heads or tails of Chinese medicine and gongfu anatomy or physiology, fengshui geomantics and xingshu astrology or mingshu destiny calculation.

How the yijing is used in daoist alchemy

Y in-Yang and yijing provide important concept in the ideas of Chinese alchemy. It is often pointed out that the ideas of them are pervasive throughout alchemical theory, as the metals were categorized as being male or female, and mercury and sulphur especially were thought to have powers relating to lunar and solar respectively. Yijing and yin yang provide bridging terminology and can help see similarities between different situations or materials.

Prior to the Daoist tradition, the Chinese already had very definitive notions of the natural world, especially involving the wuxing (5 forms) which were Water-like, Fire-like, Earth-like, Metal-like and Wood-like. See for the full explanation of this concept the IOC Daoland online course on Basic Theories in Chinese culture. The wuxing is discussed in about 250 pages in part three and goes accompanied with assignments to help you think from the perspectives of wuxing in a way that denies most western interpretations of the theories. The Wuxing were commonly thought to be interchangeable with one another; each is capable of becoming like the other through changes. These changes happen due to consumption. Fire eats wood, wood drinks water etc. And if overdoing things, you become what you eat. You eat a lot of dead meat and you become dead meat. It means that internally things can be consistent -but in their behaviour they might not. The concept is integral, as the belief in outer alchemy necessitates the belief in natural elements being able to change into others. The cyclical balance of the elements relates to the binary opposition of yin-yang, and so it appears quite frequently.

Trigram wuxing associations are as such:

Wuxing	metal	metal	fire	wood	wood	water	earth	earth
Trigrams	☰	☱	☲	☴	☵	☶	☷	☷
character	乾	兌	離	巽	坎	艮	坤	
Trigram	qián	duì	lí	zhèn	xùn	kǎn	gèn	kūn
Yinyang	yang	yin	yang	yang	yin	yin	yin	yang
colour	white	grey	red	green	light green	blue	orange	yellow

The division as both heaven and earth as yang is because the expeansiveness of earth and heaven are model to the required need for personality development, whicxh is supposed to become wide, accepting and all inclusive like heaven and earth as a prerequisite to transform into an immortal.

The division of the the yijing Eight Houses is a way of assigning the wuxing to the hexagrams. This method is called the Najia method. This is used to identify the line which contains the same xing as the hexagram, as a whole, and to establish an ordered relationship among the lines of the hexagram. There are various ways of arranging the houses in relation to each other.

Each house begins with a hexagram made by doubling a trigram. Then lines 1 thru 5 are changed to produce the first 6 hexagrams. Next the fourth line of hexagram 6 is changed to produce hexagram 7. Changing the first three lines of hexagram 7 produces hexagram 8. These eight hexagrams are of the same xing as the original hexagram that was made by doubling a trigram.

For example, the house of the first hexagram is:

As a result these 8 hexagrams all belong to the metal form/xing, meaning their workings are organized by being a tool (metal mirroring, forded or molded or hammered object) when yang and being a source (ore) when yin. The shared line is then the 6th line being the ruling line, showing that the eight heaxagrams in the house of qian represent the advices of heaven.

The wuxing are further developed into time markers such as the twelve branches and ten stems, moon and sun periods. Although it is called the Kingly Order (order of king wen (wen means manly), much of the commentaries and associations were formalized by Jing Fang, who assigns stem and branch elements to the lines of the trigrams. (the trigrams as a whole already had their own wuxing correspondences). The correspondences of the trigrams for the celestial stems and earthly branches below indicate the time based xing (forms) for each line of the trigrams, as opposed to the trigrams as a whole.

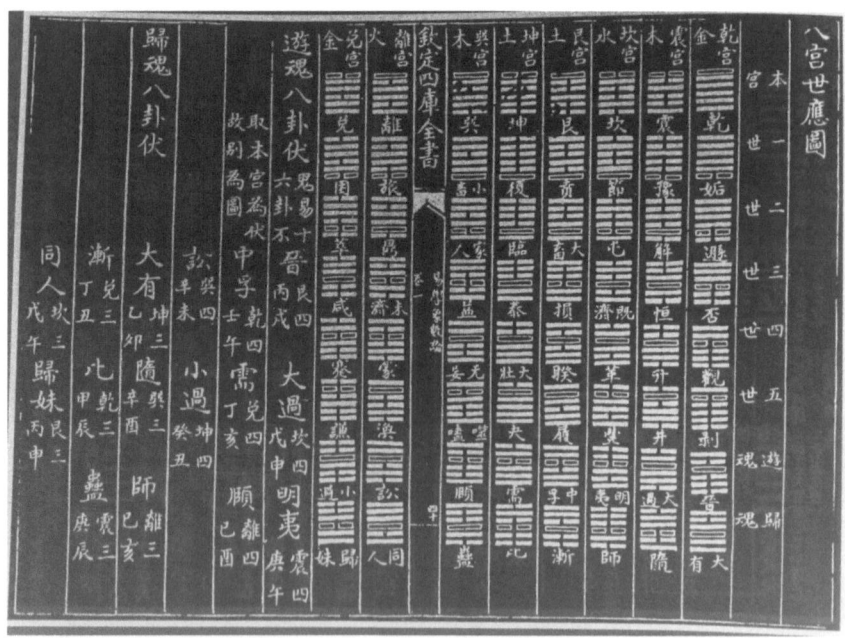

Traditional graph for the study of the 8 houses, reading from right to left

Celestial stem		Trigram	xing
Jia	甲	☰	wood
Yi	乙	☷	earth
Bing	丙	☷	fire
Ding	丁	☲	metal
Wu	戊	☷	earth
Ji	己	☲	water
Geng	庚	☷	wood
Xin	辛	☲	wood
Ren	壬	☰	metal
Gui	癸	☷	earth

The twelve branches and the trigrams are associated as follows:

Earthly Branch			animal	Trigram	Xing
1	子	zǐ	Rat	☰,☷	water
2	丑	chǒu	Ox	☷	earth
3	寅	yín	Tiger	☷	wood
4	卯	mǎo	Rabbit	☲	wood
5	辰	chén	Dragon	☷	earth
6	巳	sì	Snake	☰	fire
7	午	wǔ	Horse	yang	fire
8	未	wèi	Goat	☷	earth
9	申	shēn	Monkey	yang	metal
10	酉	yǒu	Rooster	yin	metal
11	戌	xū	Dog	yang	earth
12	亥	hài	Pig	yin	water

The joining of the stems and branches form the 60 time sequences of the greater year. There are 6 of those in a year, every day have four 60 moment cycles, etcetera. Each of these 60 are subdivided in four quadrants of 15 combinations that follow the four quadrants of heaven, being heaven, earth, helpful or not helpful. In alchemical and ritual texts these are often called:

- *xuanwu the dark warrior in the north,* ☳ rising in the lower trigram
- *the phoenix in the south* ☷ rising in the lower trigram
- *the white tiger in the west* ☱ rising in the lower trigram
- *the green dragon in the east* ☴ rising in the lower trigram

Chinese alchemy can be divided into two methods of practice which are waidan or "external alchemy" and neidan or "internal alchemy". Doctrine can be accessed to describe these methods in greater detail; the majority of Chinese alchemical sources can be found in the Daozang, the "Daoist Canon".

The meaning of waidan derives from wai (outside, exterior) and dan referring to alchemical operations, such as the preparation of chemical elixirs, made from cinnabar, realgar, and other substances generally involving mercury, sulfur, lead, and arsenic or else the animal and botanical products which are found in Chinese herbology and Traditional Chinese medicine. Waidan refers to practices relating to the process of making an elixir often containing herbal or chemical substances found outside of the body. This process involves esoteric oral instructions, building a laboratory, kindling and sustaining the special fires used in the production process, rules of seclusion and purification for the alchemist him or herself to follow, and various practices including the performance of ceremonies to protect the self and the ritual area. Waidan can also include following a dietary regimen which prescribes or proscribes certain foods. Preparing medicines and elixirs can be referred to as outer practices or weidan as these practices occur outside of the body until they are verified by the ingestion of medicines, herbs, and pills to bring about physical changes within the body, separate to the soul. For yijing study that is relevbant because it subdivides reality into alchemical substitutes. It means that every action you undertake should be undertaken within the appropriate context and with suitable attention, and not as a side dish to life.

The term Neidan can be divided into two parts Nei meaning inner and Dan referring to alchemy, elixir and cinnabar (mercury). Neidan uses techniques such as: composed meditation techniques, visualization, breathing and bodily posture exercises. Breathing exercises were used to develop and maintain jing or " essencial life construction/cultivation" and bodily postures were used to improve qi, jin, ying, wei, blood, body fluids, yin and yang flows in the body. Neidan comprises the elixir from the principles of Traditional Chinese Medicine and the cultivation of substances already present in the body, in particular the manipulation of three substances in the body known as the "Three Treasures". These three treasures are also associated with locations in the body where the alchemical firing process can take place, known as the three dantians in belly, chest and head. Daoist Yoga is a core element in this process. Yoga and alchemy are both concerned with the ultimate balancing of life. Chinese alchemical yoga depended on exercises, breathing methods and an ordered and balanced diet which was designed to increase longevity. The diet was often vegetarian, and some diets removed onion and garlic, others removed grains, and still other removed fish and other meat. The development of internalized purposeful existence was the core goal, because it was seen as a mirror through which the will of heaven can be understood. Also the developed vitality serves to act with care. The developed sensitivities serve to help analyse things irrespective of oneself, so that thoughts are not coloured by personal needs, desires, angers or fears. The yijing and its symbols and transformations serve the development process. In most cases one will need a proper teacher to introduce you to the skills as well as helping you to finetune you to the meaningful siode of your experiences. Daoism and the yijing agree on the fact that having experiences has no consequences. We all have them, having expereiences does not make them meaningful. By referring them as meaningful because you have them you fill in the de-facto emptiness of the experience with theatrical value. The expereicne then is about you and your self-judgement of self-need for self-confirmation. As a core acceptance people need to work on accepting is the likely fact that they are not special, exceptional or anything. Brilliance comes from modesty and the willingness to be of no consequence. Laozi asks his readers if they are willing to be the last in line, instead of putting themselves on the foreground. Daoists are required to always let others go or take first and live by the leftovers to help life forward. Having -, or being involved with frontline experiences etc are recognized as hindrances to progress in one's development. Likewise, it is not enough to think one's self lowly. One should at the same time feel like being a king. But as Mozi and Zhuangzi both suggested true kings are not known by their peoples, they just rule by goodness and example, not by rules and decrees.

The yijing and Daoist deities

Daoism seems to hold on to many different kinds of gods. Daoism also has been developed after the Yijing had been established firmly at the heart of all Chinese developments. As such we see that Daoism as a religion has always been both historical and a-historical. The daoist pantheon and its construction has continuously been added to and altered becaseu it has always been a devise to help the ascension from the person from commonality to immortality.

The Daoist universe and the body both house a large phletora of deities, ghosts, spirits, demons and so on. Though developing aliances during ritual and ritualized meditations, hierarchy, co-operation bodily functions are established, having to lead to acceptance in heavenly paradises, or the 36 grott's as they are called. The 36 grotto's primarily are the extrapolations on the diagrams of the yijing and follow a mohist process of division. They are represented by the heaven diagram in the post natal bagua diagram.

First of all let us discuss the 36 grotto's. we start with pointing towards hexagram 36, which is called "darkening of brightness/brilliance". In its main text it gives the advice to first rise to heaven to find access to earth. With earth the grotto's are intended. We further see that all the lines are associated with hexagrams that are considered positive. But when we reverse all the lines it turns into litigation. Therefore, hexagram 36 outlines the way to do things right.

Then, what about the number 36? The number 36 is an extrapolation from the daoist verbatim: from the dao comes the one, from the one ciome the two, from two come the three and from the three come the ten thousand things. We know that meditation on the one is essential for daoists. The daoist alchemical text revolving about yijing Baopuzi states that when we can hold on to the one all the ten thousand litigations will be resolved. The 10.000 litigations referrs to the many issues we face in daily life that hinder us in doing our cultivation smoothly.

The one to hold on to is also the three in one. The three in one originates in Mohist thought. Mozi proposed to organize government from the emoperor to three ministers, who each had three advisors, and they had each four envoys and so on. This gives us a calculation like this: The one x3=3, x3=9, 4x9=36. Its essence is in the number three, which is the number of pure yang, following the pure yin, represented by 2: Dao is one yin or one yang, togheter is liang 兩 which are practiced. A daoist practices yin (the feminine, pliancy, following) to hold one to the three in one, the yang at both sides of the yin. This is trigram number 9, the eye or fire.

The one though is the three in one. Heaven is the one and heaven is the "supreme being", called Taiyi, the greater one. It is the embodiment of heaven and has many forms and can be found everywhere. As such Taiyi is the face of Dao. Taiyi is also represented as deathlessness. It is for this reason why Taiyi gongfu forms rank so highly in the neiquan repertoire of Wudang daoist gongfu monks. The there in one mirror the division in three of Confucianism:

Heaven and earth moreover are depicted as the male one and the feminine one[1]. Different from the Confucian triad we see that in Confucianism the earth is following heaven. In higher heaven the male one follows the female one. For completeness I added the offices on the left aqnd right of Yudi high lord. The jade emperor rules ofcourse all under heaven, the human affairs. Zhenwu great god as an emanation of jade emperor high god, is also the black or dark one. He is the ruler of faiths, queller

---

[1] For an extensive discussion of the relationship between the male and female I refer to Isbelle Robinet: Taoist meditation, the maoshan tradition of great purity. The version I use here of this vision is based on teachings on cosmology given at wudang shan, which ofcourse puts its own mountain at the center of the universe, like all other holy mountains do.

of demons and the master of cultivation. Wen Chang great god is the god of status, he is responsible for who is granted which title and which postion. Yudi is like Taiyi supreme god a controller. But taiyi knows no death, yudi on the other hand is limited in its time of existence. The three layers together form a heavenly square of nine positions.

These upper three are the three lines of the heaven trigram. The lower line is the feminine one, it is the root. The middle one is taiyi, the unchanging one with many faces. And the upper one is the male one, the one that follows and perceives. From here we see that fire is the male one and the feminine one mediated by yin, resulting in brightness and understanding. The water trigram we see that taiyi leads the yin, the world of manifestations. Again we see that here brightness is hidden. We see here that hexagram 36 shows how dao works, when Laozi explains that when the ordinary person sees dao he would not understand and dismiss it.

The three also display a verticalness in the placement of the person in the world. On the left we see how Zhenwu represents the male one, but sits on mount wudang, or a mountain. We see that Wenchang mediates in one's relationship with the feminine one, sometimes represented as Xiwangmu (grandmother west, living in the western heavenly mount Kunlun [昆仑]), the goddess mother of all gods. Her command to elevate you to immortal state brings the daoist to the 36 heavenly grottos. Wenchang commands the ritual court and elevation in social status as well as one's relationship to the divinities. Wenchang high god therefore also is the one that registers scripture attribution. He is frequently prayed to and offered ceremonial bribes by common people at the temple courts in the hope to develop a better life or career.

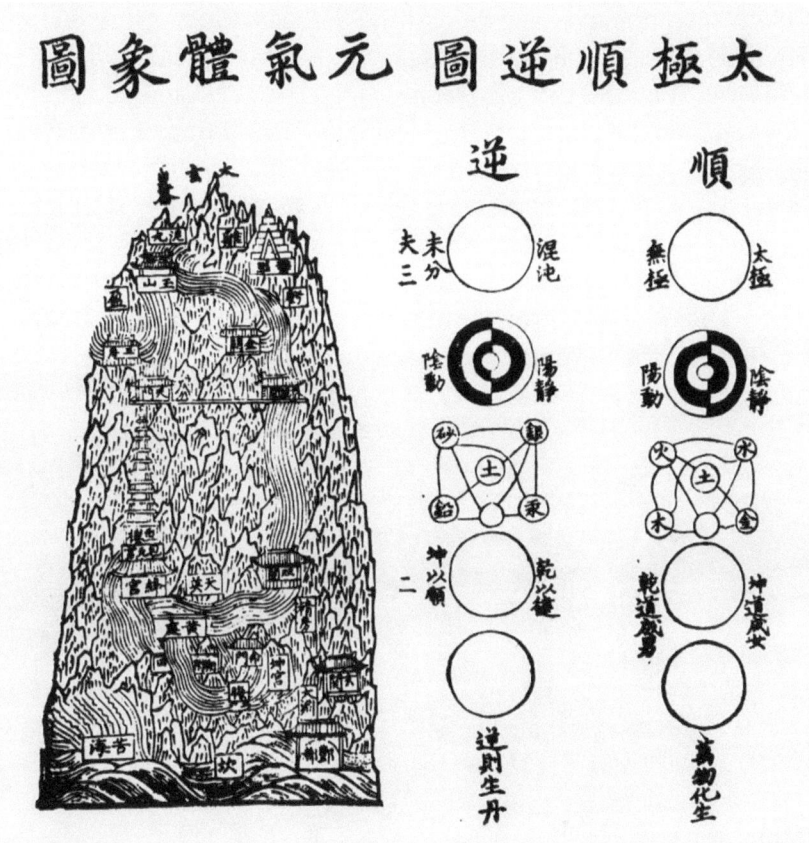

These divinities and relationship are a framework for the daoist to develiop his alchemical work towards heaven. It explains why heaven is so close to humanity. Heaven is a grotto. It is hidden, a dimension tucked away from reality but not non-existent. Likewise, a person can always enter a mountain and dedicate him or her-self/personhood to cultivation, emulating the life path zhenwu/xuanwu showed for his own ascension.

Another short history of the yijing

We already mentioned some exiting aspects of the yijing. But there is so much more to the yijing. Traditionally, the yijing and its hexagrams were thought to pre-date recorded history, and based on traditional Chinese accounts, its origins trace back to the 3rd to the 2nd millennium BC.

Modern scholarship suggests that the earliest layers of the text may date from the end of the 2nd millennium BC, but place doubts on the mythological aspects in the traditional accounts. Some consider the yijing the oldest extant book of divination, dating from 1,000 BC and before. The oldest manuscript that has been found, albeit incomplete, dates back to the Warring States Period (475–221 BC). In geernal it is suggested that the Yijing came about or became possible due to the integration of yinyang and wuxing cosmogonies, that could together more coherently explain the shifting taking place through time and space complicating the farmers' calendar and thus rulership of the worldly realms. It produced the Guangzi, Huangdineijing.

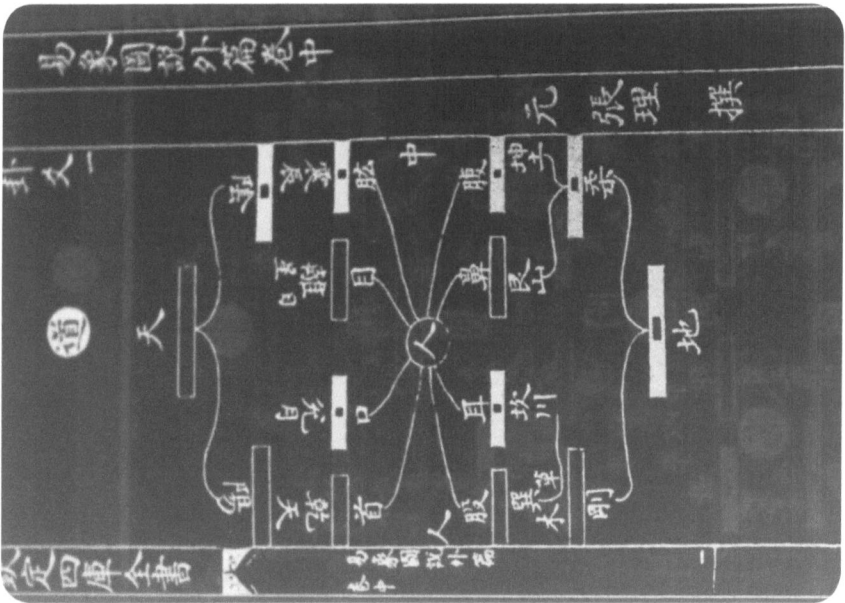

During the Warring States Period, the text was re-interpreted as a system of cosmology and philosophy that subsequently became intrinsic to Chinese culture. It centered on the ideas of the dynamic balance of opposites, the evolution of events as a process, and acceptance of the inevitability of change.

The standard text originated from the Old Text version (古文經) transmitted by Fei Zhi (费直, c. 50 BC-10 AD) of the Han Dynasty, which survived Qin's book-burning. During the Han Dynasty this version competed with the New Text (今文經) version transmitted by Tian He at the beginning of the Western Han. However, by the time of the Tang Dynasty the Old Text version became accepted as standard.

Traditionally it was believed that the principles of the yijing originated with the mythical ruler Fu Xi (伏羲 Fú Xī). He is granted the development of the trigrams and scripture from these trigrams. In this respect he is seen as an early culture hero, one of the earliest legendary rulers of China (traditional dates 2800 BC-2737 BC), reputed to have had the 8 trigrams (八卦 bā guà) revealed to him supernaturally. By the time of the legendary Yu (禹 Yǔ) 2194 BC – 2149 BC, the trigrams had supposedly been developed into 64 hexagrams (六十四卦 lìu shí sì gùa), which were recorded in the scripture Lian Shan (《連山》 Lián Shān; also called Lian Shan Yi). Lian Shan, meaning "continuous mountains" in Chinese, begins with the hexagram Bound (艮 gèn), which depicts a mountain (☶) mounting on another and is believed to be the origin of the scripture's name.

After the traditionally recorded Xia Dynasty was overthrown by the Shang Dynasty, the hexagrams are said to have been re-deduced to form Gui Cang (《歸藏》 Gūi Cáng; also called Gui Cang Yi), and the hexagram responding (坤 kūn) became the first hexagram. Gui Cang may be literally translated into "return and be contained", which refers to earth as the first hexagram itself indicates. At the time of Shang's last king, Zhou Wang, King Wen of Zhou is said to have deduced the hexagram and discovered that the hexagrams beginning with Initiating (乾 qián) revealed the rise of Zhou. He then gave each hexagram a description regarding its own nature, thus Gua Ci (卦辭 guà cí, "Explanation of Hexagrams"). This ordering has remained the core of Yijing use since that time.

When King Wu of Zhou, son of King Wen, toppled the Shang Dynasty, his brother Zhou Gong Dan is said to have created Yao Ci (爻辭 yáo cí, "Explanation of Horizontal Lines") to clarify the significance of each horizontal line in each hexagram. It was not until then that the whole context of Yijing was understood. Its philosophy heavily influenced the literature and government administration of the Zhou Dynasty (1122 BC-256 BC). Later, during the time of Spring and Autumn Period (722 BC-481 BC), Confucius is traditionally said to have written the Shi Yi (十翼 shí yì, "Ten Wings"), a group of commentaries on the yijing. By the time of Han Wu Di (漢武帝 Hàn Wǔ Dì) of the Western Han Dynasty (c. 200 BC), Shi Yi was often called Yi Zhuan (易傳 yì zhùan, «Commentary on the yijing"). Together with the commentaries by Confucius, yijing is also often referred to as Zhou Yi (周易 zhōu yì, "Exchanges of Zhou"). All later texts about Zhou Yi were explanations only, due to the classic's deep meaning.

In the past 50 years a "Modernist" history of the yijing emerged based on research into Shang and Zhou dynasties' oracle bones, Zhou bronze inscriptions and other sources (Marshall 2001, Rutt 1996, Shaughnessy 1993, Smith 2008). In the 1970s, Chinese archaeologists discovered intact Han dynasty-era tombs in Mawangdui near Changsha, Hunan province. One of the tombs contained the Mawangdui Silk Texts, a 2nd century BC new text version of the yijing, the Daodejing and other works, which are mostly similar yet in some ways diverge from the received, or traditional texts preserved historically. This version of the yijing, despite its textual form, belongs to the same textual tradition as the standard text, which suggests it was prepared from an old text version for the use of its Han patron.

Rather than being the work of one or several legendary or historical figures, the core divinatory text is now thought to be an accretion of Western Zhou divinatory concepts. According to Daniel Woolf, the text reached a "definitive form" at the end of the 2nd millennium BC. As for the Shi Yi commentaries traditionally attributed to Confucius, scholars from the time of the 11th century AD scholar Ouyang Xiu onward have doubted this, based on textual analysis, and modern scholars date most of them to the Warring States period (475 BC-256 or 221 BC), with some sections perhaps being as late as the Western Han period (206 BC-9 AD).

The general structure of the layers of the text, in a modern edition will look like the following layers:

Hexagram:

1) *Hexagram - Warring States manuscript*
2) *Hexagram name - Warring States manuscript*
3) *Hexagram statement - Warring States manuscript*

4) *Judgment commentary*
5) *Greater Image Commentary*
6) *Line statements - Warring States manuscript*
7) *Lesser Image Commentary (line by line)*

Overview whole text:

1) *Main body of text*
2) *Great Appendix (Upper & Lower sections)*
3) *Explications of the Hexagrams*
4) *Ordering the Hexagrams*
5) *Miscellanea of the Hexagrams*

From this we can see that the yijing as a principle doesn't leave out anything. Anything can be relevant in the context of the yijing. Like the yijing we are asked to keep track of our pasts and plans for the future in a likewise fashion. It is part of ritualizing life. It serves to prevent making life a random event. Having a place or book in your life that commemorates the things you achieved and initiated in your life is an important contribution to understand your life options and life goals.

There are several ways to understand the line relationships. One we have already discussed above. In addition, we give the following:

	From the ten wings	*Daoist description*
Line 6	Ancestral temple and temple of heaven	Will of heaven. In the body representing the body form
Line 5	Son of heaven, mediator	Imperial pivot, interpreting heaven and serving by example, in the body representing the heart
Line 4	Feudal dukes, descendants	Ministerial line, advising the king, executing orders of the emperor, servants of the empire, in the body representing the lungs

Line 3	Messengers of heaven, earth and water, communication	Aristocracy line from which generals and ministers are drawn to serve the empire. In the body representing the stomach and sanjiao[2]
Line 2	Senior official, manager	General line, or war king, the line of teaching and strategy. In the body representing the liver
Line 1	Senior servant/ servant manager	Soil line, or producing line, the first reaching to heaven. In the body representing the sea of water and grains

	From the dao of heaven earth and men	Home related order
Line 6	Yin	Elder
Line 5	Yang	Patriarch
Line 4	Benevolence	Wife
Line 3	Rigtheousness	Neighbour/guest
Line 2	Soft/gentle	Teens
Line 1	Hard/strong	Children/lastborns/newborns

From the Song dynasty onward descriptions of the 8 diagrams became the description of combined values of yin yang and wuxing studies.

---

[2] This is especially interesting in understanding sanjiao in the context of the body in Chinese medicine studies. Sanjiao is hotly disputed and few know how to hit the mark on what the sanjiao is for, mostly dividing the san jiao as three localities in stead as three interwoven functionalities of water, grain and qi. The fact that the third linje represents sanjiao may be perceived as not coincidental but as purposefull, since it is in the cusp between heaven and earth.

Part 2

The actual Yijing

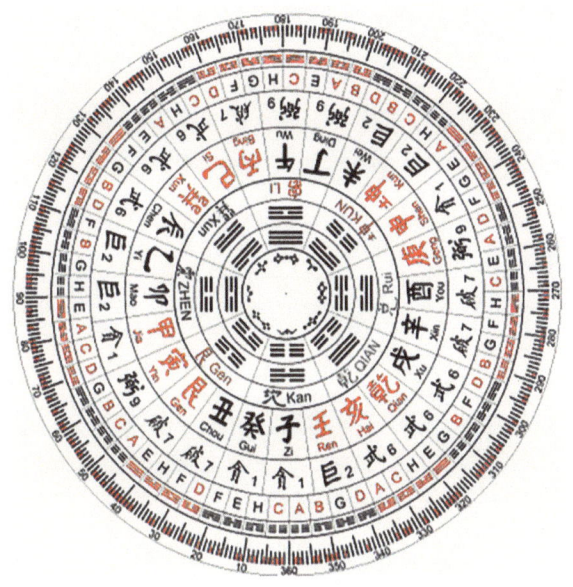

*From the Song dynasty onward descriptions of
the 8 diagrams became the description
of combined values of yin yang and wuxing studies,
but it also became the description
of the 360 degrees circumference of a circle,
matching the bagua with the 8 directions
more closely as sectors such as the 4 mountains
and 4 directions converging in the
center. This map is a modernized rendering
including the pinyin names. The first ring*

are the eight major star houses, then the preheaven
and post heaven diagams then the
stems and branches. I have no idea what the letters
mean as non classical addition, but
considering the colours they must be indicators
for kinds of good and bad luck. The
next rings are the mirrored yin and yang trigrams
through the vertical axis between
heaven and earth, north and south, and the
360 degree sectors of luck and bad luck.

How to cast a relevant hexagram

The text of the yijing is a set of statements representing 64 sets of six lines each called hexagrams (卦 guà). Each hexagram is a figure composed of six stacked horizontal lines (爻 yáo), starting counting from the bottom because all lines reach to heaven. Each line is either Yang (an unbroken, or solid line), or Yin (broken, an open line with a gap in the center). With six such lines stacked from bottom to top there are 26 or 64 possible combinations, and thus 64 hexagrams represented. The order of hexagrams suggests different forms of interlinked paired-ness, receding and increasing diversification and confusion etc.

The hexagram diagram is composed of two three-line arrangements called trigrams (卦 guà). Each trigram is a merging of two emblems. This means that the relationship of emblems to trigrams is similar as that of trigrams to hexagrams, most notably when we talk of the inner trigrams, where the core four lines of a hexagram are split and split again in trigrams from the top and the bottom to unfold the essential trend of the hexagram. The trigrams then every time share the core lines in a similar way as emblems share core lines when they form trigrams. This interlinked-ness shows there are often more options to come to an outcome.

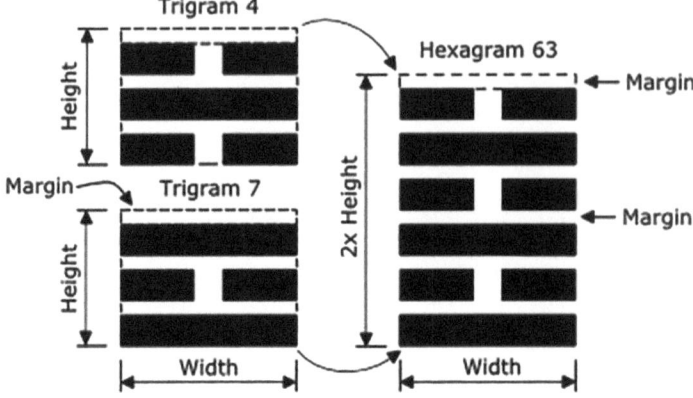

The traditional view is that hexagrams were originally not thought of, but a later development and resulted from combining two trigrams. However, in the earliest relevant archaeological evidence, groups of numerical symbols on many Western Zhou bronzes and a very few Shang oracle bones, such groups already usually appear in sets of six. A few have been found in sets of three numbers, but these are somewhat later. Numerical sets greatly predate the groups of broken and unbroken lines, leading modern scholars to doubt the mythical early attributions of the hexagram system, (Edward Shaugnessy 1993). Since Yijing graphs clearly belong to the oldest remnants of written language they also crossover the boundaries between pictograph and semiotics. The essential difference between pictograms and visual symbols is that pictograms are visually standardized and intended to be independent of their cultural context to transfer meaning. In addition, pictograms are scalable -- capable of being presented at a range of scales without loss of information. Symbols on the other hand are sharing cultural information. The yijing gua do not transfer information persé, but how information can be ordered. As such it stimulates understanding by association.

In fact, like any word or character -which is a pictograph, we can say that the 8 gua are a form of shorthand, placing knowledge in categories. As such they do convey information, but the information they convey is the information people naturally know, such as: what is a mountain, what is specific on mountain range, what is rain, what is the moon etc These 8 pictorial/symbolic categories further are placed in a circle of four harmonizing pairs, or placed in a flow of developing yin and yang. In all cases a twofold division of four is part of this graphic, forming a mandala of four pillars and four doors as is already extensively discussed in the discussion of the yin yang theory. As a shorthand, the graphs catalogues knowledge into similarities to 8 basic environmental iconographic presences such as the plains, mountains, clouds, rain, fire etc. the symbols can be placed in a variety of meaningful settings. One we can call vertical and one horizontal. The two directions reflect the plane in which we can see association based on the placement of ourselves in the center of existence, as the king of our own realm. Above is heaven and below is earth and the six other symbols move between them, such as the rising sun and moon, wind and clouds, mountains and thunder. In the horizontal order the sun is in the south and the cold in the north, thunder rumbles in the east and marshes are found in the west, between the northeast and the south west we find an earthly axis, separating and connecting the clear and the unclear radicalizing g the yin yang and incorporating the wuxing.

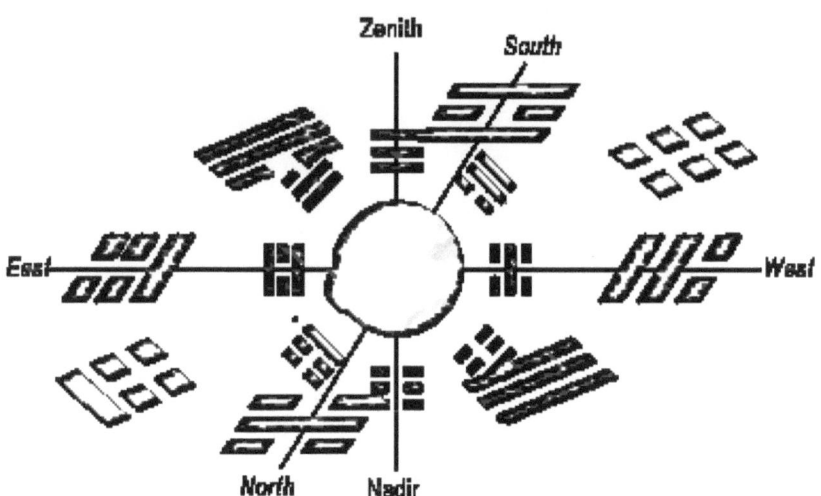

Then it should be reminded that yin is nothing more than a broken yang or two yang pressing onto each other. It means that the yijing shows the forms of yang and the formulation of yin through density of meeting yangs.

Then, a question should be properly analyzed. The answer should not be already suggested in the question. Yes/no answers also do not exist. Questions should provide a mapmaking answer, in the sense that answers are descriptive, associative. Learning to understand the nature of one's question makes most questions redundant. It shows also the difference between when asking the yijing for answers is useful and when not.

Opening yourself for an answer or inspiration is not required but can be helpful to develop sincerity. When one's mind is not focused and one's hart is not clear, for instance because you are emotional; or otherwise preoccupied, rushed or obsessed the answers are comparably fuzzy. The fault for unclear answers therefore is in the questioner, not in the yijing. A system is by nature infallible, even when it doesn't function properly. If it would be fallible it would not be a system. It is in the dedication of a user to use the system according to its rules if a system is useful or not. Hence western science is infallible, and so is Chinese pre-western science. Chinese cosmology sees reality as a system and Yijing is its expression. That is similar like Dao: if there is Dao, also is there it's Qi. "If no Dao also no qi". So when practicing taijiquan or qigong or yoga and people say they feel their qi, that means they are perfect, because perfection, the will of heaven and Dao arrive more or less simultaneously. Since most people are not perfect but they feel things it must follow that what they feel is not qi. The western concept of energy might apply, but qi certainly not. Similar a yang line or a yin line represent yinqi and yangqi and therefore the dao of yin and the dao of yang. Differentiation then always follows a preset pattern, starting with wuji or hundun, then yin and yang, then the four emblems and then the eight trigrams:

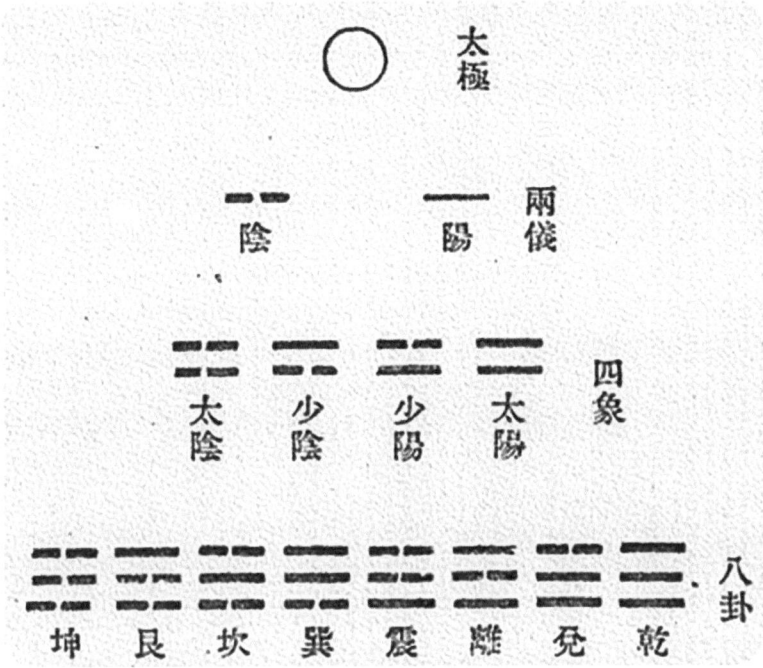

When a hexagram is cast using one of the traditional processes of divination with yijing, each yin and yang line will be indicated as either moving (that is, changing), or fixed (unchanging). Sometimes called old lines, a second hexagram is created by changing moving lines to their opposite. Each line of a hexagram determined with these methods is either stable ("young") or changing ("old"). These are referred to in the text by the numbers six through nine as follows:

- *Nine is old yang, an unbroken line (—ϑ—) changing into yin, a broken line (— —);*
- *Eight is young yin, a broken line (— —) without change;*
- *Seven is young yang, an unbroken line (———) without change;*
- *Six is old yin, a broken line (—X—) changing into yang, an unbroken line (———).*

The oldest method for casting the hexagrams, the yarrow stalk method, was gradually replaced during the Han Dynasty by the three coins method and the yarrow stalk method was lost. With the coin method, the probability of yin or yang is equal while with the recreated yarrow stalk method of Zhu Xi (1130–1200), the probability of old yang is three times greater than old yin. In old times this higher probability was called the natural prevalence of the will of heaven.

Once a hexagram is determined, each line has been determined as either changing (old) or unchanging (young). Old yin is seen as more powerful than young yin, and old yang is more powerful than young yang. Any line in a hexagram that is old ("changing") adds additional meaning to that hexagram.

Daoism holds that strong yin will eventually turn to yang (and vice versa), so a new hexagram is formed by transposing each changing yin line with a yang line, and vice versa. Thus, further insight into the process of change is gained by reading the text of this new hexagram and studying it as the result of the current change.

How the coins are tossed

1) use three coins with distinct "head" and "tail" sides
2) for each of the six lines of the hexagram, beginning with the first (bottom) line and ending with the sixth (top) line
3) toss all three coins, assign the value 3 to each "head" result, and 2 to each "tail" result,
4) write down the resulting line
5) total all the coin values, the total will be six, seven, eight or nine
6) determine the current line of the hexagram from this number: 6 = old yin, 7 = young yang, 8 = young yin, 9 = old yang.
7) once six lines have been determined, the hexagram is formed
8) To find which number belongs to your hexagram you can find in the graph below the combinations of the trigrams. Combine the upper and the lower trigram in the legenda.

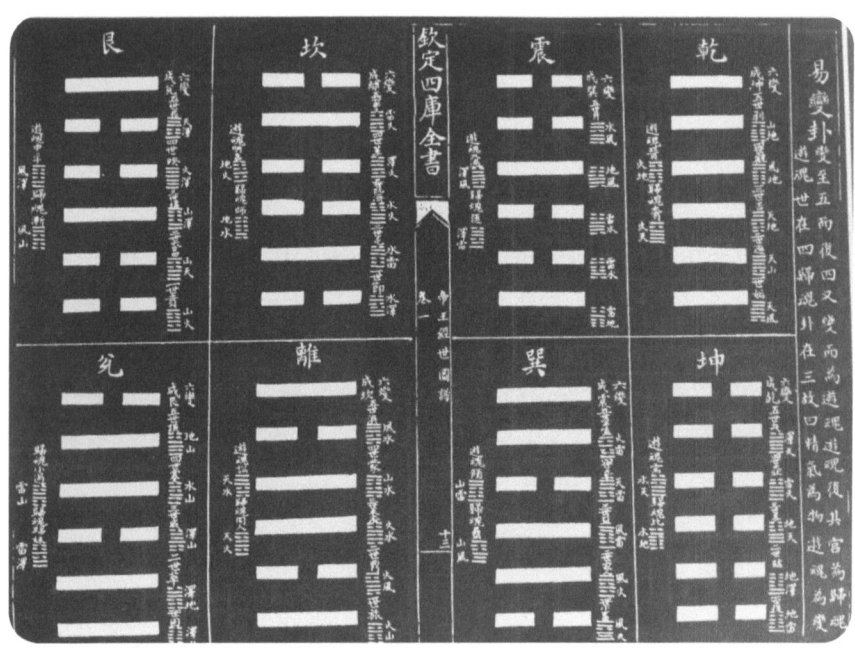

Traditionele associatie hexagramlijnen met bijbehorende hexagram. Voor verklaring betekenis lijn als voorbeeld hoe deze yijing ook opgezet is.

How to read the diagrams in the book

A s you might have noticed If you leaved forward, the diagrams in the book seem a bit complicated. Every hexagram is being put in a table and each table has 7 lines and 6 collumns. It takes a bit of adjustment, but the diagrams are this way self clarifying. You can immediately see all the natural predispositions of every line inn relationship to yinyang, wuxing, textual meaning and associated heaxagram. What it doesn't mention is from the inner wuxing association of the hexagrams what hexagram belongs there, but that is easy to find. In the explanation of the 4 bigrams we have also concluded that the middle two lines are the root of the hexagram, and it belongs to the human realm and how we relate to heaven and earth. The hexagrams are themselved piled up from the bottom upwards. The first line is the upcoming influencer and the last line is the outgoing adviser.

The top line point to the comparative texts of the line and the corresponding hexagram. In the translation I took attention to the need of the lines and the hexagram meanings to correspond in some way. Because many characters have multiple meanings when transferred to the western cultural languages it was a search for corresponding meanings. Ofcourse a character in Chinese just means what it means. You cannot take the various options in English as an explanation for variation in meaning in Chinese. But through cultural drift meanings in general change due to variation in use. How that works is easy to explain: When you spoke of love when 4 years old, that was not the same as when 18, 30 or 50 years of age. Drift of meaning already occurs during your life. Meanings are fluid and not fixed, and because your understanding grows meaning individually changes. In cultures likewise meanings can change due to the changes in the culture, maturation, aging.

It also means that a translation of the yijing requires to stay close to its own intent and that means choosing for not translating, as my daoist teachers suggested or doing a cultural descriptive translation. You should neve r translate towards concepts of the receiving culture. It provides false comparison. Like with the Wilhelm translation, or the legge translation, or all the other ones that are based on them.

People often think thst translation as the translation of words is literal. But far from it. Language is not a mental phenomenon, but one of habitual use of reference between members of a cultural group. Change the language and you change the culture. Like the Japanese, the Korean and the Chinese have done in various ways, also the Taiwanese. We have changed our culture significantly in the centuries since Kant's 'kritik der Reinen vernumft'.

I happened to meet about 2009 with Li Zhangxi, by accident. He gave me his book 'relevance and adjustability'. It is about the translation process. He is part of a group that likes to translate cultural values, and unlike Charles Leblanc's Huinanzi he doesnot wish to put his text full of footnotes. And that is a dilemma. He was on his way to a conference about this issue.

He follows translation psychologists as Serber, Wildon and Verschuren, from whom he takes the title of his book. A core idea is that the translator stands at a crossing between cultures nand predigests texts on the basis of relevance and in what way meanings should be adjusted to suit te reader or to maintain loyalty to the original giving culture. Ofcourse, the original Yijing culture doesn't exist anymore. We only know the yijing from its characters, its comments, and its edits over time to adapt to newer iterations of the Chinese culture. Cultural drift.

You understand the dilemma. The issue is that line texts and hexagram texts are holisticly bound in the idea that the yijing as a moral map has to help find the way to heaven back. This idea became more emphasized in later time, but Even Confucius in his 'ten wings' commentaries was already aware of the cosmological origins and intentions of the book. Then seeing it in the light of the myth of Fuxi, offering the 8 diagrams to teach people language and meaning, and king Wen in writing the texts, and his son adding the texts of the lines, as a filial son not allowed to betray the work of his father by deviating meaning. The yijing would not have been accepted with internal errors. This is ofcourse not the historical sequence of events, you might say, but nonetheless, the myths of the yijing are the truth aspect directionality of the yijing, offering clues as the how and why of the yijing and its use.

So in the second column you find the yijing text of the line. They are piled from the bottom to the top, representing the diagrams. The third column offers the related heaxagrammic diagramsn and their meaning of origin. The piled up texts of the hexagrams reflext the 6 lines and their functions in the six lines, such as start, master line, general line etc.

The next 3 collumns show the interactions of the internal and external diagrams. Each line has 1 or more con nec tions with the wuxing value of each hexagram. It shows the complexity of a line value. You see line 3 of hexagram three has three values, one yin wood, one yin earth and one yang earth. This means the line is overly yin but yang controls it or moves it. It is also overly earth, so the wood is sparse on the earth. A single seedling. The text goes:

> Approaching the deer[3] without gamekeeper,
> entering the middle of the forest.
> In giving alms[4] the gentleman can almost not be compared with.
> Distress leaves.

It means that earth receptivity is helping the seedling.

In this way the diagrams help you to recognize the ultimate values of the line as either yinyang and wuxing, that the peripheral lines as foundational

---

[3] The deer is a symbol of a creature with strong sexual potency that can nourish one's yang very deeply but it can also be dangerous, that is why use of a gamekeeper/experienced person is adviced

[4] Generosity is the core of a true person

or admonishing are one of each, and the center are three values. Below in the diagram you find the yin yang wuxing values from heaxagram 3 from top to bottom.

WUXING

6		
5	5	
4	4	4
3	3	3
2		2
1		
Outer upper and lower diagram	Upper inner diagram	Lower inner diagram

YINYANG

6	Yin broken	
5	Yang whole	
4	Yin broken	
3	Yin broken	
2	Yin broken	
1	yang whole	

Bagua nine houses Legenda:

Yin wood	Yinyang fire	Yang earth
Yang wood		Yin metal
Yin earth	Yinyang water	Yang metal

Bagua colour legenda

Wuxing	Trigrams	Character	name	Yinyang	Colour
metal	☰	乾	qián	yang	white
metal	☱	兌	duì	yin	grey
fire	☲	離	lí	yang	red
wood	☳	巽	zhèn	yang	green
wood	☴	坎	xùn	yin	light-green
water	☵	艮	kǎn	yin	blue
earth	☶	坤	gèn	yin	yellow
earth	☷		kūn	yang	gold

In the text the ordering of the wuxing I have given:

Outer: ...under.... / layered....
Inner: ...in....

The outer diagrams represent a piling of factors, while the inner diagrams represent an intertwinement of factors. The earlier mentioned hexagram number 3 states:

> **3 Zhun: birththrows[5]**
>
> Smooth origin, beneficial determination
> Do not use! Have a place to go to
> Favourable to establish an official
>
> Outer: Thunder under rain
> Inner: mountain on earth

It does not discuss yin or yang in the inner or outer wuxing. The yin and yang belong to the gua, not to the xing. In case offering the yinyang wuxing relationship it would be

---

[5] Birthtrows because of the growing influence of heaven because of one's return to heaven. Similar like how in excerice pain and difficulty are signs of what one redevelops in oneself after having it lost. One first has to learn to be receptive like the earth is before one can recognize the will of heaven and use it as a guiding light

Outer: water in yang wood
Inner: yin earth in yang earth

When we speak of water or fire we cannot really speak of yin or yang. Fire in respect to water seems yang, but to be honest the strength of water can also be tremendous and as such also can it be yang. Fire and water are mystical xing because they can both be yin and yang, depending on circumstances. If there were separate yin and yang fire/water, there would have been two more gua and it would have been 10gua instead of 8gua, which is a whole different set of esthetics. The symmetry would be perfect, but the complexity of interaction would become unatractice because it would exclude a certain randomness. It would become unnatural.

In the following diagram map you can relate the top and bottom bagua or the inner trigrams to each other, their opposites etc, and find the number of the hexagram that the combination belongs to.

Upper trigram >>	Ch'ien	Chen	K'an	Kên	K'un	Sun	Li	Tui
Ch'ien	1	34	5	26	11	9	14	43
Chen	25	51	3	27	24	42	21	17
K'an	6	40	29	4	7	59	64	47
Kên	33	62	39	52	15	53	56	31
K'un	12	16	8	23	2	20	35	45
Sun	44	32	48	18	46	57	50	28
Li	13	55	63	22	36	37	30	49
Tui	10	54	60	41	19	61	38	58

Translation and interpretation

Note:

The first part of the Yijing text has been annotated to give an impression of the many layers of meaning. In time this will be completed and given further extrapolated on.

1 Qian: sky

Smooth origin,
Favourable determination

Outer: Layered sky
Inner: sky in sky

6 branches comparison:

	Zhou linetext[6]	Wen'gua text			
Line 6 **Advice** **Mystery**	Dragon[7] in the gully[8], there will be trouble	**43 Quai/Jue: decide, determine, to cleanse, open out** Display a capture at the kings court[9] There be threatening reports from the town A violent aproach is unfavourable[10] Favourable to have roots in the past[11]			

---

[6] The linetext are addded to the gua as a textual nuance to the meaning that the gua has. The textual nuance is based on analysis of the gua text in whcioh the dague would change if it moved. Moved would mean yin turns in yang or yang turns into yin.

[7] Dragons are compared with cloud forces, cloud qi, the subtle qi of heaven and dao manifest in clouds en enbula's, moving a bout and affecting nourishment. They are also the unexpected aspects of/ movements in the sky

[8] Yin presses on heaven like clouds in the sky forming bad weather

[9] The kings court reflect's heaven. In the yijing 1gua stands at the bright center of all the other gua. All the other gua either move towards or away from 1gua. In our body the heart is the court and all our life's content moves towards or away from our heart. In the kingdom all look for the court or look away from it in their actions

[10] Violence means disruption of heaven's harmony. 1gua is heaven's harmony reflected in the graphic display of the gua. The text shows the possible disharmonies and thus which different other gua can arise as situations away from the 1 gua. This movement is the foundation of the yi

[11] No actions stand on themselves. If one acts rooted in the past one acts with the support of the past

Line 5 *King* *Sun*	Dragon flies in the sky, favourable to see a big master[12]	**14 Da you: great having** Grand having greatly Behave accordingly			
Line 4 *Minster* *(yin)* *General* *(yang)*	Some leap in the deep, no misfortune	**9 xiao chu: small livestock**[13] Small livestoch behaves like dense clouds No rain from the western outskirts[14] Retrieve one's dao, what misfortune is this? Auspicious.			
Line 3 *Messenger* *Legal* *court* *Mediator* *Conflict*	The noble[15] ends the day vigourous, is wary-like at night as if under thread, no misfortune	**10 Lu: shoe, footstep, honour, carry out, to walk on** Honouring the tigers[16] tail It does not bite the cultivated Behave accordingly			

---

[12] Big master is a person of greater cultivation, one who has reached a status of perfection in being human and humane. It is also a reference to the 6th line

[13] Small livestock are heard animals that might be stubborn at times but allows itself to be lead or need leadership

[14] Place of offering

[15] Behavioural guidance for proper noble behavior, always on guard and not allowing tiredness to force into rest or distraction on wht is one's role in life/society

[16] The tiger is an animal of fierce strength but highly grumpy and unpredictable. It needs to be treated as high official or a king to avoid backlash

Line 2 *General* *Popular* *leader*	Dragon is seen in the field[17], favourable to see a big master	**13 Tong Ren: similar cultivated (persons)**[18] Gather cultivated ones in the open country Behave accordingly Favourable to wade accros the big river Favourable determination for the gentleman			
Line 1 *Rising* *force*	Do not use a submerged dragon[19]	**44 Gou: to meet, to encounter, female ruler, intercourse** *Strong woman* Has no use to marry a women[20]			
All lines *change in* *opposition*	Auspicious to see a group of dragons with no head[21]	**2 Kun: middle earth.** Smooth origin. A mare is determined as noble. Have a place to go; first lose your way, get a host later. West is favourable. Get a friend in south. Lose one in north. Auspicious determination for security matters.			

---

17   Earth is a reflection and executer of the will of heaven and field in chinese sounds similar to heaven and thus is a holy placy where things can happen
18   Belonging to the same social group, sharing likewise level of understanding of things
19   A submerged dragon has its own plan
20   The meeting of yin anchoring the movement of yang. If a woman in ancient times dared to do that on her own volition (bottom line) then she would have to know she is backed up by mightier forces than you.
21   A yang line is a dragon. A yin line is two dragons but without a head, so the yang of yin doesn't know where to go to. Yin then is an unguided movement or conflicting yang movements, describiong location and density

2 Kun: middle earth

Smooth origin
A mare[22] is determined as noble
Have a place to go; first lose your way, get a host later
West[23] is favourable.
Get a friend in south[24]. Lose one in north[25].
Auspicious determination for security[26] matters.

Outer: Earth piled on earth
Inner: earth in earth

6 branches comparison:

	Zhoulinetext	*Wen'guatext*			
Line 6	Dragons battle in the open country, Blood is dark and bright yellow.	**23 Bo: foretelling by elimination, stripping away, flaying** Not favourable to have roots in the past[27]			

---

22   Chinese cultures often praised the horse for its immaculate strength but strength that could be harnessed by a good rider. Qi and blood in the body are compared with it. The blood is the horse, and the qi is the rider that knows where to go. The rider is then the stallion replacement. One's behaviour should be yin in comparison to heaven.
23   West is yin metal, where the sun sets and the po goes with the earth spirits of the body after death
24   The bright, fire
25   The dark (xuan, mystery), water
26   Security comes from following the yang of heaven and allowing dao to play itself out
27   If you bind the ends together you can see that the past here is not in support, it is better to try something new. All lines either are supported or conflicted by the past.

Line 5	Yellow skirt[28]. Primary auspiciousness	**8 Bi: emulate, copy, model after** Original auspiciousness Manipulate the (millifoil) stalks (oracle)[29] Behave accordingly grand for a long-term determination. No misfortune. Not a peacefull method-state (tranquility meditation) Ominous for the man/ husband that comes late.			
Line 4	Bind the pouch Without misfortune and without honor	**16 Yu: giving an elephant[30] away, pleased** Favourablre to establish a high official Mobilize the army			
Line 3	Hold a jade talisman in the mouth[31], it can be determined. Some follow the king in service Have an ending without completion.	**15 Qian: modesty (speech in contention, the sound of modesty)** Behave accordingly The gentleman has an end (conclusion)			

---

28   Act out the way of earth symbolically/ceremonially
29   Divine the will of heaven so that you can follow it
30   The elephant was a symbol of greatness and expenses. Giving things away is seen as a way to enrich yourself
31   Act of confession to the high god of heaven by confessing sins while bounded and with some piece of jade on the tongue to hinder one's clarity of speech. The sound of confession is the sound of modesty

Line 2	Straight square. Big, not doubled. Nothing unfavourable	**7 Shi: teacher, master, skilled one, army**[32] Determination for the greatly cultivated one is auspicious. No misfortune.			
Line 1	Stepping on frost: solid ice arrives[33]	**24 Fu: turn around, answer, recover/resume, revenge, again**[34] Going out, coming in; behave accordingly (and there'll be) no illness Friend comes, no misfortune Oppose resuming of the Dao and after seven suns comes the answer Favourable to have roots in the past			
All lines change in opposition	benificial and perpetual clarity[35]	**1 Qian: sky.** Smooth origin, Favourable determination			

---

[32] The teacher is the one that helps one in one's cultivation and is thus the greatest one to you after heaven itself, that is why the master is seen as heaven in one's life, different from the kind

[33] The cycle if yin and yang transforming or becoming each other shows that everything is foreshadowed by portents and thet everhything is a protent of what comes. By observing reality as it happens one will likewiuse as with frost and ice gradually develop the clarity of perception to recognize dao at work after a long time or ripening.

[34] Retracing one's origin is the movement of dao

[35] Kun is the turbid and the opposite of the turbid is the clear, so heaven and earth as the two extremes are represented by the dust under our feet and the wideness of heaven. But as such they are not opposties but intertwined in an endless cycle of giving and giving. Heaven gives its clarity and earth receives it. Earth uses the clarity and gives the creatures that bent to the willof heaven and grow to reunite with it.

3 Zhun: birththrows[36]

Smooth origin, benificial determination
Do not use! Have a place to go to
Favourable to establish an official

Outer: Thunder under rain
Inner: mountain on earth

6 branches comparison:

	Zhoulinetext	*Wen'guatext*			
Line 6	Drive horses as if arrayed Weep as if blood streams[37]	**42 Yi; increasing, overflow (of liquid), benefit** Favourable to have roots in the past Favourable to cross the big plain/river[38]			

---

[36] Birthtrows because of the growing influence of heaven because of one's return to heaven. Similar like how in excerice pain and difficulty are signs of what one redevelops in oneself after having it lost. One first has to learn to be receptive like the earth is before one can recognize the will of heaven and use it as a guiding light

[37] Conflict is at the root of change, but it not something to rejoice about. Think forward about what you go achieve with your actions does it harmonize with the past?

[38] Rivers and plains both are areas where the landscape separates two areas, so if one crosses the river/plain, one moves from one reality to another

Line 5	Hoarding fat[39] Auspicious to determine the small Ominous to determine the big	*24* **Fu: turn around, answer, recover/resume, revenge, again** Going out, coming in; behave accordingly (and there'll be) no illness Friend comes, no misfortune Oppose resuming of the Dao and after seven suns comes the answer Favourable to have roots in the past			
Line 4	Drive horses as if arrayed Seek the wife's kin, matching[40] goes auspicious. Nothing unfavourable	*17* **Sui: follow, comply** Primary smoothness (succes) Enjoy the favourable determination No fault (blame)			
Line 3	Approaching the deer[41] without gamekeeper, entering the middle of the forrest. In giving alms[42] the gentleman can almost not be compared with. Distress leaves.	**63 Ji Ji: already/now that cross a river/be of help** **Smooth, little favourable determination Auspicious at the beginning, disorder at the end**			

---

[39] Fat is associated with good health/wealth

[40] One cannot match with a person or organization without having permission of its context/background

[41] The deer is a symbol of a creature with strong sexual potency that can nourish one's yang very deeply but it can also be dangerous, that is why use of a gamekeeper/experienced person is adviced

[42] Generosity is the core of a true peson

Line 2	As if bundled together, as if turning around, as if driving the horses around arrayed. They are not bandits, they are family of the wife reaching agreement over their daughter[43]. The determination is no pregnancy for ten years, then pregnancy	**60 Jie: joint, node, knot** **Smooth** **Bitter node (as in bamboo)** [44] **Cannot be determined** **Get its tail wet** **Distress**	🟩		🟨
Line 1	A huge rock, a birch tree Favourable to abide with for divination Favourable to appoint a marquis	*8* **Bi: emulate, copy, model after** Original auspiciousness Manipulate the (millifoil) stalks (oracle) Behave accordingly grand for a long-term determination. No misfortune. Not a peacefull method-state (tranquility meditation) Ominous for the man/ husband that comes late.	🟩		

---

43 If you learn to differentiate the real behind the wind that blows up dust to make it look like mountians, things are not so threatening. Being defenisve and agressive doesn't work.

44 Bamboo is sign of pliancy due to its amazing node structure and elegant leaves. It is the behaviour of a gentleman, to be pliant and never break and never be uprooted

All lines change in opposition		**50 Ding: sacrificial vessel (Tripod)**[45] Primary auspiciousness Smooth			

4 Meng: blindfolded[46]

Smooth: we do not seek the dodder[47], the dodder seeks us first.
Manipulate the stalks and it will tell twice.
The third time is an insult.

Outer: River under mountain
Inner: heaven in wood

6 branches comparison:

	Zhoulinetext	*Wen'guatext*			
Line 6	Beating dodder Not favourable to become a bandit Favourable to fend off bandits	**7 Shi: teacher, master, skilled one, army** Determination for the greatly cultivated one is auspicious. No misfortune.			

---

45   The opposite of birth is to alchemically generate it (life) in a cooking vessel: exactly what people practice in neidan

46   Blindfolded means not knowing where to go to and having to learn read signs

47   Viral creeper plant. Dodder provides stalks that are supposed to contain much earthqi and thus can represent best the will of heaven which earth follwos in its generation of living creatures

Line 5	Auspicious dodder	**59 Huan: to melt, vanish** Smooth The artificial king[48] has a temple Favorable to wade across the great river Favourable determination			
Line 4	Pounding the dodder. Distress.	**64 Wei Ji: have not / did not cross a river / be of help** Smooth Small fox[49] at the point of crossing the streamgets his tail wet Not at all favourable			
Line 3	Do not take a girl for wife See metal (golden) husband without a body[50] Without favour.	*18* **Gu: (legendary) venomenous insect**[51] Primary smoothness Go through the big plains before Jia (yang wood heavenly stem) sun and after jia sun/period[52] (jia sun was considered unlucky)			

---

[48] By acting as a king one gradually gains nobility and understanding of the will of heaven

[49] Foxes were perceived as seductive fairies, often showing themselves as beautiful women who seduced travelers or came to live in temples and households posing as immortals. Older fox fairies actually often became enlightened guiodes for people

[50] An immature person only sees one's ideas about that person, not the person itself. That behaviour is likened to the fickleness of girls

[51] used in black magic. Here it refers to the fickleness of an immature girl given the status of wife

[52] Time is divided on the basis of recurrence of yin, yang and the wuxing. The yijing itself is a reflection of that: four heavenly directions 1,2, 29,30 (or 63/64) and sixty recurring mixes of 10 heavenly stems and 12 earthly branches, each combining wuxing and yin yang stages reconbining in beneficial periods and not so beneficial periods

Line 2	Carry the dodder Auspicious to bring in a wife Auspicious: a son can make a clan.	**23 Bo: foretelling by elimination, stripping away, flaying** Not favourable to have roots in the past			
Line 1	Dislodge the dodder Favourable to use punishment Use a master to remove the leg's shackles Restraint makes distress go.	**41 Sun: decrease, empty the vessel (of libation liquid)** Have a very auspicious capture No misfortune can be determened Favourable to have roots in the past What to use? Two tureens[53] can be used for the offering			
All lines change in opposition		**49 Ge: leather, hide, transform, change[54]** Capture great smoothness at sacrificial day Favourable determination Troubles go away			

---

53   A particular type of vase
54   Because skin is worked at it becomes leather, thus being one of the yijing metaphors of change. That is the opposite of being blindfolded. Blindfolded means not knowing where you go to. In that sense blindfolded follows on 3 birththrows

5 Xü: needing, wanting

Have a glorious capture and act accordingly
The determination is auspicious
It is favourable to wade across the big river

Outer: The river of heaven
Inner: fire in metal

6 branches comparison:

	Zh oulinetext	*Wen'guatext*			
Line 6	There is no urge to enter the cave[55]. There will be guests: three persons[56] come Respect them and it ends auspicious	**9 xiao chu: small livestock** Small livestock behaves like dense clouds No rain from the western outskirts Retrieve one's dao, what misfortune is this? Auspicious.			
Line 5	Wanting in drinks and food Auspicious determination[57].	**11 Tai: safe, peacefull, tranquil, extreme, most** The small goes, the big comes Auspicious, behave accordingly			

---

[55] Caves are centers of mystery. In Daoism caves are seen as entrances to paradises. From ancient times onward people did seek the darkness of caves to emulate the womb and to find understanding about the nature and purpose of reality. In neidan they speak of inner cavities as location of inner treasure.

[56] Morality, affinity and clarity

[57] Auspicious because one waits without urgent needs

Line 4	Wanting in blood[58] Come out from the hole/cave.	**43 Quai/Jue: decide, determine, to cleanse, open out** Display a capture at the king's court There be threatening reports from the town A violent aproach is unfavourable Favourable to have roots in the past			
Line 3	Wanting in mud[59] This brings on the arrival of bandits	**60 Jie: joint, node, knot** Smooth Bitter node (as in bamboo) Cannot be determined Get its tail[60] wet Distress			
Line 2	Wanting at small grit Have a talk It ends auspicious.	**63 Ji Ji: already/now that cross a river/be of help** Smooth, little favourable determination Auspicious at the beginning, disorder at the end			

[58] Waiting in conflict, creating oneself a dangerous situation, don't firce yourself
[59] Mud is metaphor for what drags one back and holds one immobile or stationary, that makes one attractive to be used, such as bamboo
[60] Reference to the fox fairy in 63/64 gua

Line 1	Wanting at the suburban altar. The use is for a long time favourable[61]. No misfortune	48 Jing: (a) well Change a town but not change a well No loss no gain Go, come in perfect order Nearly reaches but not drawing water The well damages the earthen Jug Ominous			
All lines change in opposition		35 Jin: to enter, advance, promote[62] Lord of Kang (Health) uses giving of many (mated numbers) horses[63] During light of day three joinings			

6 Song: arguing, lawsuit[64]

Have a capture and they will be zhi-ti frightened
Middle stage auspicious, end ominous
Favourable to see the big cultivated one
Not favourable to wade a big river.

Outer: Rain under the sky
Inner: rain in fire

---

[61] A heavenly omen for the king at a suburban altar is compared to a well, which is very important for any community. It will not stop having a good affect if properly respected and taken care off

[62] The opposite of wanting and waiting is getting promoted and receiving blessings

[63] Mated horses are a gift in a gift, because they can breed and make more horses

[64] Reasoning always follows the format of an argument. So the skill of adressing issues is a very important one. If one is not skillful in arguing one will lose an argument easily and resort to more emotional approaches, or false arguments to force a deal. A true person always considers the fairness of a situation in arguing, if need be even at his/her own expense.

6 branches comparison:

	Zhoulinetext	*Wen'guatext*			
Line 6	Some bestow him a leather belt[65]. At the end of the morning it is taken away three times	**47 Kun: stranded, surrounded, tired, pinned down, bothered** Smooth determination for a greatly cultivated one Auspicious, no misfortune There'll be unreliable talk			
Line 5	Original argument[66] Auspicious	**64 Wei Ji: have not / did not cross a river / be of help** Smooth Small fox at the point of crossing the streamgets his tail wet Not at all favourable			
Line 4	No arguing Return as an aproach to charge a change for the worse[67] [68]Auspicious determination for security	**59 Huan: to melt, vanish** Smooth The artificial king has a temple Favorable to wade across the great river Favourable determination			

---

[65] A leather belt is a sign of office

[66] The argument is clear and cannot be refuted. The counter argument cannot find a foothold

[67] Although you try to stay out of the argument, you will understand that without your support the situation will only get worse. Although you have no leadership position here it will be good to act as if you have.

[68] The purpose of arguing is to generate clarity, so its opposite is the darkening of the light where clarity and brightness are concealed

Line 3	Eating something old. A threatening determination that is in fact auspicious[69]. Some follow the kings service No completion	**44 Gou: to meet, to encounter, female ruler, intercourse** Strong woman Has no use/need to marry a women			
Line 2	No arguing. Return to make 300 towndwellers flee through their doors[70]. No calamity.	**12 Pi: negative/not mouth** Bad his/her unperson, not favourable for the gentleman Determination: big goes, small comes			
Line 1	Do not prolong that which serves the small[71] Have a talk to make it end auspicious.	**10 Lu: shoe, footstep, honour, carry out, to walk on** Honouring the tigers tail It does not bite the cultivated Behave accordingly			
All lines change in opposition		**36 Ming yi: safe/ darkening of brightness/ brilliance** Favourable in a hardship determination			

---

[69] Old things have ripened and collected qi in itself due to being used long time with purpose.
[70] Door is a reference to mountain diagram, which also can be seen as a door. Doors here are the two mountains of hexagram 12.
[71] The small is that what doesnot serve heaven or dao or return to the harmony of 1 gua

7 Shi: teacher, master, skilled one, army[72]

Determination for the greatly cultivated one is auspicious.
No misfortune.

Outer: Rain under earth
Inner: heaven in wood

6 branches comparison:

	Zhoulinetext	*Wen'guatext*			
Line 6	The big ruler has a charge Establishes a state Receives a feudal house[73]. No use for one of little cultivation[74]	**4 Meng: blindfolded** Smooth: we do not seek the dodder, the dodder seeks us first. Manipulate the stalks and it will tell twice. The third time is an insult.			
Line 5	Have game in the hunt. Favourable to seize prisoners for questioning No misfortune. The elder son commands the army, the younger carts corpses Ominous determination.	**29 (Xi) kan: (review / be used to) bank, ridge** Have a prisoner safeguard the heart Smooth Travel has esteem			

---

[72] The 7 gua teacher is the diagram of self empowerment of the people. If everyone is a master (greatly cultivated one) everyone will know what to do to make the world or keep the world harmonious
[73] Becomes a dynasty
[74] Check yourself if you are of big or little cultivation before you enter an adventure

Line 4	Army. Camps to the left[75]. No misfortune	**40 Jie: divide, seperate, untie, undo, explain, solve, comprehend, relieve oneself** Favourable: southwest No place to go to therefore turning back, auspicious Have a place to go to since long, auspicious
Line 3	Army. Some cart corpses. Ominous.[76]	**46 Sheng: ascending, going upwards** Primary smoothness Visit the greatly cultivated one (priest) Don't worry Attacking the south is auspicious
Line 2	Enter the army in the middle. Auspicious, no misfortune. The king three times bestows a charge	**2 Kun: middle earth** Smooth origin A mare is determined as noble Have a place to go; first lose your way, get a host later West is favourable. Get a friend in south. Lose one in north. Auspicious determination for security matters.

---

[75] The left is the yang side. For the army that is the agressors side. An army should –like the liver- be on the right- and just be busy with peaceful things. In this case it means the army takes control

[76] Seek advice because things do not go as planned, but things are not lost yet

Line 1	The army marches using pitchpipes. Not good. Ominous.	**19 Lin: face, overlook, befall, arrive, on the point of** Grand smoothness Favourable determination that extends to the eight moon Have an act of violence			
All lines change in opposition		**13 Tong Ren: similar cultivated (persons)**[77] Gather cultivated ones in the open country Behave accordingly Favourable to wade accros the big river Favourable determination for the gentleman			

8 Bi: emulate, copy, model after

Original auspiciousness
Manipulate the (millifoil) stalks (oracle)
Behave accordingly grand for a long-term determination.
No misfortune.
Not a peacefull method-state (tranquility meditation)
Ominous for the man/husband that comes late.

Outer: Earth under rain
Inner: earth in heaven

---

[77] A master is a group of one, the opposite is the grouping of people with similar backgrounds

6 branches comparison:

	Zhoulinetext	Wen'guatext			
Line 6	Emulating them without head[78] Ominous	**20 guan: conception of the nature of things, observe, view, (monestary)** Washing but no offering Have faith and sincerety captured			
Line 5	Show emulation. The king uses three drive horses to lose game ahead. City people are not frightened. Auspicious.[79]	**2 Kun: middle earth** Smooth origin A mare is determined as noble Have a place to go; first lose your way, get a host later West is favourable. Get a friend in south. Lose one in north. Auspicious determination for security matters.			

---

[78] See also 1 gua, without head means also without consideration of consequences
[79] Leadership shows itself in allowing escape/choice though which leaders are followed or refused withour fear.

Line 4	Emulate them who are outside Auspicious determination.	**45 Cui: to gather together** Smooth The king goes into his temple Favourable to visit the greatly cultivated one (priest) Smooth and favourable determination Auspicious to use large sacrificial animal Favourable to have roots in the past			
Line 3	Emulate the uncultivated[80].	**39 Jian: lame, trouble** Favourable: the southwest (kun) Not favourable: the northeast (gen) Favourable to be exposed to a considerably (large) cultivated one Auspicious determination			
Line 2	Emulate them who are inside. Auspicious determination	**29 (Xi) kan: (Review / be used to) bank, ridge** Have a prisoner safeguard the heart[81] Smooth Travel has esteem			

---

80 The uncultivated are the one's who make errors without understanding why they are errors.
81 This saying refers to the court that is being kept safe by means of a prisoner/hostage. In reality that could mean by means of a false argument or other means that are not appropriate

Line 1	Have a capture, emulate them. No misfortune, there will be a capture. Fill the earthen vessel[82] Comes the end; there will be a disaster[83]. Auspicious.	3 Zhun: birththrows Smooth origin, benificial determination Do not use! Have a place to go to Favourable to establish an official			
All lines change in opposition		35 Jin: to enter, advance, promote Lord of Kang (Health) uses giving of many (mated numbers) horses During light of day three joining			

9 xiao chu: small livestock

Small livestock behaves like dense clouds[84]
No rain from the western outskirts
Retrieve one's dao, what misfortune is this?[85]
Auspicious.

Outer: Sky under wind
Inner: fire in metal

---

[82] Since this is a bottom line it must refer to an earthen pit filled with water, and this line is its bottom. It could refer to the bottom of a womb.
[83] Indicates the birthing process, which is both risky and painful, but also a happy event.
[84] Small lifestoch shows herd mentality and thus clits together, much like dense clouds. As a result the individual cannot be separated from the group
[85] Going back to the natural order of things

6 branches comparison:

	Zhoulinetext	*Wen'guatext*			
Line 6	Already rain, already stopped still[86]. The matron gets to plant. Threatening determination: Moon is almost full. Attack is ominous for the cultivated	**5 Xü: needing, wanting** Have a glorious capture and act accordingly The determination is auspicious It is favourable to wade across the big river			
Line 5	Have capture as if tied together. Rich thanks to a neighbor	**26 Da Chu: large livestock** Beneficial determination Auspicious to not eat with your clan Favourable to cross the wide plain (swomp gua can also mean plain, there is no xiaogua refereing to water)			
Line 4	Have a capture. Remove blood (substance). Go out watchfull. No misfortune	**1 Qian: sky** Smooth origin, Favourable determination			

---

[86] Things already worked themselves out

Line 3	Spokes come of from the carriage Husband and wife reverse their eyes[87]	**61 Zhong Fu: center/ middle/attained/inner faith, inner sincerity** Young pig, fish: auspicious Favourable to cross the great plain Favourable determination			
Line 2	Lead to return. Auspicious[88]	**37 Jia ren: domestication, cultivated family/clan person, cultivated professional person** Favourable feminine determination			
Line 1	Ones own dao returning. What auspicious misfortune is this?[89]	**57 Xun (Zhuan): calculation** Little smooth Favourable to have roots in the past. Favourable to see the largely cultivated one			
All lines change in opposition		**16 Yu: giving an elephant away, pleased** Favourablre to establish a high official Mobilize the army			

---

[87] It seems that the situation here is based on misplaced trust, or maybe a loss of trust, while the situation is essentially a good one, but requires work, in this case the ore being melted into metal tools.

[88] Reference seems to be falling back onn one's upbringing and not on one's opinion.

[89] One's own dao returning is the influence of one's action (producing yang metal) for which a plan is needed.

10 Lu: shoe, footstep, honour, carry out, to walk on

Honouring the tigers tail[90]
It does not bite the cultivated
Behave accordingly

Outer: Swomp under the sky
Inner: wood in fire

6 branches comparison:

	Zhoulinetext	*Wen'guatext*			
Line 6	Watching footsteps. Inspect the omens[91] return. Very fortunate	**58 Dui (Yue): exchange, conversion** (Common meaning: pleasure, lake modeled after the similar sounding name of the double gua) Smooth. Favourable determination			
Line 5	Honour splitted open. Threatening determination[92]	**38 Kui: (meditative) gazing** A small affair, Auspicious			

---

[90] The tiger's tail is a geneal reference to danger. The tiger in all its ferocipousness is the root metaphor for demons, generals and gongfu masters alike. From a cultivated master it is said that his inner peace is so large that when he steps on the tiger's tail it will not bite him. Ingeneral it sais that inner peace makes one impevious to tiger and rhinoceros attacks.

[91] Omens are signs embedded in reality that give us clues about unfolding events omens are much like footsteps.

[92] A person honourability is usually the cause for one's inner peace. When someone doubts your honojurability then we easily get upset

Line 4	Honouring the tiger tail that has a panicky appearance[93]. It ends fortunate	**61 Zhong Fu: center/ middle/attained/inner faith, inner sincerity** Young pig, fish: auspicious Favourable to cross the great plain Favourable determination			
Line 3	The feeble sighted is able to see. The lame is able to take footsteps to honour the tiger tail[94]. Ominous for it bites the cultivated one. The martially cultivated one acts as a big gentleman.	**1 Qian: sky** Smooth origin, Favourable determination			
Line 2	Honouring the flat-smooth Dao[95]. Auspicious determination for the confined cultivated one.	**25 Wu wang: without presumption** Primary enjoyment Favourable determination If not straight (punctual, centered); have calamety Not favourable to have roots in the past			

---

93   Nerveous tiger

94   There is no excuse to get yourself into trouble, even when you are handicapped, you can still practice self cultivation

95   Dao is here compared to the tiger's tail, revealing a nuclear assumption of the Yijing, namely that the good and the evil are two faces of the same event, it depends on the mood/ judgements of the observer which one is experienced.

Line 1	Plain white honour[96] Go without misfortune	**6 Song: arguing, lawsuit** Have a capture and they will be zhi-ti frightened Middle stage auspicious, end ominous Favourable to see the big cultivated one Not favourable to wade a big river.
All lines change in opposition[97]		**15 Qian: modesty** **(speech in contention,** **the sound of modesty)** Behave accordingly The gentleman has an end (conclusion)

11 Tai: safe, peacefull, tranquil, extreme, most

The small goes, the big comes
Auspicious, behave accordingly

Outer: Sky under earth[98]
Inner: Wood in metal

---

[96] The tiger is classified in wuxing as metal, so is honour
[97] The opposite of trying to get yourself out of danger is trying to avoid to get into danger through modest behavior. Chinese culture never elevated heroes, it advised against heroics, different than in modern China.
[98] Peace is based on movement supporting substance and thus communication between yang and yin. Dagua 11, 12, 63 and 64 need to be compared to comprehend this.

6 branches comparison:

	Zhoulinetext	Wen'guatext			
Line 6	The city wall collapses in a dry moat. Don't use army. From town comes report to charge. Distressing determination[99]	**26 Da Chu: large livestock** Beneficial determination Auspicious to not eat with your clan Favourable to cross the wide plain (swomp gua can also mean plain, there is no xiaogua refereing to water)	yellow		
Line 5	Di Yi[100] is happy because he sends his daughter in marriage. Primary fortune	**5 Xü: needing, wanting** Have a glorious capture and act accordingly The determination is auspicious It is favourable to wade across the big river	yellow	green	
Line 4	Fluttering (flying) about[101], No wealth thanks to neighbour. Capture is due to lack of caution	**34 Da Zhuang: big force, big health (stoutness)** Sharp determination	yellow	green	grey

---

99 Things are not what they are supposed to be, they seem to contradict each other. The real situation is that things are just decrepit, but from a distance it seems someone is trying to do harm

100 Emperor Yi. The line is one of developing clairty

101 Lack of coherent strategy

Line 3	Not level, no slope. No go, no return. Hardship determination, not misfortune. Don't worry: a capture while eating. Have a blessing	**19 Lin: face, overlook, befall, arrive, on the point of** Grand smoothness Favourable determination that extends to the eight moon Have an act of violence		🟩	⬜
Line 2	Use a hollow gourd[102] to ford the He-river Your friend is not left far behind, Disappear to get reward in the middle line	**36 Ming yi: safe/ darkening of brightness/ brilliance** Favourable in a hardship determination			⬜
Line 1	Pull out the mao-grasshalms together with their roots[103] Fortunate attack	**46 Sheng: ascending, going upwards** Primary smoothness Visit the greatly cultivated one (priest) Don't worry Attacking the south is auspicious			

---

[102] The concept of gourd, or hulu is that of the human body with the head. Here the gourd is used to ford a torrent river. If you follwo advice it is not needed to worry

[103] Maograss roots are intertwined, so that if you pluch one bunch many others come with it. It is also very fragile, so carefulness is adviced

All lines change in opposition		**12 Pi: negative/not mouth**[104] Bad his/her unperson, not favourable for the gentleman Determination: big goes, small comes			

12 Pi: negative/not mouth

Bad his/her unperson, not favourable for the gentleman
Determination: big goes, small comes

Outer: Earth under sky
Inner: wood in earth

6 branches comparison:

	Zhoulinetext	**Wen'guatext**			
Line 6	First bad for a short time, later joy[105].	**45 Cui: to gather together** Smooth The king goes into his temple Favourable to visit the greatly cultivated one (priest) Smooth and favourable determination Auspicious to use large sacrificial animal Favourable to have roots in the past			

---

[104] The opposite of peace is the force of demons at work, that is why the opposite for peace is when heaven and earth move each on different directions and go their own way.

[105] The advice to heaven and earth is to come back together

Line 5	Stop the boogyman (the greatly cultivated one with no mouth / bad spirit, or maybe Pan Gu). Auspicious. (it) Runs away, runs away: tie it to the thickly leaved mulberry tree[106]	**35 Jin: to enter, advance, promote** Lord of Kang (Health) uses giving of many (mated numbers) horses During light of day three joinings		green	
Line 4	No misfortune to have a charge. A plowed field and lia-birds: happiness[107]	**20 guan: conception of the nature of things, observe, view, (monestary)** Washing but no offering Have faith and sincerety captured		green	orange
Line 3	Wrap the offering of prepared food[108]	**33 Dun: little pig, conceal, hide** Smooth, Determination a little favourable	yellow	green	orange

---

[106] The mulberry tree at the other side of earth is where the sun at night rests. If we understand this, we receive a great gift

[107] Good timing because of understanding the nature of the event

[108] Try to avoid spilling

Line 2	Wrap the offering of steamed meat. For the one with little cultivation good. Bad for the greatly cultivated one[109]. Behave accordingly	**6 Song: arguing, lawsuit** Have a capture and they will be zhi-ti frightened Middle stage auspicious, end ominous Favourable to see the big cultivated one Not favourable to wade a big river.			
Line 1	Pull out the mao-grasshalms together with their roots. Auspicious determination. Behave accordingly[110]	**25 Wu wang: without presumption** Primary enjoyment Favourable determination If not straight (punctual, centered); have calamety Not favourable to have roots in the past			
All lines change in opposition		**11 Tai: safe, peacefull, tranquil, extreme, most[111]** The small goes, the big comes Auspicious, behave accordingly			

---

[109] The offering of food is not in its food-ness but in its qi, which is related to its fragrance. The offering can only be appreciated through its fragrance.the one of small cultivation doesnot comprehend that part.

[110] See note 91

[111] The opposite of bad advice is good advice. Good advice requires the communication of heaven and earth, therefore the opposite of the unperson is peace.

13 Tong Ren: similar cultivated (persons)

Gather cultivated ones in the open country
Behave accordingly
Favourable to wade accros the big river
Favourable determination for the gentleman

Outer: Sun under sky
Inner: metal in wood

6 branches comparison:

	Zhoulinetext	*Wen'guatext*			
Line 6	Gather cultivated ones at the suburban altar. No trouble[112]	49			
Line 5	Gather cultivated ones. First weep and wail, later laugh. Big armies can meet each other[113]	30 Li: to leave, part from Favourable determination Smooth to raise cows Auspicious			
Line 4	Mounting the wall, it cannot attack. Auspicious[114]	**37 Jia ren: domestication, cultivated family/clan person, cultivated professional person** Favourable feminine determination			

---

[112] Connect with people like yourself so that transformation and improvement can be brought forth

[113] To get cultivated people together is a hard task since they tend to be quite individualistic and seem to repel each other similar like big armies do. It is partly the force of their following that causes the replling force

[114] Self cultivation is much like raidsing lifestock or being part of a family, you have to know your place and paurpose in the whole

Line 3	The war charriot is hidden in tall weeds Climbing the high hill: for three years no uprising[115]	**25 Wu wang: without presumption** Primary enjoyment Favourable determination If not straight (punctual, centered); have calamety Not favourable to have roots in the past			green
Line 2	Gather cultivated ones at the ancestral hall[116]	**1 Qian: sky** Smooth origin, Favourable determination			green
Line 1	Gather cultivated ones at the gate. No misfortune[117]	**33 Dun: little pig, conceal, hide** Smooth, Determination a little favourable	orange		
All lines change in opposition		**7 Shi: teacher, master, skilled one, army[118]** Determination for the greatly cultivated one is auspicious. No misfortune.			

---

115   Aggression is forgotten for now
116   Having cultivated people together makes more clear what is the will iof heaven
117   To make connection with cultivation is neither good nor bad, it also means you hide yourself a bit.
118   The opposite of a forum of cultivated ones is the singular master

14 Da you: great having

Grand having greatly
Behave accordingly

Outer Sky under fire[119]
Inner: metal in metal

6 branches comparison:

	Zhoulinetext	Wen'guatext			
Line 6	From sky divine help for them. Auspicious, not unfavourable[120]	**34 Da Zhuang: big force, big health (stoutness)** Sharp determination			
Line 5	Their capture as if crossed. As if terrified[121]. Auspicious	**1 Qian: sky** Smooth origin, **Favourable determination**			
Line 4	The peng sacrifice (water splashing sacrefice) of a bandit[122]. Without misfortune	**26 Da Chu: large livestock** Beneficial determination Auspicious to not eat with your clan Favourable to cross the wide plain (swomp gua can also mean plain, there is no xiaogua refereing to water)			

---

[119] The sun is the king of heaven, so here heaven supports the king.
[120] The great force that seems to support is because you act in accord with the will of heaven
[121] The yin leads the yang by keeping the movements of yang captive, tied up
[122] Repentance. Even criminals can be moral people

Line 3	The duke used to behave according to heaven[123] The son of a small cultivated one is not able	**38 Kui: (meditative) gazing** A small affair, Auspicious
Line 2	Have a transport by a big carriage. Have a place to go to. No misfortune	**30 Li: to leave, part from** Favourable determination Smooth to raise cows Auspicious
Line 1	Not coming across harm there will be no misfortune[124] If hardship, in that case no misfortune	**50 Ding: sacrificial vessel (Tripod)** Primary auspiciousness Smooth
All lines change in opposition		**8 Bi: emulate, copy, model after[125]** Original auspiciousness Manipulate the (millifoil) stalks (oracle) Behave accordingly grand for a long-term determination. No misfortune. Not a peacefull method-state (tranquility meditation) Ominous for the man/husband that comes late.

---

[123] Serves as an example of how we should behave: always act as a responsible person ruling the greater kingdom, even if you are not. That is alarge part of being a cultivated person.

[124] Some sacrifice may be required, but is not misforutne

[125] The opposite iof having it greatly is having nothing, therefore the opposite of having it greatly is copying those who do have it greatly

15 Qian: modesty (speech in contention, the sound of modesty)

Behave accordingly
The gentleman has an end (conclusion)

Outer: Mountain under earth[126]
Inner: wood in water

6 branches comparison:

	Zhoulinetext	Wen'guatext			
Line 6	Calling hamster[127]. Favourable for using the mobilized army to attack the town-state. (or: to annex the town-state)	**52 Gen: stopping, stilling (associations with root, source, base)** Stilling the back but not capturing the structure Traveling the court but not showing evidence of being a cultivated one No misfortune			
Line 5	Not rich thanks to the neighbour[128]. Beneficial to use an invading attack. Not unfavourable	**39 Jian: lame, trouble** Favourable: the southwest (kun) Not favourable: the northeast (gen) Favourable to be exposed to a considerably (large) cultivated one Auspicious determination			

---

[126] A hidden mountain is a powerful object not withstanding its relative invisibility. That is why modesty is so highly prized in the Yijing.
[127] The hamster is a methaphor for being of little cultivation
[128] No support

Line 4	Not unfavourable to tear the hamster[129]	**62 Xiao Guo: small pass, small life/time, going a little beyond, small finish (a bit of ending), a small betterment, smallness.** Smooth and favourable determination Approval for small matter, no approval for big matter A flying (fluttering) bird leaves his sound behind Not suitable to rise, suitable to descent Large benefit
Line 3	Toiling hamster[130], The gentleman has an end (conclusion). Auspicious	**2 Kun: middle earth** Smooth origin A mare is determined as noble Have a place to go; first lose your way, get a host later West is favourable. Get a friend in south. Lose one in north. Auspicious determination for security matters.

---

129   Here the hamster is compared to a fluttering burd, both symypbols of indecisiveness, nerveaousness and little cultivation
130   The toiling hamster is a hamster that tries to change its faith by following what needs to be done

Line 2	Hamster call[131]. Auspicious determination	**46 Sheng: ascending, going upwards** Primary smoothness Visit the greatly cultivated one (priest) Don't worry Attacking the south is auspicious			
Line 1	Crunch-crunch. The gentlemean uses wading across the big river[132]. Auspicious	**36 Ming yi: safe/ darkening of brightness/ brilliance** Favourable in a hardship determination			
All lines change in opposition		**10 Lu: shoe, footstep, honour, carry out, to walk on**[133] Honouring the tigers tail It does not bite the cultivated Behave accordingly			

16 Yu: giving an elephant away, pleased[134]

Favourable to establish a high official
Mobilize the army

Outer: Earth under wood
Inner: water in earth

---

[131] Understanding one's lack of cultivation is made visible, it will take away danger.
[132] Using what one needs to do to teach the environment
[133] The opposite of modesty is putting oneself in danger because of lack of oversight
[134] The act of generosity ios highly praised in the yijing

6 branches comparison:

	Zhoulinetext	**Wen'guatext**			
Line 6	Pleasure turns dark. Have a change for the worse.[135] No misfortune	**35 Jin: to enter, advance, promote** Lord of Kang (Health) uses giving of many (mated numbers) horses During light of day three joinings			
Line 5	Determining chronic illness. No death	**45 Cui: to gather together** Smooth The king goes into his temple Favourable to visit the greatly cultivated one (priest) Smooth and favourable determination Auspicious to use large sacrificial animal Favourable to have roots in the past			

---

[135] The advice is about a gift with a hidden darker side

Line 4	Having big catch because of giving an elephant away (pleasure). No doubt, gather friends in a link	**2 Kun: middle earth** Smooth origin A mare is determined as noble Have a place to go; first lose your way, get a host later West is favourable. Get a friend in south. Lose one in north. Auspicious determination for security matters.
Line 3	A staring elephant[136] (that is given away). Trouble. Walk slowly or have hesitation	**62 Xiao Guo: small pass, small life/time, going a little beyond, small finish (a bit of ending), a small betterment, smallness.** Smooth and favourable determination Approval for small matter, no approval for big matter A flying (fluttering) bird leaves his sound behind Not suitable to rise, suitable to descent Large benefit

---

[136] A staring elephant is an angry elephant and therefore dangerous. It is better to not make yourself to visible

| Line 2 | A border in stone inscription will not last a day.[137] Auspicious determination | **40 Jie: divide, seperate, untie, undo, explain, solve, comprehend, relieve oneself**

Favourable: southwest
No place to go to therefore turning back, auspicious
Have a place to go to since long, auspicious | | | |
| Line 1 | Crying elephant (that is given away)[138]. Ominous | **51 Zhen: shake, shock, quake, vibrate, greatly exited, deeply astonished**

Smooth,
Shock comes 'crackcrack!!!'
Laughing, talking 'yakyak'
Shock frigthens an area 100 li around
Do not drop the ladle (spoon) with aromatic spirits
(aromatic spirits pictographicly refering to the container of the Po souls) | | | |

[137]   A border stone inscription is to mark a permanent border. Here a border is made that will not last
[138]   Elephants are feeling creatures with strong sentimental attachments. To give one away that attached to you might break his heart.

All lines change in opposition		9 xiao chu: small livestock[139] Small livestoch behaves like dense clouds No rain from the western outskirts Retrieve one's dao, what misfortune is this? Auspicious.			

17 Sui: follow, comply

Primary smoothness (succes)
Enjoy the favourable determination
No fault (blame)

Outer: wood under metal
Inner: wood in earth

6 branches comparison:

	Zhoulinetext	Wen'guatext			
Line 6	Limit relation with them, then let the tie loose.[140] The king uses smoothness with/ on the western mountain (Kunlun)[141]	25 Wu wang: without presumption Primary enjoyment Favourable determination If not straight (punctual, centered); have calamety Not favourable to have roots in the past			

---

[139] The opposite of a large elephant is a herd of small animals, lie sheep, therefore the opposite of an elephant that is given away is herding small livestock.
[140] The advice is to gradually untie your bond with them/it
[141] The western mountian is the area of the immortals ascending to heaven, normal people's ghosts depart to the underworld following the sun.

Line 5	Captured in praise[142]. Auspicious	**51 Zhen: shake, shock, quake, vibrate, greatly exited, deeply astonished** Smooth, Shock comes 'crackcrack!!!' Laughing, talking 'yakyak' Shock frigthens an area 100 li around Do not drop the ladle (spoon) with aromatic spirits (aromatic spirits pictographicly refering to the container of the Po souls)
Line 4	Persuit has a catch[143]. Ominous determination. Have a capture in the Dao, Make a covenant with that. What misfortune?	**3 Zhun: birththrows** Smooth origin, benifical determination Do not use! Have a place to go to Favourable to establish an official

---

142   Praise is compared to the effect of thunder
143   An outcome with an unexpected catch that brings you closer to dao.

Line 3	Relate to the true man, vow to the little child[144]. Persue and there'll be that you get what you seek. Favourable determination for storage	**49 Ge: leather, hide, transform, change** Capture great smoothness at sacrificial day Favourable determination Troubles go away			
Line 2	Relate to the little child, vowing the true man[145]	**58 Dui (Yue): exchange, conversion** (Common meaning: pleasure, lake modeled after the similar sounding name of the double gua) Smooth. Favourable determination			
Line 1	Organ (official) hall (probably fu organ but mental aspect) has a change[146]. Genuine luck, Open the door outwards to turn over done deeds	**45 Cui: to gather together** Smooth The king goes into his temple Favourable to visit the greatly cultivated one (priest) Smooth and favourable determination Auspicious to use large sacrificial animal Favourable to have roots in the past			

---

[144] Understanding true reason but preferring childish choices changes one from hide to leather
[145] Understanding childish motivation but preferring true reasonable choices opens oneself up
[146] To experience change indicated by activity within becoming visible outwardly

All lines change in opposition		18 Gu: (legendary) venomenous insect[147] (used in black magic) Primary smoothness Go through the big plains before Jia (yang wood heavenly stem) sun and after jia sun (jia sun was considered unlucky)			

18 Gu: (legendary) venomenous insect[148]

Primary smoothness
Go through the big plains before Jia (yang wood heavenly stem) sun/period and after jia sun/period[149]

Outer: Wood under earth
Inner: wood in metal

---

[147] The effect of following is growth and change, which is a form of magic in itself. The opposite of following is forcing your way, therefore following is opposed with/by (black) magic.

[148] The gu is appropriated by putting 5 varying killing animals together, such as snake, spider, scorpio etc. The one that survives is the Gu. The Gu was widely used as part of dark magical practices in which the naturalness of things was forced to alter to the will of the performer of the magic.

[149] jia sun/period was considered unlucky. Refer also to note ...

6 branches comparison:

	Zhoulinetext	*Wen'guatext*			
Line 6	Not serving kingly noblemen (There is/in spite of) high reward for sevice[150]	**46 Sheng: ascending, going upwards** Primary smoothness Visit the greatly cultivated one (priest) Don't worry Attacking the south is auspicious			
Line 5	Gu bites a father in the trunk Apply a Yu eulogy[151]	**57 Xun (Zhuan): calculation** Little smooth Favourable to have roots in the past. Favourable to see the largely cultivated one			
Line 4	Loads of Gu go towards father He shows evidence of distress[152]	**50 Ding: sacrificial vessel (Tripod)** Primary auspiciousness Smooth			
Line 3	Small Gu bites a father in the trunk Have trouble, but no big misfortune[153]	**4 Meng: blindfolded** Smooth: we do not seek the dodder, the dodder seeks us first. Manipulate the stalks and it will tell twice. The third time is an insult.			

---

[150] This advice is similar to the remarks of Zhuangzi that dragging one's tail in the mud like a tortoise has its own rewards.

[151] Death will result as result of black magic

[152] A dangerous attac k is eminent and now clear

[153] The poisonous bite is not life threatening

Line 2	Gu bites a mother in the trunk This can not be determined[154]	**52 Gen: stopping, stilling (associations with root, source, base)** Stilling the back but not capturing the structure Traveling the court but not showing evidence of being a cultivated one No misfortune			
Line 1	Gu bites a father in the trunk He has a son, so the dead father has no misfortune threatening It ends auspicious[155]	**26 Da Chu: large livestock** Beneficial determination Auspicious to not eat with your clan Favourable to cross the wide plain (swomp gua can also mean plain, there is no xiaogua refereing to water)			
All lines change in opposition		**17 Sui: follow, comply[156]** Primary smoothness (succes) Enjoy the favourable determination No fault (blame)			

---

[154] If the gu bites the mother then that is not a good attack strategy
[155] If the father /leader is killed suitable descendants will take over
[156] The opposite of magic is compliance with the way things develop

19 Lin: face, overlook, befall, arrive, on the point of

Grand smoothness
Favourable determination that extends to the eight moon
Have an act of violence

Outer: meatal under earth
Inner: earth in wood

6 branches comparison:

	Zhoulinetext	Wen'guatext			
Line 6	Sincere chanting of eulegy, auspicious Without misfortune	**41 Sun: decrease, empty the vessel (of libation liquid)** Have a very auspicious capture No misfortune can be determened Favourable to have roots in the past What to use? Two tureens can be used for the offering			
Line 5	Be aware of ceremonial wailing from the grand gentleman (to the earthgod) Suitable auspiciousness	**60 Jie: joint, node, knot** Smooth Bitter node (as in bamboo) Cannot be determined Get its tail wet Distress			
Line 4	Extreme chanting of eulegy No misfortune	**54 Gui Mei: returning younger sister** Ominous for an expedition Favourable for nothing			

Line 3	Sweet chanting of eulegy Without friendly favor, already grieved him No misfortune	**11 Tai: safe, peacefull, tranquil, extreme, most** The small goes, the big comes Auspicious, behave accordingly
Line 2	Salty chanting of eulegy, auspicious Not without favor	**24 Fu: turn around, answer, recover/resume, revenge, again** Going out, coming in; behave accordingly (and there'll be) no illness Friend comes, no misfortune Oppose resuming of the Dao and after seven suns comes the answer Favourable to have roots in the past
Line 1	Salty chanting of eulegy Auspicious determination	**7 Shi: teacher, master, skilled one, army** Determination for the greatly cultivated one is auspicious. No misfortune.
All lines change in opposition		**33 Dun: little pig, conceal, hide** Smooth, Determination a little favourable

20 guan: conception of the nature of things, observe, view, (monestary)

Washing but no offering
Have faith and sincerety captured

Outer: Earth under wood
Inner: earth in earth

6 branches comparison:

	Zhoulinetext	Wen'guatext			
Line 6	Conception of the nature of former growth. For the gentleman sage no error	8 Bi: emulate, copy, model after Original auspiciousness Manipulate the (millifoil) stalks (oracle) Behave accordingly grand for a long-term determination. No misfortune. Not a peacefull method-state (tranquility meditation) Ominous for the man/ husband that comes late.	🟩		
Line 5	Observe my growth. For the gentleman (sage) no error	23 Bo: foretelling by elimination, stripping away, flaying Not favourable to have roots in the past	🟩	🟧	

Line 4	Have a grasp of the nation's brilliance. Favourable use to be guest of the ruler	**12 Pi: negative/not mouth** Bad his/her unperson, not favourable for the gentleman Determination: big goes, small comes
Line 3	Observe my growth advance and withdraw	**53 Jian: to advance, gradually melting, reaching** Woman sent in marriage Auspicious Favourable determination
Line 2	Peeking at the conception of the nature of things Favourable if a woman does this	**59 Huan: to melt, vanish** Smooth The artificial king has a temple Favorable to wade across the great river Favourable determination
Line 1	The pupil (of the eye) has a grasp of the one with little cultivation No blame The gentleman sage has disstress	**Yi; increasing, overflow (of liquid), benefit** Favourable to have roots in the past Favourable to cross the big plain/river
All lines change in opposition		**34 Da Zhuang: big force, big health (stoutness)** Sharp determination

21 Shi He: biting through, the sounding voice of oracular speach, biting through a sounding voice

Smooth, favourable to use locking up/putting in jail, lawsuit

Outer: wood under fire
Inner: water in earth

6 branches comparison:

	Zhoulinetext	Wen'guatext			
Line 6	Wearing stocks over the shoulders, the ears are destroyed. Ominous	**51 Zhen: shake, shock, quake, vibrate, greatly exited, deeply astoished** Smooth, Shock comes 'crackcrack!!!' Laughing, talking 'yakyak' Shock frigthens an area 100 li around Do not drop the ladle (spoon) with aromatic spirits (aromatic spirits pictographicly refering to the container of the Po souls)			
Line 5	Biting dry meat, get yellow metal. Threatening determination. Without misfortune	**25 Wu wang: without presumption** Primary enjoyment Favourable determination If not straight (punctual, centered); have calamety Not favourable to have roots in the past			

Line 4	Biting in vain at bone inside the meat. Get a metal arrow. Favourable if hardship is determined. Auspicious	**27 Yi: jaws, nourishing** (character suggesting eating appropiately [something between the jaws], or the nourishing of a person whom cultivates appropiate behaviour, the second part as a whole is the character for zhen, that is mostly translated as determination/ determined) Auspicious determination Observe the jaws (conciousness) itself seeking substance for the mouth
Line 3	Oracular speech from past moon The fruitmeat/ pulp receives poison. Small disstress, no misforune	**30 Li: to leave, part from** Favourable determination Smooth to raise cows Auspicious
Line 2	Biting at the skin, destroying the nose. No misfortune	**38 Kui: (meditative) gazing** A small affair, Auspicious

Line 1	Wearing stocks on the ankels, his feet are destroyed. No misfortune	**35 Jin: to enter, advance, promote** Lord of Kang (Health) uses giving of many (mated numbers) horses During light of day three joining			
All lines change in opposition		**48 Jing: (a) well** Change a town but not change a well No loss no gain Go, come in perfect order Nearly reaches but not drawing water The well damages the earthen Jug Ominous			

22 Bi: bright, decoration

Behave accordingly small
Favourable to have roots in the past

Outer: fire under earth
Inner:

6 branches comparison:

	Zhoulinetext	*Wen'guatext*			
Line 6	White decoration. No misfortune	**36 Ming yi: safe/ darkening of brightness/ brilliance** Favourable in a hardship determination			

Line 5	The decorated go to the hill (western mountain of kunlun) with bundles of silk. Scanty distress but it ends auspicious	**37 Jia ren: domestication, cultivated family/clan person, cultivated professional person** Favourable feminine determination
Line 4	As if whitishly decorated. As if a white horse with long manes. Not a robber, but family of the wife to make an agreement	**30 Li: to leave, part from** Favourable determination Smooth to raise cows Auspicious
Line 3	As if decorated glossy-wet like. Auspicious for long term determination	**27 Yi: jaws, nourishing** (character suggesting eating appropiately [something between the jaws], or the nourishing of a person whom cultivates appropiate behaviour, the second part as a whole is the character for zhen, that is mostly translated as determination/ determined) Auspicious determination Observe the jaws (conciousness) itself seeking substance for the mouth

Line 2	Decorated beard	26 Da Chu: large livestock Beneficial determination Auspicious to not eat with your clan Favourable to cross the wide plain (swomp gua can also mean plain, there is no xiaogua refereing to water)			
Line 1	Decorated feet. Abandon carriage and walk	52 Gen: stopping, stilling (associations with root, source, base) Stilling the back but not capturing the structure Traveling the court but not showing evidence of being a cultivated one No misfortune			
All lines change in opposition		47 Kun: stranded, surrounded, tired, pinned down, bothered Smooth determination for a greatly cultivated one Auspicious, no misfortune There'll be unreliable talk			

23 Bo: foretelling by elimination, stripping away, flaying

Not favourable to have roots in the past

Outer Earth under earth
Inner:

6 branches comparison:

	Zhoulinetext	*Wen'guatext*			
Line 6	Large fruit uneaten. Gentleman gets the carriage The one of small cultivation flayes the cottage	**2 Kun: middle earth** Smooth origin A mare is determined as noble Have a place to go; first lose your way, get a host later West is favourable. Get a friend in south. Lose one in north. Auspicious determination for security matters.			
Line 5	Eating fish on a string. Favor of the palace people Not without favor	**20 Guan: conception of the nature of things, observe, view, (monestary)** Washing but no offering Have faith and sincerety captured			

Line 4	Flaying the bed's surface. Ominous	**35 Jin: to enter, advance, promote** Lord of Kang (Health) uses giving of many (mated numbers) horses During light of day three joinings			
Line 3	Flay this, no misfortune	**52 Gen: stopping, stilling (associations with root, source, base)** Stilling the back but not capturing the structure Traveling the court but not showing evidence of being a cultivated one No misfortune			
Line 2	Flaying the bed apart. Ominous for exorcism determination	**4 Meng: blindfolded** Smooth: we do not seek the dodder, the dodder seeks us first. Manipulate the stalks and it will tell twice. The third time is an insult.			

Line 1	Flaying the bed's legs. Ominous for exorcism determination	**27 Yi: jaws, nourishing** (character suggesting eating appropiately [something between the jaws], or the nourishing of a person whom cultivates appropiate behaviour, the second part as a whole is the character for zhen, that is mostly translated as determination/ determined) Auspicious determination Observe the jaws (conciousness) itself seeking substance for the mouth			
All lines change in opposition		**43 Quai/Jue: decide, determine, to cleanse, open out** Display a capture at the kings court There be threatening reports from the town A violent aproach is unfavourable Favourable to have roots in the past			

24 Fu: turn around, answer, recover/resume, revenge, again

Going out, coming in; behave accordingly (and there'll be) no illness
Friend comes, no misfortune
Oppose resuming of the Dao and after seven suns comes the answer
Favourable to have roots in the past

Outer: wood under earth
Inner: earth in earth

6 branches comparison:

	Zhoulinetext	*Wen'guatext*			
Line 6	Confused turning around, trouble. Have terrible disaster Mobilize your army and have a great defeat because of bad rulership of the nation. For over ten years attack is impossible	**27 Yi: jaws, nourishing** (character suggesting eating appropiately [something between the jaws], or the nourishing of a person whom cultivates appropiate behaviour, the second part as a whole is the character for zhen, that is mostly translated as determination/determined) Auspicious determination Observe the jaws (conciousness) itself seeking substance for the mouth			
Line 5	Sincere turning around without regret	**3 Zhun: birththrows** Smooth origin, benificial determination Do not use! Have a place to go to Favourable to establish an official			

Line 4	Turn around on your own to the middle path (middle line, could mean yellow brick road)	**51 Zhen: shake, shock, quake, vibrate, greatly exited, deeply astonished** Smooth, Shock comes 'crackcrack!!!' Laughing, talking 'yakyak' Shock frigthens an area 100 li around Do not drop the ladle (spoon) with aromatic spirits (aromatic spirits pictographicly refering to the container of the Po souls)			
Line 3	Turn around to the riverbank. Threatening, but no misfortune	**36 Ming yi: safe/ darkening of brightness/ brilliance** Favourable in a hardship determination			
Line 2	Stop turning around. Auspiciousness	**19 Lin: face, overlook, befall, arrive, on the point of** Grand smoothness Favourable determination that extends to the eight moon Have an act of violence			

Line 1	Do not keep the return away. Not cultivating trouble. Basic auspiciousness	**2 Kun: middle earth** Smooth origin A mare is determined as noble Have a place to go; first lose your way, get a host later West is favourable. Get a friend in south. Lose one in north. Auspicious determination for security matters.			
All lines change in opposition		**44 Gou: to meet, to encounter, female ruler, intercourse** Strong woman Has no use to marry a women			

25 Wu wang: without presumption

Primary enjoyment
Favourable determination
If not straight (punctual, centered); have calamity
Not favourable to have roots in the past

Outer: metal under metal
Inner: wood in earth

6 branches comparison:

	Zhoulinetext	**Wen'guatext**			
Line 6	Not presuming calamity while traveling Without benefits from the past	**17 Sui: follow, comply** Primary smoothness (succes) Enjoy the favourable determination No fault (blame)			
Line 5	Not presuming illness Warning against medical treatment and have joy	**21 Shi He: biting through, the sounding voice of oracular speach, biting through a sounding voice** Smooth, favourable to use locking up/putting in jail, lawsuit			
Line 4	Determinations without misfortune	**Yi; increasing, overflow (of liquid), benefit** Favourable to have roots in the past Favourable to cross the big plain/river			
Line 3	Without presuming a disaster, someone tied it to the ox Traveler's gain, townsman's disaster	**13 Tong Ren: similar cultivated (persons)** Gather cultivated ones in the open country Behave accordingly Favourable to wade accros the big river Favourable determination for the gentleman			

Line 2	No ploughing benefits Not breaking ground but tilling old field, Then favourable to have roots in the past	**10 Lu: shoe, footstep, honour, carry out, to walk on** Honouring the tigers tail It does not bite the cultivated Behave accordingly			
Line 1	Auspicious going without presumptions	**10 Lu: shoe, footstep, honour, carry out, to walk on** Honouring the tigers tail It does not bite the cultivated Behave accordingly			
All lines change in opposition		**46 Sheng: ascending, going upwards** Primary smoothness Visit the greatly cultivated one (priest) Don't worry Attacking the south is auspicious			

26 Da Chu: large livestock

Beneficial determination
Auspicious to not eat with your clan
Favourable to cross the wide plain
(swomp gua can also mean plain, there is no xiaogua refereing to water)

Outer: heaven under earth
Inner: wood in metal

6 branches comparison:

	Zhoulinetext	**Wen'guatext**			
Line 6	(rhetorically:) Granted favour (responsebility) as a blessing from heaven. (Behave accordingly:) enjoy	**11 Tai: safe, peacefull,tranquil, extreme, most** The small goes, the big comes Auspicious, behave accordingly			
Line 5	Auspicious fangs of a gelded pig	**9 xiao chu: small livestock** Small livestoch behaves like dense clouds No rain from the western outskirts Retrieve one's dao, what misfortune is this? Auspicious.			
Line 4	A thwart on the young ox to protect the horns. Primary benefit	**14 Da you: great having** Grand having greatly Behave accordingly			
Line 3	Favourable to persue a fine horse. Favourable if hardship is determined. Form a barrier with charriots for protection Beneficial to have roots in the past	**41 Sun: decrease, empty the vessel (of libation liquid)** Have a very auspicious capture No misfortune can be determened Favourable to have roots in the past What to use? Two tureens can be used for the offering			

Line 2	Axle support comes off the carriage	**22 Bi: bright, decoration** Behave accordingly small Favourable to have roots in the past			
Line 1	Have a threat, beneficial to stop	**18 Gu: (legendary) venomenous insect** (used in black magic) Primary smoothness Go through the big plains before Jia (yang wood heavenly stem) sun and after jia sun (jia sun was considered unlucky)			
All lines change in opposition		**45 Cui: to gather together** Smooth The king goes into his temple Favourable to visit the greatly cultivated one (priest) Smooth and favourable determination Auspicious to use large sacrificial animal Favourable to have roots in the past			

27 Yi: jaws, nourishing

(character suggesting eating appropiately [something between the jaws], or the nourishing of a person whom cultivates appropiate behaviour, the second part as a whole is the character for zhen, that is mostly translated as determination/determined)

Auspicious determination
Observe the jaws (conciousness) itself seeking substance for the mouth

Outer:
Inner:

6 branches comparison:

	Zhoulinetext	*Wen'guatext*			
Line 6	Because of threatening fangs it is auspicious to cross the plains	**24 Fu: turn around, answer, recover/resume, revenge, again** Going out, coming in; behave accordingly (and there'll be) no illness Friend comes, no misfortune Oppose resuming of the Dao and after seven suns comes the answer Favourable to have roots in the past			
Line 5	Flinking the shin-bone/touch the classics. Auspicious determination for dwelling. No change(!)/ cannot(!) cross the plains	**Yi; increasing, overflow (of liquid), benefit** Favourable to have roots in the past Favourable to cross the big plain/river			

Line 4	Stuffed jaws, auspicious The tiger's apearance is the glaring staring look of far-reaching desire No misfortune	**21 Shi He: biting through, the sounding voice of oracular speach, biting through a sounding voice** Smooth, favourable to use locking up/putting in jail, lawsuit	
Line 3	Manage the jaws, the determination is ominous. Do not apply for ten years. Favor taken away by the past	**22 Bi: bright, decoration** Behave accordingly small Favourable to have roots in the past	
Line 2	Stuffed jaws, endure flinking of the shin bone. The jaw attacks the hillock (might be part of militairy movement) Ominous (*first line*: receiving a verbal beating, cursing the ancestors [burrial hill]/ *or*:touch/flink classic/undergo/ pass through/ manage/deal in/endure (shin bone) at/up to mound jaw attack	**41 Sun: decrease, empty the vessel (of libation liquid)** Have a very auspicious capture No misfortune can be determened Favourable to have roots in the past What to use? Two tureens can be used for the offering	

Line 1	Abandon your turtle spirit/soul/ fairy. I observe jaws hanging Ominous	**23 Bo: foretelling by elimination, stripping away, flaying** Not favourable to have roots in the past			
All lines change in opposition		**28 Da Guo: enlargening** Yielding support Favourable to have roots in the past Smooth			

28 Da Guo: enlargening

Yielding support
Favourable to have roots in the past
Smooth

Outer: wood under metal
Inner: metal in metal

6 branches comparison:

	Zhoulinetext	*Wen'guatext*			
Line 6	Experiencing immersion of the head in water. Ominous but no misfortune	**44 Gou: to meet, to encounter, female ruler, intercourse** Strong woman Has no use to marry a women			

Line 5	Withered poplar tree gives birth to flowers, Old woman finds bachelor husband: No misfortune, no honor	**50 Ding: sacrificial vessel (Tripod)** Primary auspiciousness Smooth
Line 4	Thriving support, auspicious; Have it stingy	**48 Jing: (a) well** Change a town but not change a well No loss no gain Go, come in perfect order Nearly reaches but not drawing water The well damages the earthen Jug Ominous
Line 3	Yielding support:Ominous	**47 Kun: stranded, surrounded, tired, pinned down, bothered** Smooth determination for a greatly cultivated one Auspicious, no misfortune There'll be unreliable talk
Line 2	Withered poplar tree gives birth to shoots, Old man receives a maiden for a bride Not unfavourable	**31 Xian / Gan: salty, to move/influence** Smooth, favourable determination, Take a maiden for wife Auspicious

Line 1	Apply offering of white cogongrass. Without harm	**43 Quai/Jue: decide, determine, to cleanse, open out** Display a capture at the kings court There be threatening reports from the town A violent aproach is unfavourable Favourable to have roots in the past			
All lines change in opposition		**27 Yi: jaws, nourishing** (character suggesting eating appropiately [something between the jaws], or the nourishing of a person whom cultivates appropiate behaviour, the second part as a whole is the character for zhen, that is mostly translated as determination/ determined) Auspicious determination Observe the jaws (conciousness) itself seeking substance for the mouth			

29 (Xi) kan: (review / be used to) bank, ridge

Have a prisoner safeguard the heart
Smooth
Travel has esteem

Outer: layers of water
Inner: earth in wood

6 branches comparison:

	Zhoulinetext	Wen'guatext			
Line 6	Use tying a 3-strand braid and 2-strand cord Hide (put) a group of people in the bushes Ominous for three years	**59 Huan: to melt, vanish** Smooth The artificial king has a temple Favorable to wade across the great river Favourable determination			
Line 5	Not filled to the ridge. Earth spirit is already calm No misfortune	**7 Shi: teacher, master, skilled one, army** Determination for the greatly cultivated one is auspicious. No misfortune.			
Line 4	Zun-flask, liqour, double gui-tureen Use earthen vessel Send them in bound together and through the window It ends without misfortune	**47 Kun: stranded, surrounded, tired, pinned down, bothered** Smooth determination for a greatly cultivated one Auspicious, no misfortune There'll be unreliable talk			

Line 3	Bring ridges Steep and deep, Entering the pitfall. Inhibit the use	**48 Jing: (a) well** Change a town but not change a well No loss no gain Go, come in perfect order Nearly reaches but not drawing water The well damages the earthen Jug Ominous			
Line 2	Ridge drops steeply Seek small gain	**8 Bi: emulate, copy, model after** Original auspiciousness Manipulate the (millifoil) stalks (oracle) Behave accordingly grand for a long-term determination. No misfortune. Not a peacefull method-state (tranquility meditation) Ominous for the man/ husband that comes late.			
Line 1	Review the ridge, entering the pitfall. Ominous	**60 Jie: joint, node, knot** Smooth Bitter node (as in bamboo) Cannot be determined Get its tail wet Distress			

All lines change in opposition		30 Li: to leave, part from[157]			
		Favourable determination Smooth to raise cows Auspicious			

30 Li: to leave, part from

Favourable determination
Smooth to raise cows
Auspicious

Outer: layers of fire
Inner: metal in wood

6 branches comparison:

	Zhoulinetext	Wen'guatext			
Line 6	The king uses going out and attack Have celebration chopping of heads Capture the ugly bandit Not unfortunate	55 Feng: plentifull, great Smooth. King fakes the inhibition of worry/sorrow Appropiate for the middle of sun (day)			

---

157 When you leave the darkness of the valleys and the cliffs of the mountain ranges you can get to see much more of the true outstretch of the world.

Line 5	Produce flowing of tears, as if grieved, as 'alas!' Auspicious	**13 Tong Ren: similar cultivated (persons)** Gather cultivated ones in the open country Behave accordingly Favourable to wade accros the big river Favourable determination for the gentleman
Line 4	If sudden, such be as good as it comes, like burning as if abandoned and in accordance with death	**22 Bi: bright, decoration** Behave accordingly small Favourable to have roots in the past
Line 3	Parting with sun sinking in the west If not drumming on earthen vessel and singing then the great ancestor says 'alas!' Ominous	**21 Shi He: biting through, the sounding voice of oracular speach, biting through a sounding voice** Smooth, favourable to use locking up/putting in jail, lawsuit
Line 2	Yellow parting from Original benefit	**14 Da you: great having** Grand having greatly Behave accordingly

Line 1	Stepping crosswise[158] Respect them No misfortune	**56 Lü: travel (possibly traveler), staying away fom home, troops, force** Little smooth For travel is the determination auspicious			
All lines change in opposition[159]		**29 (Xi) kan: (review / be used to) bank, ridge** Have a prisoner safeguard the heart. Smooth Travel has esteem			

31 Xian / Gan: salty, to move/influence

Smooth, favourable determination,
Take a maiden for wife
Auspicious

Outer: earth under metal
Inner: metal in wood

6 branches comparison:

	Zhoulinetext	**Wen'guatext**			
Line 6	Moving the cheeks, jowls and tongue	**33 Dun: little pig, conceal, hide** Smooth, Determination a little favourable			

---

[158] Crosswise stepping here seems to refer to the exhausted step of a long time traveler. The foot of the hexagram is fire directly biting into the handle of an axe (metal in wood). The situation requires proper handling to control the wants of the fire.

[159] When the illumination by fire changes in its opposite the image is that of mountain ridges alternating with deep valleys with rivers to traverse.

Line 5	Influence the spinal flesh No trouble	**62 Xiao Guo: small pass, small life/time, going a little beyond, small finish (a bit of ending), a small betterment, smallness.** Smooth and favourable determination Approval for small matter, no approval for big matter A flying (fluttering) bird leaves his sound behind Not suitable to rise, suitable to descent Large benefit
Line 4	Auspicious determination Trouble goes away If unsetteld you go and come A friend follows your thoughts	**39 Jian: lame, trouble** Favourable: the southwest (kun) Not favourable: the northeast (gen) Favourable to be exposed to a considerably (large) cultivated one Auspicious determination

Line 3	Moving the tigh, holding the marrow Distress goes	**45 Cui: to gather together** Smooth The king goes into his temple Favourable to visit the greatly cultivated one (priest) Smooth and favourable determination Auspicious to use large sacrificial animal Favourable to have roots in the past			
Line 2	Moving the lower leg Ominous Auspicious to store up	**28 Da Guo: enlargening** Yielding support Favourable to have roots in the past Smooth			
Line 1	Moving the big toes[160]	**49 Ge: leather, hide, transform, change** Capture great smoothness at sacrificial day Favourable determination Troubles go away			

---

[160] By moving the big toes you change the solid mountain into a moment of clarity and activity, That is an indication af a grand transfiormation, much like how a shapeshifter would do during a ritual by dressing with hides or masks and taking the nature of the animal or spirit to be intransfored as a cloth to help establish the transformation.

All lines change in opposition[161]		18 Gu: (legendary) venomenous insect (used in black magic) Primary smoothness Go through the big plains before Jia (yang wood heavenly stem) sun and after jia sun (jia sun was considered unlucky)			

32 Heng: permanent, lasting

Smooth, no misfortune
Favourable determination
Favourable to have roots in the past

Outer: layers of wood
Inner: metal in metal

6 branches comparison:

	Zhoulinetext	Wen'guatext			
Line 6	Lasting shaking: ominous	50 Ding: sacrificial vessel (Tripod) Primary auspiciousness Smooth			

---

[161] The opposite of influencing a situation is taking drastic measures.

Line 5	Lasting determination of the mind The maried woman a cultivated one: auspicious Male son: ominous	**28 Da Guo: enlargening** Yielding support Favourable to have roots in the past Smooth			
Line 4	No birds in the field	**46 Sheng: ascending, going upwards** Primary smoothness Visit the greatly cultivated one (priest) Don't worry Attacking the south is auspicious			
Line 3	The mind perhaps can't hold the shame permanently Determining distress	**40 Jie: divide, seperate, untie, undo, explain, solve, comprehend, relieve oneself** Favourable: southwest No place to go to therefore turning back, auspicious Have a place to go to since long, auspicious			

Line 2	Regret passes away	**62 Xiao Guo: small pass, small life/time, going a little beyond, small finish (a bit of ending), a small betterment, smallness.** Smooth and favourable determination Approval for small matter, no approval for big matter A flying (fluttering) bird leaves his sound behind Not suitable to rise, suitable to descent Large benefit			
Line 1	Permanent dredging Ominous determination Favourable for nothing	**34 Da Zhuang: big force, big health (stoutness)** Sharp determination			
All lines change in opposition		**Yi; increasing, overflow (of liquid), benefit** Favourable to have roots in the past Favourable to cross the big plain/river			

33 Dun: little pig, conceal, hide

Smooth,
Determination a little favourable

Outer: earth under metal
Inner: metal in wood[162]

6 branches comparison:

	Zhoulinetext	Wen'guatext			
Line 6	Fat piglet Not unfavourable	**31 Xian / Gan: salty, to move/influence** Smooth, favourable determination, Take a maiden for wife Auspicious			
Line 5[163]	Hide the piglet Auspicious determination	**56 Lü: travel (possibly traveler), staying away fom home, troops, force** Little smooth For travel is the determination auspicious			

---

[162] Because we talk here of yang metal on top of yin earth we could speak of a mountain under heaven. But the inner diagrams show yin wood around the metal, which could be a reference to a tool in the bushes. In the 3rd line this idea comes best to expression when there is talk of a piglet, a yin pig (small). In disease theory we speak of piglet disease, which is a disease rummaging around due to interation of the liver and the intestines.

[163] In line 56 there is talk of losing an axe. Travel here might be the activity of hiding the axe, where the inner and outer qi of the lines is yang metal, metal in a form

Line 4[164]	Fine piglet Auspicious for the gentleman Bad for the one of little cultivation	**53 Jian: to advance, gradually melting, reaching** Woman sent in marriage Auspicious Favourable determination			
Line 3[165]	Tie up the piglet Has threatening illness Auspicious to keep bondservant (m/f)	**12 Pi: negative/not mouth** Bad his/her unperson, not favourable for the gentleman Determination: big goes, small comes			
Line 2	Take charge of the yellow-brown ox hide not to let it escape	**6 Song: arguing, lawsuit** Have a capture and they will be zhi-ti frightened Middle stage auspicious, end ominous Favourable to see the big cultivated one Not favourable to wade a big river.			

---

[164] Line 4 works out the effects of line 156, in that self cultivation can help weaken the impact of the problem.

[165] Line three speaks of inner turmois which could be reference to ghost activity inside the person's belly

Line 1	Piglet's tail Threatening Do not use this Have roots in the past	**13 Tong Ren: similar** **cultivated (persons)** Gather cultivated ones in the open country Behave accordingly Favourable to wade accros the big river Favourable determination for the gentleman			
All lines *change in* *opposition*		**19 Lin[166]: face, overlook,** **befall, arrive, on the** **point of** Grand smoothness Favourable determination that extends to the eight moon. Have an act of violence			

---

[166] The revesal of a hidden tool is the ore still hidden in the earth, underground. The 8th moon is the beginning of September mostly, and thus the season of metal-autum. The storm season of yang rising up from the earth as thunder, the act of violence as a natural occurring resulting event.

34 Da Zhuang: big force, big health (stoutness)[167]

Sharp determination

Outer: metal under wood
Inner: metal in metal

6 branches comparison:

	Zhoulinetext	Wen'guatext			
Line 6	Ram buts the fence Not able to withdraw, not able to push through Good for nothing Hardship, later auspicious	**14 Da you: great having** Grand having greatly Behave accordingly			
Line 5	Loosing sheep at transformation (change) Without trouble	**43 Quai/Jue: decide, determine, to cleanse, open out** Display a capture at the kings court There be threatening reports from the town A violent aproach is unfavourable Favourable to have roots in the past			

---

[167] Due to the dominance of metal holding ore and carrying wood we see here a stron sense of purposefull behavior. Metal is in the wuxing the sign of human interference to complete the cycle of wuxing. A strong argument is that the wuxing without human intervention would lack yang metal, so there would be no mirrors to produce water vapour for human use, and thus a lot slower progression in nature's evolution.

Line 4	Auspicious determination, troubles go Breaking through the fence without being weakened Stout on the axle support of big carrier	**11 Tai: safe, peacefull, tranquil, extreme, most** The small goes, the big comes Auspicious, behave accordingly			
Line 3	Small cultivated one uses stout gentleman This is a determination without auspiciousness Threatening Ram butts the fence, his horns weaken	**54 Gui Mei: returning younger sister** Ominous for an expedition Favourable for nothing			
Line 2	Determination auspicious	**55 Feng: plentifull, great** Smooth. King fakes the inhibition of worry/sorrow Appropiate for the middle of sun (day)			
Line 1	Stout foot attack, ominous Have capture	**32 Heng: permanent, lasting** Smooth, no misfortune Favourable determination Favourable to have roots in the past			

All lines change in opposition		**20 guan[168]: conception of the nature of things, observe, view, (monestary)** Washing but no offering Have faith and sincerety captured			

35 Jin: to enter, advance, promote

Lord of Kang (Health) uses giving of many (mated numbers) horses
During light of day three joinings

Outer: earth under fire[169]
Inner: water in earth[170]

6 branches comparison:

	Zhoulinetext	*Wen'guatext*			
Line 6	Advancing his/her horns For using attack of the town threat is auspicious	**16 Yu: giving an elephant away, pleased** Favourablre to establish a high official Mobilize the army			

---

[168] The natural opposite of action is observation
[169] The character for fire relates to the heart. The heart radical resembles the running of a horse in the character for horse. The horse runs over the earth. In the context of the original language of the yijing to resemble imagery with horses is completely natural.
[170] The wuxing combination of water in the mountain is a symbol of fertility. Many rivers start from mountains.

Line 5	Trouble goes away Whatever gets lost, don't worry. Auspicious to go. Nothing unfavourable.	**12 Pi: negative/not mouth** Bad his/her unperson, not favourable for the gentleman Determination: big goes, small comes			
Line 4	Advancing like a rat animal Threatening determination	**23 Bo: foretelling by elimination, stripping away, flaying** Not favourable to have roots in the past			
Line 3	The multitude has faith Trouble go away	**56 Lü: travel (possibly traveler), staying away fom home, troops, force** Little smooth For travel is the determination auspicious			
Line 2	Advancing when grieved Auspicious determination Receive this great blessing from the king's mother	**64 Wei Ji: have not / did not cross a river / be of help** Smooth Small fox at the point of crossing the streamgets his tail wet Not at all favourable			

Line 1	Advancing when urged Auspicious determination Be without trouble; abundant capture No misfortune	**21 Shi He: biting through, the sounding voice of oracular speach, biting through a sounding voice** Smooth, favourable to use locking up/putting in jail, lawsuit			
All lines change in opposition[171]		**5 Xü: needing, wanting** Have a glorious capture and act accordingly The determination is auspicious It is favourable to wade across the big river			

36 Ming yi: safe/darkening of brightness/brilliance

Favourable in a hardship determination

Outer: fire under earth[172]
Inner: wood in water[173]

---

[171] The opposite of initiating change is waiting for the accumulation of momentum until the opportune moment for change happens with only a slight effort or none at all. Here the wanting of change works like a magical formula, intiating a process of incremental changes until it happens almost invisibly arriving or through historical necessity you generated through your wanting.

[172] The wuxing combination of fire under the earth is that of a hidden lava lake.

[173] The image of wood in water is that of a plant absorbing life giving water to grow. The qi of the plant seems to come from below thee earth.

6 branches comparison:

	Zhoulinetext	Wen'guatext			
Line 6	Not brillant: dark First rise into sky, than enter the earth	**22 Bi: bright, decoration** Behave accordingly small Favourable to have roots in the past	🟨		
Line 5	Master Ji darkens the brilliance Favourable determination	**63 Ji Ji: already/now that cross a river/be of help** Smooth, little favourable determination Auspicious at the beginning, disorder at the end		🟩	
Line 4	Enter through the left side, Catch the dark briljant pheasant's heart Take out through the courtgate	**55 Feng: plentifull, great** Smooth. King fakes the inhibition of worry/sorrow Appropiate for the middle of sun (day)	🟨	🟩	🟦
Line 3	Dark briljant pheasant got wounded at the southern hunt Got his big head Not worth an urgent determination	**24 Fu: turn around, answer, recover/resume, revenge, again** Going out, coming in; behave accordingly (and there'll be) no illness Friend comes, no misfortune Oppose resuming of the Dao and after seven suns comes the answer Favourable to have roots in the past	🟧	🟩	🟦

Line 2	Dark briljant pheasant wounded in the left tigh For healing use balls of horse Auspicious	**11 Tai: safe, peacefull, tranquil, extreme, most** The small goes, the big comes Auspicious, behave accordingly			
Line 1	Dark brilliant pheasant goes flying, droops his wings The gentleman goes to travel: three days no food Have a place to go to, have a talk with the owner (a cultivated one)	**15 Qian: modesty (speech in contention, the sound of modesty)** Behave accordingly The gentleman has an end (conclusion)			
All lines change in opposition		**6 Song: arguing, lawsuit**[174] Have a capture and they will be zhi-ti frightened Middle stage auspicious, end ominous Favourable to see the big cultivated one Not favourable to wade a big river.			

---

[174] The image of rain coming from heaven seems an affron and sudden argument in the context of a hidden lava lake or the nourishment from plants form a lake or river.

37 Jia ren[175]: domestication, cultivated family/ clan person, cultivated professional person

Favourable feminine determination

Outer: fire under wood[176]
Inner: the fire in water[177]

6 branches comparison:

	Zhoulinetext	Wen'guatext			
Line 6[178]	Have terrefying capture Ends auspicious	**63 Ji Ji: already/now that cross a river/be of help** Smooth, little favourable determination Auspicious at the beginning, disorder at the end			
Line 5[179]	King supposes to have family Don't worry, auspicious	**22 Bi: bright, decoration** Behave accordingly small Favourable to have roots in the past			

---

175 The hexagram of fire under wood and fire in water is often taken to mean family, or at best as clan. But for Chinese culture it is the implications of being a passive or active participant in the clan is of importance. To be active means cultivating the designated role you have and thus is being member of a clan by necessity a matter of self cultivation if you you do not want eventually to be the lowest rank in a community.

176 Fire under wood is a matchstick situation. It is the best nourishment fire can get.

177 Fire in water is the symbol of self cultivation, of meditative gathering of inner power even. The dantian in the belly is situated above and in front of the bladder and kidneys, both water organs controlling the descending fire of the heart. Also the belly is the sea of water and grain, and for bigu the grains are avoided so that the belly does not hinder the self-cultivation process. On top of the wood above a fire situation, that ofcourse desires a balancing act to control the finishing of the wood and thus extinguish the fire. It also reveals that every situation by nature is ending, all the human relationships come with an eventual end. The trick is to maintain them as good as you can by managing yourself.

178 The wood here has the prospect of going to be burned, so it is going to be helpful as food for the fire, but it will also come to its demise.

179 The fire here can consume the wood freely, offering the brightness of its bliss.

Line 4[180]	Wealthy family Most auspicious	**13 Tong Ren: similar cultivated (persons)** Gather cultivated ones in the open country Behave accordingly Favourable to wade accros the big river Favourable determination for the gentleman
Line 3[181]	Cultivated family person sighs The threat of trouble; auspicious If wife and child giggle distress ends	**Yi; increasing, overflow (of liquid), benefit** Favourable to have roots in the past Favourable to cross the big plain/river
Line 2	Not a distant satisfaction Be in the center of foodserving Auspicious determination	**9 xiao chu: small livestock** Small livestoch behaves like dense clouds No rain from the western outskirts Retrieve one's dao, what misfortune is this? Auspicious.

---

180   In line 4 the interaction between wood, fire and water is most balanced and harmonious, thus the recognized wealth of the situation.

181   In line 3 the fire has full control over the water it steams up.

Line 1[182]	Close the gate of ones house Trouble go away	53 Jian: to advance, gradually melting, reaching Woman sent in marriage Auspicious Favourable determination			
All lines change in opposition		40 Jie[183]: divide, seperate, untie, undo, explain, solve, comprehend, relieve oneself Favourable: southwest No place to go to therefore turning back, auspicious Have a place to go to since long, auspicious			

38 Kui: (meditative) gazing

A small affair[184],
Auspicious

Outer: metal under fire
Inner: water in metal

---

[182] Here the fire tries to generate effects from self cultivation, but the fire here only can lean on itself yet. It can see thewood, but not yeat eat it. It can feel the water but not yet steam it.

[183] The opposite of cultivation as part of a plan or community is the moving out of the pressure of the cultivation process as to relieve oneself of it.

[184] A major part of the starting process in daoist meditation is decreasing oneself and recognizing the in significance of large portions of what you call your self. The example of meditation is containing yourself, not by repression but by minimal effort, in this case by controlling fire with ore, the ore here might refer to chokes. The fire nonetheless will warm up the steam of the yangqi as in hexagram 63. The root of the hexagram is the alternation of water and fire, so understandin g the fire -water process is essential.

6 branches comparison:

	Zhoulinetext	*Wen'guatext*			
Line 6	Gazing fox sees a pig carrying mud on the back One carriage transports gohsts First draw a bow taut on them, later loosening the bow on them They aren't bandits but family of the wife for the wedding If meeting with rain it is auspicious	**54 Gui Mei: returning younger sister** Ominous for an expedition Favourable for nothing			
Line 5	Regret goes away Faint in the ancestrall hall Bite the skin What misfortune goeas away?	**10 Lu: shoe, footstep, honour, carry out, to walk on** Honouring the tigers tail It does not bite the cultivated Behave accordingly\			

Line 4	Gazing fox meets primary/basic man Turns over prisoner of war Threatening, no misfortune	**41 Sun: decrease, empty the vessel (of libation liquid)** Have a very auspicious capture No misfortune can be determened Favourable to have roots in the past What to use? Two tureens can be used for the offering			
Line 3	See the cart dragged by a bovine, one horn up, one horn down. His cultivated one has a tattoo on his forehead and a cut off nose. Have an ending without beginning	**14 Da you: great having** Grand having greatly Behave accordingly			
Line 2	Meet the master/ god of a lane No misfortune	**21 Shi He: biting through, the sounding voice of oracular speach, biting through a sounding voice** Smooth, favourable to use locking up/putting in jail, lawsuit			

Line 1	Regret goes away, Do not persue a lost horse: It will return by itself	**64 Wei Ji: have not / did not cross a river / be of help** Smooth Small fox at the point of crossing the streamgets his tail wet Not at all favourable			
All lines change in opposition		**39 Jian: lame, trouble** Favourable: the southwest (kun) Not favourable: the northeast (gen) Favourable to be exposed to a considerably (large) cultivated one Auspicious determination			

39 Jian: lame, trouble

Favourable: the southwest (kun)
Not favourable: the northeast (gen)
Favourable to be exposed to a considerably (large) cultivated one
Auspicious determination

6 branches comparison:

	Zhoulinetext	Wen'guatext			
Line 6	Going lame because of leisure Auspicious Favourable to be exposed to person of considerably cultivated one	**53 Jian: to advance, gradually melting, reaching** Woman sent in marriage Auspicious Favourable determination			

Line 5	Very lame; friend comes	**15 Qian: modesty (speech in contention, the sound of modesty)** Behave accordingly The gentleman has an end (conclusion)
Line 4	Going lame because of connections	**31 Xian / Gan: salty, to move/influence** Smooth, favourable determination, Take a maiden for wife Auspicious
Line 3	Going lame because of opposition	**8 Bi: emulate, copy, model after** Original auspiciousness Manipulate the (millifoil) stalks (oracle) Behave accordingly grand for a long-term determination. No misfortune. Not a peacefull method-state (tranquility meditation) Ominous for the man/ husband that comes late.

Line 2	The King's bondservant appears lame The cause is not in the body	48 Jing: (a) well Change a town but not change a well No loss no gain Go, come in perfect order Nearly reaches but not drawing water The well damages the earthen Jug Ominous			
Line 1	Going lame because of honor	63 Ji Ji: already/now that cross a river/be of help Smooth, little favourable determination Auspicious at the beginning, disorder at the end			
All lines change in opposition		38 Kui: (meditative) gazing A small affair, Auspicious			

40 Jie: divide, seperate, untie, undo, explain, solve, comprehend, relieve oneself

Favourable: southwest
No place to go to therefore turning back, auspicious
Have a place to go to since long, auspicious

6 branches comparison:

	Zhoulinetext	Wen'guatext			
Line 6	The duke has shot a hawk on top of a high wall, caught it Not unfavourable	**64 Wei Ji: have not / did not cross a river / be of help** Smooth Small fox at the point of crossing the streamgets his tail wet Not at all favourable			
Line 5	Have the gentlemans safeguard untied: Auspicious. Have capture by the little cultivated one	**47 Kun: stranded, surrounded, tired, pinned down, bothered** Smooth determination for a greatly cultivated one Auspicious, no misfortune There'll be unreliable talk			
Line 4	Relax your thumbs and toes; A friend arrives. Capture him	**7 Shi: teacher, master, skilled one, army** Determination for the greatly cultivated one is auspicious. No misfortune			
Line 3	Both carrying stuff on the back and riding Brings on the arrival of bandits Determination of distress	**32 Heng: permanent, lasting** Smooth, no misfortune Favourable determination Favourable to have roots in the past			

Line 2	Hunt and catch three foxes Receive golden arrow Auspicious determination	**16 Yu: giving an elephant away, pleased** Favourablre to establish an high official Mobilize the army			
Line 1	No error	**54 Gui Mei: returning younger sister** Ominous for an expedition Favourable for nothing			
All lines change in opposition		**37 Jia ren: domestication, cultivated family/clan person, cultivated professional person** Favourable feminine determination			

41 Sun: decrease, empty the vessel (of libation liquid)

Have a very auspicious capture
No misfortune can be determened
Favourable to have roots in the past
What to use?
Two tureens can be used for the offering

6 branches comparison:

	Zhoulinetext	*Wen'guatext*			
Line 6	No decrease; increase it! No determination of misfortune; auspicious Favourable to have roots in the past Get yourself bondservant, not family	**19 Lin: face, overlook, befall, arrive, on the point of** Grand smoothness Favourable determination that extends to the eight moon Have an act of violence			
Line 5	Maybe benefitting his ten friends with turtle None can refuse Very auspicious	**61 Zhong Fu: center/ middle/attained/inner faith, inner sincerity** Young pig, fish: auspicious Favourable to cross the great plain Favourable determination			
Line 4	To decrease his suffering quickly causes to have joy No misfortune	**38 Kui: (meditative) gazing** A small affair, Auspicious			
Line 3	If three persons travel they will be decreased by one If one person travels then get his/her companion	**26 Da Chu: large livestock** Beneficial determination Auspicious to not eat with your clan Favourable to cross the wide plain (swomp gua can also mean plain, there is no xiaogua refering to water)			

Line 2	Favourable determination for attack Ominous: no decrease; increase it!	**27 Yi: jaws, nourishing** (character suggesting eating appropiately [something between the jaws], or the nourishing of a person whom cultivates appropiate behaviour, the second part as a whole is the character for zhen, that is mostly translated as determination/determined) Auspicious determination Observe the jaws (conciousness) itself seeking substance for the mouth			
Line 1	Quicly go for sacreficial service No misfortune Decrease the libation	**4 Meng: blindfolded** Smooth: we do not seek the dodder, the dodder seeks us first. Manipulate the stalks and it will tell twice. The third time is an insult			
All lines change in opposition		**31 Xian / Gan: salty, to move/influence** Smooth, favourable determination, Take a maiden for wife Auspicious			

42 Yi; increasing, overflow (of liquid), benefit

Favourable to have roots in the past
Favourable to cross the big plain/river

6 branches comparison:

	Zhoulinetext	*Wen'guatext*			
Line 6	Non increase this one, some strike him Take heart, but not for long: Ominous	**3 Zhun: birththrows** Smooth origin, benificial determination Do not use! Have a place to go to Favourable to establish an official			
Line 5	Have a capture wich is heartfelt; don't ask! Very auspicious There is a capture we might receive	**27 Yi: jaws, nourishing** (character suggesting eating appropiately [something between the jaws], or the nourishing of a person whom cultivates appropiate behaviour, the second part as a whole is the character for zhen, that is mostly translated as determination/determined)			
Line 4	The duke follws the report at the middle of the road Favourable to earnestly use moving of the nation	**25 Wu wang: without presumption** Primary enjoyment Favourable determination If not straight (punctual, centered); have calamety Not favourable to have roots in the past			

Line 3	Increase their use, Ominous to serve No misfortune to have a capture at the middle of the road To report the duke uses a gui tablet (register)	**37 Jia ren: domestication, cultivated family/clan person, cultivated professional person** Favourable feminine determination
Line 2	Maybe benefit his ten friends with turtle None can refuse Auspicious for long term determination King has pleasure from the supreme being Auspicious	**61 Zhong Fu: center/ middle/attained/inner faith, inner sincerity** Young pig, fish: auspicious Favourable to cross the great plain Favourable determination
Line 1	Favorable to use serving in a big project Very auspicious, no misfortune	**20 guan: conception of the nature of things, observe, view, (monestary)** Washing but no offering Have faith and sincerety captured
All lines change in opposition		**32 Heng: permanent, lasting** Smooth, no misfortune Favourable determination Favourable to have roots in the past

43 Quai/Jue: decide, determine, to cleanse, open out

Display a capture at the kings court
There be threatening reports from the town
A violent aproach is unfavourable
Favourable to have roots in the past

6 branches comparison:

	Zhoulinetext	Wen'guatext			
Line 6	Ominous if in the end have no outcry	**1 Qian: sky** Smooth origin, Favourable determination			
Line 5	The mountain goat lands most determined at the middle of the road No misfortune	**34 Da Zhuang: big force, big health (stoutness)** Sharp determination			
Line 4	Buttocks without skin make travel hardgoing Lead the sheep away from troubles Hear unreliable talk	**5 Xü: needing, wanting** Have a glorious capture and act accordingly The determination is auspicious It is favourable to wade across the big river			
Line 3	It is ominous to have strength in the cheeckbone Gentleman decides to open out Travel alone and encounter rain There'll be displeasure if getting wet, no misfortune	**58 Dui (Yue): exchange, conversion** (Common meaning: pleasure, lake modeled after the similar sounding name of the double gua) Smooth. Favourable determination			

Line 2	Cries out warily in the evening At night there'll be violence Do not worry	**49 Ge: leather, hide, transform, change** Capture great smoothness at sacrificial day Favourable determination Troubles go away			
Line 1	Strength in the front of the foot Goes but does not overcome Misfortune	**28 Da Guo: enlargening** Yielding support Favourable to have roots in the past Smooth			
All lines change in opposition		**23 Bo: foretelling by elimination, stripping away, flaying** Not favourable to have roots in the past			

44 Gou: to meet, to encounter, female ruler, intercourse

Strong woman
Has no use to marry a women

6 branches comparison:

	Zhoulinetext	*Wen'guatext*			
Line 6	Interlocking their horns: Distress, no misfortune	**28 Da Guo: enlargening** Yielding support Favourable to have roots in the past Smooth			

Line 5	Wrap melon with purple willow, Hold a jade talisman in the mouth: Have fallen from sky due to sky (refers to Qian)	**50 Ding: sacrificial vessel (Tripod)** Primary auspiciousness Smooth			
Line 4	Unwrapped fish, Ominous to remove	**57 Xun (Zhuan): calculation** Little smooth Favourable to have roots in the past. Favourable to see the largely cultivated one			
Line 3	Buttocks without skin make travel hardgoing Threatening but no large misfortune	**6 Song: arguing, lawsuit** Have a capture and they will be zhi-ti frightened Middle stage auspicious, end ominous Favourable to see the big cultivated one Not favourable to wade a big river.			
Line 2	Have the fish wrapped, No misfortune, Unfavourable to be guest	**33 Dun: little pig, conceal, hide** Smooth, Determination a little favourable			

Line 1	Tied to a metal spindle, Determined (that it is) auspicious to have roots in the past An ominous sight: the capture of an emaciated pig; it plants its feet (in the ground) and balks when moved	1 Qian: sky Smooth origin, Favourable determination			
All lines change in opposition		24 Fu: turn around, answer, recover/resume, revenge, again Going out, coming in; behave accordingly (and there'll be) no illness Friend comes, no misfortune Oppose resuming of the Dao and after seven suns comes the answer Favourable to have roots in the past			

45 Cui: to gather together

Smooth
The king goes into his temple
Favourable to visit the greatly cultivated one (priest)
Smooth and favourable determination
Auspicious to use large sacrificial animal
Favourable to have roots in the past

6 branches comparison:

	Zhoulinetext	*Wen'guatext*			
Line 6	Sighing, sobbing, tears and snot No misfortune	**12 Pi: negative/not mouth** Bad his/her unperson, not favourable for the gentleman Determination: big goes, small comes			
Line 5	Tossed together and have seniority (high rank) No misfortune and not being captured Primary auspiciousness Troubles go away in case of a longterm determination	**16 Yu: giving an elephant away, pleased** Favourablre to establish an high official Mobilize the army			
Line 4	Very auspicious No Misfortune	**8 Bi: emulate, copy, model after** Original auspiciousness Manipulate the (millifoil) stalks (oracle) Behave accordingly grand for a long-term determination. No misfortune. Not a peacefull method-state (tranquility meditation) Ominous for the man/ husband that comes late.			

Line 3	Sighing as if bundled together, not favourable for anything No misfortune in going Small Distress	**31 Xian / Gan: salty, to move/influence** Smooth, favourable determination, Take a maiden for wife Auspicious
Line 2	Auspicious to draw the bow taut No misfortune in capture and then favourable to use a yue (sacrifice)	**47 Kun: stranded, surrounded, tired, pinned down, bothered** Smooth determination for a greatly cultivated one Auspicious, no misfortune There'll be unreliable talk
Line 1	Have a capture, no death and then a mess then wailing as if trossed together A cackling sound becomes a laugh Don't worry, no misfortune in going	**17 Sui: follow, comply** Primary smoothness (succes) Enjoy the favourable determination No fault (blame)
All lines change in opposition		**46 Sheng: ascending, going upwards** Primary smoothness Visit the greatly cultivated one (priest) Don't worry Attacking the south is auspicious

46 Sheng: ascending, going upwards

Primary smoothness
Visit the greatly cultivated one (priest)
Don't worry
Attacking the south is auspicious

6 branches comparison:

	Zhoulinetext	Wen'guatext			
Line 6	Dark ascending Favourable to be determined not to stop	**18 Gu: (legendary) venomenous insect** (used in black magic) Primary smoothness Go through the big plains before Jia (yang wood heavenly stem) sun and after jia sun (jia sun was considered unlucky)			
Line 5	Auspicious determination Ascending stairs	**48 Jing: (a) well** Change a town but not change a well No loss no gain Go, come in perfect order Nearly reaches but not drawing water The well damages the earthen Jug Ominous			

Line 4	The king smoothly goes to mount Qi (rough) Auspicious and no misfortune	**32 Heng: permanent, lasting** Smooth, no misfortune Favourable determination Favourable to have roots in the past
Line 3	Going upwards in a hilltown	**7 Shi: teacher, master, skilled one, army** Determination for the greatly cultivated one is auspicious. No misfortune.
Line 2	A capture; then favourable to use yue (sacrifice) No misfortune	**15 Qian: modesty (speech in contention, the sound of modesty)** Behave accordingly The gentleman has an end (conclusion)
Line 1	A fair ascending Greatly auspicious	**11 Tai: safe, peacefull, tranquil, extreme, most** The small goes, the big comes Auspicious, behave accordingly

All lines change in opposition		**45 Cui: to gather together** Smooth The king goes into his temple Favourable to visit the greatly cultivated one (priest) Smooth and favourable determination Auspicious to use large sacrificial animal Favourable to have roots in the past			

47 Kun: stranded, surrounded, tired, pinned down, bothered

Smooth determination for a greatly cultivated one
Auspicious, no misfortune
There'll be unreliable talk

6 branches comparison:

	Zhoulinetext	*Wen'guatext*			
Line 6	6 Pined down by vine (vitis flexuosa, climber) at tree supporter Sun changes regret Have regret Attacking is auspicious	**6 Song: arguing, lawsuit** Have a capture and they will be zhi-ti frightened Middle stage auspicious, end ominous Favourable to see the big cultivated one Not favourable to wade a big river			

Line 5	5 Cut of nose Cut of feet Pinned down by red kneeshields and slowly have them removed Favourable to use devotional sacrefice	**40 Jie: divide, seperate, untie, undo, explain, solve, comprehend, relieve oneself** Favourable: southwest No place to go to therefore turning back, auspicious Have a place to go to since long, auspicious			
Line 4	4 Coming slowly, pinned down by metal cart The distress has an ending	**29 (Xi) kan: (review / be used to) bank, ridge** Have a prisoner safeguard the heart Smooth Travel has esteem			
Line 3	3 Pinned down by rocks, grabs at vine (tribulus terestris, earth creeper) Entering his house, not seeing his wife Ominous	**28 Da Guo: enlargening** Yielding support Favourable to have roots in the past Smooth			

Line 2	2 Pinned down by liquid food Vermilion kneeshield party comes Favourable for using smooth sacrifice Ominous for attack No misfortune	**45 Cui: to gather together** Smooth The king goes into his temple Favourable to visit the greatly cultivated one (priest) Smooth and favourable determination Auspicious to use large sacrificial animal Favourable to have roots in the past			
Line 1	1 Buttocks pinned down by tree supporter, numbed Enter the dark valley (coma) For three years not seeing counciousness (face to face)	**58 Dui (Yue): exchange, conversion** (Common meaning: pleasure, lake modeled after the similar sounding name of the double gua)			
All lines change in opposition		**48 Jing: (a) well** Change a town but not change a well No loss no gain Go, come in perfect order Nearly reaches but not drawing water The well damages the earthen Jug Ominous			

48 Jing: (a) well

Change a town but not change a well
No loss no gain
Go, come in perfect order
 Nearly reaches but not drawing water
The well damages the earthen Jug
Ominous

6 branches comparison:

	Zhoulinetext	*Wen'guatext*			
Line 6	6 Do not take up the well and put it away Cover it and there'll be a very auspicious capture	**57 Xun (Zhuan): calculation** Little smooth Favourable to have roots in the past. Favourable to see the largely cultivated one			
Line 5	5 A well with clear cold spring Drink	**46 Sheng: ascending, going upwards** Primary smoothness Visit the greatly cultivated one (priest) Don't worry Attacking the south is auspicious			
Line 4	4 Well lined with tiles No misfortune	**28 Da Guo: enlargening** Yielding support Favourable to have roots in the past Smooth			

Line 3	3 An unsettled well, no drinking Becomes our heart sorrow If used to draw water by the bright king's covenant, together (we) would receive its blessings	**29 (Xi) kan: (review / be used to) bank, ridge** Have a prisoner safeguard the heart Smooth Travel has esteem			
Line 2	2 Silver carp shoots away in the depth of the well The earthen jar is ruined and leaks	**3 Zhun: birththrows** Smooth origin, benificial determination Do not use! Have a place to go to Favourable to establish an official			
Line 1	1 Muddy well; no drinking An old well; no game	**5 Xü: needing, wanting** Have a glorious capture and act accordingly The determination is auspicious It is favourable to wade across the big river			
All lines change in opposition		**47 Kun: stranded, surrounded, tired, pinned down, bothered** Smooth determination for a greatly cultivated one Auspicious, no misfortune There'll be unreliable talk			

49 Ge: leather, hide, transform, change

Capture great smoothness at sacrificial day
Favourable determination
Troubles go away

6 branches comparison:

	Zhoulinetext	*Wen'guatext*			
Line 6	6 Leopard transformation of the gentleman A little cultivated one with a rawhide face (mask) Ominous for an expedition	**13 Tong Ren: similar cultivated (persons)** Gather cultivated ones in the open country Behave accordingly Favourable to wade accros the big river Favourable determination for the gentleman			
Line 5	5 Tiger transformation of the greatly cultivated one Not yet prognosticated to have a capture	**55 Feng: plentifull, great** Smooth. King fakes the inhibition of worry/sorrow Appropiate for the middle of sun (day)			
Line 4	4 Trouble go away Have a capture Auspicious for a transforming charge	**63 Ji Ji: already/now that cross a river/be of help** Smooth, little favourable determination Auspicious at the beginning, disorder at the end			

Line 3	3 Ominous for an expedition Threatening determination Have a capture of a rawhide harness with three girdlings	**17 Sui: follow, comply** Primary smoothness (succes) Enjoy the favourable determination No fault (blame)	🟧		🟩
Line 2	2 Change it on sacrificial day Auspicious for an expedition/solicit No misfortune	**43 Quai/Jue: decide, determine, to cleanse, open out** Display a capture at the kings court There be threatening reports from the town A violent aproach is unfavourable Favourable to have roots in the past	🟧		🟩
Line 1	1 For consolidation use the hide of yellow-brown bovine	**31 Xian / Gan: salty, to move/influence** Smooth, favourable determination, Take a maiden for wife Auspicious	🟧		
All lines change in opposition		**50 Ding: sacrificial vessel (Tripod)** Primary auspiciousness Smooth			

50 Ding: sacrificial vessel (Tripod)

Primary auspiciousness
Smooth

6 branches comparison:

	Zhoulinetext	*Wen'guatext*			
Line 6	6 Sacrificial vessel with jade carryingbar Very auspicious Not unfavourable	**32 Heng: permanent, lasting** Smooth, no misfortune Favourable determination Favourable to have roots in the past			
Line 5	5 Sacrificial Vessel with yellowbrown ears and a metal carryingbar Favourable determination	**44 Gou: to meet, to encounter, female ruler, intercourse** Strong woman Has no use to marry a women			
Line 4	4 Foot of sacrificial vessel snaps Overturns the dukes stew His body soaked Ominous	**18 Gu: (legendary) venomenous insect** (used in black magic) Primary smoothness Go through the big plains before Jia (yang wood heavenly stem) sun and after jia sun (jia sun was considered unlucky)			

Line 3	3 Transformation of the sacrificicial vessel's ear His walk is blocked Fatty peasant meat not eaten Just rain will make trouble lost Ends auspicious	**64 Wei Ji: have not / did not cross a river / be of help** Smooth Small fox at the point of crossing the streamgets his tail wet Not at all favourable		
Line 2	2 Sacrificial vessel has content My mate has an illness that cannot aproach me Auspicious	**56 Lü: travel (possibly traveler), staying away fom home, troops, force** Little smooth For travel is the determination auspicious		
Line 1	1 Sacrificial vessel tossed upside down Favourable to expel evil Get female slave with her child No Misfortune	**14 Da you: great having** Grand having greatly Behave accordingly		
All lines change in opposition		**49 Ge: leather, hide, transform, change** Capture great smoothness at sacrificial day Favourable determination Troubles go away		

51 Zhen: shake, shock, quake, vibrate, greatly exited, deeply astonished

Smooth,
Shock comes 'crackcrack!!!'
Laughing, talking 'yakyak'
Shock frigthens an area 100 li around
Do not drop the ladle (spoon) with aromatic spirits
(aromatic spirits pictographicly refering to the container of the Po souls)

6 branches comparison:

	Zhoulinetext	*Wen'guatext*			
Line 6	Shake, ask, demand Glare (with a ferocious look) Ominous for attack The shake doesn't go to your body, goes to neighbour No misfortune, have a talk at the wedding	**21 Shi He: biting through, the sounding voice of oracular speach, biting through a sounding voice** Smooth, favourable to use locking up/putting in jail, lawsuit			
Line 5	5 Shock comes, goes Threat does not suggests loss Have work	**17 Sui: follow, comply** Primary smoothness (succes) Enjoy the favourable determination No fault (blame)			

Line 4	4 Vibration fulfills plastering	**24 Fu: turn around, answer, recover/resume, revenge, again** Going out, coming in; behave accordingly (and there'll be) no illness Friend comes, no misfortune Oppose resuming of the Dao and after seven suns comes the answer Favourable to have roots in the past			
Line 3	3 Shock thunders into the conciousness (`becomes concious becomes concious' as the result of rolling thunder) Shock travels No calamity	**55 Feng: plentifull, great** Smooth. King fakes the inhibition of worry/sorrow Appropiate for the middle of sun (day)			
Line 2	2 Shock comes as a thread Losing your cowry shells Climb up on the nine hills (burial mounds) Do not persue, in seven suns you receive	**54 Gui Mei: returning younger sister** Ominous for an expedition Favourable for nothing			

Line 1	1 Shock comes 'crackcrack!!!' Later there is laughing, talking 'yakyak' Auspicious	16 Yu: giving an elephant away, pleased Favourablre to establish an high official Mobilize the army			
All lines change in opposition		52 Gen: stopping, stilling (associations with root, source, base) Stilling the back but not capturing the structure Traveling the court but not showing evidence of being a cultivated one No misfortune			

52 Gen: stopping, stilling (associations with root, source, base)

Stilling the back but not capturing the structure
Traveling the court but not showing evidence of being a cultivated one
No misfortune

6 branches comparison:

	Zhoulinetext	Wen'guatext			
Line 6	Sincere stilling Auspicious	15 Qian: modesty (speech in contention, the sound of modesty) Behave accordingly The gentleman has an end (conclusion)			

Line 5	5 Stilling the jaw Have ordered talk and trouble goes away	**53 Jian: to advance, gradually melting, reaching** Woman sent in marriage Auspicious Favourable determination			
Line 4	4 Stilling the structure No misfortune	**56 Lü: travel (possibly traveler), staying away fom home, troops, force** Little smooth For travel is the determination auspicious			
Line 3	3 Stilling the waist, lining up the spinal flesh Stricktly burning the heart	**23 Bo: foretelling by elimination, stripping away, flaying** Not favourable to have roots in the past			
Line 2	2 Stilling the lower leg, not removing the marrow. The heart not gratified	**18 Gu: (legendary) venomenous insect** (used in black magic) Primary smoothness Go through the big plains before Jia (yang wood heavenly stem) sun and after jia sun (jia sun was considered unlucky)			
Line 1	1 Stilling the foot, no misfortune Does good to long-term determination	**22 Bi: bright, decoration** Behave accordingly small Favourable to have roots in the past			

| All lines change in opposition | | 51 Zhen: shake, shock, quake, vibrate, greatly exited, deeply astonished

Smooth,
Shock comes 'crackcrack!!!'
Laughing, talking 'yakyak'
Shock frigthens an area 100 li around
Do not drop the ladle (spoon) with aromatic spirits
(aromatic spirits pictographicly refering to the container of the Po souls) | | | |

53 Jian: to advance, gradually melting, reaching

Woman sent in marriage
Auspicious
Favourable determination

6 branches comparison:

	Zhoulinetext	Wen'guatext			
Line 6	6 Wild goose advances to land His feathers can be used for ceremonial attire Auspicious	39 Jian: lame, trouble Favourable: the southwest (kun) Not favourable: the northeast (gen) Favourable to be exposed to a considerably (large) cultivated one Auspicious determination			

Line 5	5 Wild goose advance to the Burrial mound For three years the wife doesn't get pregnant Death; some overcome it Auspicious	**52 Gen: stopping, stilling (associations with root, source, base)** Stilling the back but not capturing the structure Traveling the court but not showing evidence of being a cultivated one No misfortune
Line 4	4 Wild goose advances to the tree Perhaps gets his nest No misfortune	**33 Dun: little pig, conceal, hide** Smooth, Determination a little favourable
Line 3	3 Wild goose advances to high ground Husband goes on expedition but does not return The wife is pregnant but does not give birth Ominous Favourable to fend off bandits	**20 guan: conception of the nature of things, observe, view, (monestary)** Washing but no offering Have faith and sincerety captured
Line 2	2 Wild goose advances to a boulder Drinks, eats and happily honks Auspicious	**57 Xun (Zhuan): calculation** Little smooth Favourable to have roots in the past. Favourable to see the largely cultivated one

Line 1	1 Wild goose (or swan) advances to the riverbank. A small child threatens to have a word. No Misfortune	37 Jia ren: domestication, cultivated family/clan person, cultivated professional person Favourable feminine determination			
All lines change in opposition		54 Gui Mei: returning younger sister Ominous for an expedition. Favourable for nothing			

54 Gui Mei: returning younger sister[185]

Ominous for an expedition
Favourable for nothing

6 branches comparison:

	Zhoulinetext	Wen'guatext			
Line 6	6 The woman holds an empty basket in her outstretched arm. The man stabs a bloodless sheep. Favourable for nothing	38 Kui: (meditative) gazing A small affair, Auspicious			

---

[185] Recent linguistic research has shown that the returning younger sister is a story of war movements. Hexagram 53 an d 54 as a unit then both deal with conflict resolvin g methodology.

Line 5	5 Supreme Being Yi (the second) returns the younger sister to the Supreme Ruler. Her sleeves are not comparable to the good sleeves of his secondary wife. The moon is almost full. Auspicious	**58 Dui (Yue): exchange, conversion** (Common meaning: pleasure, lake modeled after the similar sounding name of the double gua) Smooth. Favourable determination
Line 4	4 Return of the younger sister exceeds timing Slow in going to the new home Have delay	**19 Lin: face, overlook, befall, arrive, on the point of** Grand smoothness Favourable determination that extends to the eight moon Have an act of violence
Line 3	3 Return of the younger sister with bondservant. She opposes coming together with secondary wife	**34 Da Zhuang: big force, big health (stoutness)** Sharp determination

Line 2	2 The feeble sigthed *can* examine the determination of cultivated one from the netherworld that does do good (deeds)	**51 Zhen: shake, shock, quake, vibrate, greatly exited, deeply astonished** Smooth, Shock comes 'crackcrack!!!' Laughing, talking 'yakyak' Shock frigthens an area 100 li around Do not drop the ladle (spoon) with aromatic spirits (aromatic spirits pictographicly refering to the container of the Po souls)			
Line 1	1 Return of the younger sister as secondary wife	**40 Jie: divide, seperate, untie, undo, explain, solve, comprehend, relieve oneself** Favourable: southwest No place to go to therefore turning back, auspicious Have a place to go to since long, auspicious			
All lines change in opposition		**53 Jian: to advance, gradually melting, reaching** Woman sent in marriage Auspicious Favourable determination			

55 Feng: plentifull, great

Smooth.
King fakes the inhibition of worry/sorrow
Appropiate for the middle of sun (day)

6 branches comparison:

	Zhoulinetext	Wen'guatext			
Line 6	6 Great his house Screening his home Peeking through his door Silent his unperson For three years not seen. Ominous.	**64 Wei Ji: have not / did not cross a river / be of help** Smooth Small fox at the point of crossing the streamgets his tail wet Not at all favourable			
Line 5	5 Arrival of order. Have a celebration of honor. Auspicious	**49 Ge: leather, hide, transform, change** Capture great smoothness at sacrificial day Favourable determination Troubles go away			
Line 4	4 His great screen to see the dipper at midday (ri zhong). Meet his safe god. Auspicious	**36 Ming yi: safe/ darkening of brightness/ brilliance** Favourable in a hardship determination			

Line 3	3 Great his covering. See dark spots at middle of sun (ri zhong). Breaking his arm No misfortune	**51 Zhen: shake, shock, quake, vibrate, greatly exited, deeply astonished** Smooth, Shock comes 'crackcrack!!!' Laughing, talking 'yakyak' Shock frigthens an area 100 li around Do not drop the ladle (spoon) with aromatic spirits (aromatic spirits pictographicly refering to the container of the Po souls)
Line 2	2 His great screen to see the dipper at midday (ri zhong). Previously had the illness of doubt. Auspicious to have a capture of arousal.	**34 Da Zhuang: big force, big health (stoutness)** Sharp determination

Line 1	1 To meet his worthy god, though it be in a decade. No misfortune. Go and have reward	**62 Xiao Guo: small pass, small life/time, going a little beyond, small finish (a bit of ending), a small betterment, smallness.** Smooth and favourable determination Approval for small matter, no approval for big matter A flying (fluttering) bird leaves his sound behind Not suitable to rise, suitable to descent Large benefit			
All lines change in opposition		**56 Lü: travel (possibly traveler), staying away fom home, troops, force** Little smooth For travel is the determination auspicious			

56 Lü: travel (possibly traveler), staying away fom home, troops, force

Little smooth
For travel is the determination auspicious

6 branches comparison:

	Zhoulinetext	Wen'guatext			
Line 6	6 Bird (crow) burns his nest Traveler first laughs, later howls and wails. Lost bovine at exchange (Yi as in title book) Ominous	**62 Xiao Guo: small pass, small life/time, going a little beyond, small finish (a bit of ending), a small betterment, smallness.** Smooth and favourable determination Approval for small matter, no approval for big matter A flying (fluttering) bird leaves his sound behind Not suitable to rise, suitable to descent Large benefit			
Line 5	5 Shooting a pheasant One arrow runs off Finishing it because of life reputation	**33 Dun: little pig, conceal, hide** Smooth, Determination a little favourable			
Line 4	4 traveler deals with his/her sacred axe My heart is not quick(witted)	**52 Gen: stopping, stilling (associations with root, source, base)** Stilling the back but not capturing the structure Traveling the court but not showing evidence of being a cultivated one No misfortune			

Line 3	3 The traveler burns his/her hostel (or: staying away from home Burning his/her hostel) Losing his/her child servant Threatening determination	**35 Jin: to enter, advance, promote** Lord of Kang (Health) uses giving of many (mated numbers) horses During light of day three joinings			
Line 2	2 The traveler nears inferior thinking of his/her funding (or: staying away from home nearing panicky thoughts about his/her capital) Obtain a child servant. Auspicious determination	**50 Ding: sacrificial vessel (Tripod)** Primary auspiciousness Smooth			
Line 1	1 Traveling in tiny pieces (nomadic?) Refined his place Fetches disaster	**30 Li: to leave, part from** Favourable determination Smooth to raise cows Auspicious			
All lines change in opposition		**55 Feng: plentifull, great** Smooth. King fakes the inhibition of worry/sorrow Appropiate for the middle of sun (day)			

57 Xun (Zhuan): calculation

Little smooth
Favourable to have roots in the past.
Favourable to see the largely cultivated one

6 branches comparison:

	Zhoulinetext	*Wen'guatext*			
Line 6	6 Layout (of offering or omens) exist beneeth the bed Losing the prosperity of his sacred axe Ominous determination	**48 Jing: (a) well** Change a town but not change a well No loss no gain Go, come in perfect order Nearly reaches but not drawing water The well damages the earthen Jug Ominous			
Line 5	5 Auspicious determination: trouble leaves Nothing unfavourable No beginning but have an ending Auspicious from three days before geng (heavenly stem: 7yang metal, portent of good luck) and three days after geng.	**18 Gu: (legendary) venomenous insect** (used in black magic) Primary smoothness Go through the big plains before Jia (yang wood heavenly stem) sun and after jia sun (jia sun was considered unlucky)			

Line 4	4 Trouble leaves In the field reaping the threa articles (Jing, Shen, Qi)	**44 Gou: to meet, to encounter, female ruler, intercourse** Strong woman Has no use to marry a women
Line 3	3 Repeated layout (of offering or omens) Distress	**59 Huan: to melt, vanish** Smooth The artificial king has a temple Favorable to wade across the great river Favourable determination
Line 2	2 Layout (of offering or omens) exist beneath the bed. Use witches/ wizzards if numerous/ confused No misfortune	**53 Jian: to advance, gradually melting, reaching** Woman sent in marriage Auspicious Favourable determination
Line 1	1 Advance, withdraw Favourable determination for the military person	**9 xiao chu: small livestock** Small livestoch behaves like dense clouds No rain from the western outskirts Retrieve one's dao, what misfortune is this? Auspicious.

All lines change in opposition		58 Dui (Yue): exchange, conversion (Common meaning: pleasure, lake modeled after the similar sounding name of the double gua)			

58 Dui (Yue): exchange, conversion

(Common meaning: pleasure, lake modeled after the similar sounding name of the double gua)

Smooth.
Favourable determination

6 branches comparison:

	Zhoulinetext	Wen'guatext			
Line 6	6 Drawn out conversion	**10 Lu: shoe, footstep, honour, carry out, to walk on** Honouring the tigers tail It does not bite the cultivated Behave accordingly			
Line 5	5 Capture at flaying/fortelling by elimination (Bo 23) Be strict	**54 Gui Mei: returning younger sister** Ominous for an expedition Favourable for nothing			

Line 4	4 Discussing conversion Have no tranquility Take the illness to heart(seriously) Have joy	**60 Jie: joint, node, knot** Smooth Bitter node (as in bamboo) Cannot be determined			
Line 3	3 Going to converse. Ominous	**43 Quai/Jue: decide, determine, to cleanse, open out** Display a capture at the kings court There be threatening reports from the town A violent aproach is unfavourable Favourable to have roots in the past			
Line 2	2 Capture conversion Auspicious Trouble leave	**17 Sui: follow, comply** Primary smoothness (succes) Enjoy the favourable determination No fault (blame)			
Line 1	1 Harmonious conversion. Auspicious	**47 Kun: stranded, surrounded, tired, pinned down, bothered** Smooth determination for a greatly cultivated one Auspicious, no misfortune There'll be unreliable talk			

All lines change in opposition		57 Xun (Zhuan): calculation Little smooth Favourable to have roots in the past. Favourable to see the largely cultivated one			

59 Huan: to melt, vanish

Smooth
The artificial king has a temple
Favorable to wade across the great river
Favourable determination

6 branches comparison:

	Zhoulinetext	*Wen'guatext*			
Line 6	6 His blood vanishing Flows out far No misfortune	**29 (Xi) kan: (review / be used to) bank, ridge** Have a prisoner safeguard the heart Smooth Travel has esteem			
Line 5	5 Vanishing his liver (spirit) A loud cry A vanishing royal dwelling No misfortune	**4 Meng: blindfolded** Smooth: we do not seek the dodder, the dodder seeks us first. Manipulate the stalks and it will tell twice. The third time is an insult.			

Line 4	4 His crowd vanishes. Very auspicious. Not safe to consider having a mound	**6 Song: arguing, lawsuit** Have a capture and they will be zhi-ti frightened Middle stage auspicious, end ominous Favourable to see the big cultivated one Not favourable to wade a big river.
Line 3	3 His personal vanishing. Without trouble	**57 Xun (Zhuan): calculation** Little smooth Favourable to have roots in the past. Favourable to see the largely cultivated one
Line 2	2 His pivot hurriedly vanishes Troubles leave	**20 guan: conception of the nature of things, observe, view, (monestary)** Washing but no offering Have faith and sincerety captured
Line 1	1 Use a healthy horse for gelding Auspicious	**61 Zhong Fu: center/ middle/attained/inner faith, inner sincerity** Young pig, fish: auspicious Favourable to cross the great plain Favourable determination

All lines change in opposition		60 Jie: joint, node, knot Smooth Bitter node (as in bamboo) Cannot be determined			

60 Jie: joint, node, knot

Smooth
Bitter node (as in bamboo)
Cannot be determined

6 branches comparison:

	Zhoulinetext	Wen'guatext			
Line 6	6 Bitter node Ominous determination Troubles leave	**61 Zhong Fu: center/ middle/attained/inner faith, inner sincerity** Young pig, fish: auspicious Favourable to cross the great plain Favourable determination			
Line 5	5 Sweet node Auspicious Go and have a reward	**19 Lin: face, overlook, befall, arrive, on the point of** Grand smoothness Favourable determination that extends to the eight moon Have an act of violence			

Line 4	4 Fixed node Smooth	**58 Dui (Yue): exchange, conversion** (Common meaning: pleasure, lake modeled after the similar sounding name of the double gua) Smooth. Favourable determination			
Line 3	3 Not like a node but like a sigh No misfortune	**5 Xü: needing, wanting** Have a glorious capture and act accordingly The determination is auspicious It is favourable to wade across the big river			
Line 2	2 Not leaving from the fronyard gate Ominous	**3 Zhun: birththrows** Smooth origin, benificial determination Do not use! Have a place to go to Favourable to establish an official			
Line 1	1 Not leaving from the frontyard No misfortune	**29 (Xi) kan: (review / be used to) bank, ridge** Have a prisoner safeguard the heart Smooth Travel has esteem			

All lines change in opposition		59 Huan: to melt, vanish Smooth The artificial king has a temple Favorable to wade across the great river Favourable determination			

61 Zhong Fu: center/middle/attained/ inner faith, inner sincerity

Young pig, fish: auspicious
Favourable to cross the great plain
Favourable determination

6 branches comparison:

	Zhoulinetext	Wen'guatext			
Line 6	6 Tidings of the writing brush ascending towards sky Ominous determination	**60 Jie: joint, node, knot** Smooth Bitter node (as in bamboo) Cannot be determined	🟩		
Line 5	5 Have captives contracted if without misfortune	**41 Sun: decrease, empty the vessel (of libation liquid)** Have a very auspicious capture No misfortune can be determened Favourable to have roots in the past What to use? Two tureens can be used for the offering	🟩	🟧	

Line 4	4 The moon is almost a full moon A pair of horses flee No misfortune	**10 Lu: shoe, footstep, honour, carry out, to walk on** Honouring the tigers tail It does not bite the cultivated Behave accordingly	(green)	(orange)	(green)
Line 3	3 Obtaining an enemy Some drum, some rest, some weep, some sing	**9 xiao chu: small livestock** Small livestoch behaves like dense clouds No rain from the western outskirts Retrieve one's dao, what misfortune is this? Auspicious.	(grey)	(orange)	(green)
Line 2	2 Calling crane at yin (shady northern slope) His offspring replies I have good (filled) Jue (tripod wine vessel with loop handle) I offer that to share	**Yi; increasing, overflow (of liquid), benefit** Favourable to have roots in the past Favourable to cross the big plain/river			(green)
Line 1	1 Auspicious prediction Have him (it) not calmed	**59 Huan: to melt, vanish** Smooth The artificial king has a temple Favorable to wade across the great river Favourable determination			

All lines change in opposition		62 Xiao Guo: small pass, small life/time, going a little beyond, small finish (a bit of ending), a small betterment, smallness. Smooth and favourable determination Approval for small matter, no approval for big matter A flying (fluttering) bird leaves his sound behind Not suitable to rise, suitable to descent Large benefit			

62 Xiao Guo: small pass, small life/time, going a little beyond, small finish (a bit of ending), a small betterment, smallness.

Smooth and favourable determination
Approval for small matter, no approval for big matter
A flying (fluttering) bird leaves his sound behind
Not suitable to rise, suitable to descent
Large benefit

6 branches comparison:

	Zhoulinetext	Wen'guatext			
Line 6	6 Passing him, not meeting Flying bird is netted Ominous Is meaning calamity and disaster	56 Lü: travel (possibly traveler), staying away fom home, troops, force Little smooth For travel is the determination auspicious			

Line 5	5 Dense clouds do not rain at our western outskirts Oficial Bussines to shoot a bird that depends on a cave	**31 Xian / Gan: salty, to move/influence** Smooth, favourable determination, Take a maiden for wife Auspicious			
Line 4	4 Without benefit Meeting him, not passing Dangerous to go, necessary to be cautious Do not use in long term determination	**15 Qian: modesty (speech in contention, the sound of modesty)** Behave accordingly The gentleman has an end (conclusion)			
Line 3	3 Not passing, preventing his following Maybe killed (slayed) Ominous	**16 Yu: giving an elephant away, pleased** Favourablre to establish an high official Mobilize the army			
Line 2	2 Passing his forefather, meeting his foremother Not reaching his supreme ruler, meeting his official (minister) No misfortune	**32 Heng: permanent, lasting** Smooth, no misfortune Favourable determination Favourable to have roots in the past			
Line 1	1 Ominous because of flying (fluttering) bird	**55 Feng: plentifull, great** Smooth. King fakes the inhibition of worry/sorrow Appropiate for the middle of sun (day)			

All lines change in opposition		**61 Zhong Fu: center/ middle/attained/inner faith, inner sincerity** Young pig, fish: auspicious Favourable to cross the great plain Favourable determination			

63 Ji Ji: already/now that cross a river/be of help

Smooth, little favourable determination
Auspicious at the beginning, disorder at the end

6 branches comparison:

	Zhoulinetext	*Wen'guatext*			
Line 6	6 Get his head wet Threatening	**37 Jia ren: domestication, cultivated family/clan person, cultivated professional person** Favourable feminine determination			
Line 5	5 The eastern neighbour slaughters a bovine Not comparable with western neighbour's yue purification Through sacrifice really receiving your blessings	**36 Ming yi: safe/ darkening of brightness/ brilliance** Favourable in a hardship determination			

Line 4	4 The leak is stuffed with silk floss Be cautious till the end of the sun (period)	**49 Ge: leather, hide, transform, change** Capture great smoothness at sacrificial day Favourable determination Troubles go away			
Line 3	3 The high ancestor attacks ghost Just three years to subdue it People with little cultivation no use	**3 Zhun: birththrows** Smooth origin, benificial determination Do not use! Have a place to go to Favourable to establish an official			
Line 2	2 The matron looses her hairpin and (that clips her) false hair Do not persue, obtain it in seven days	**5 Xü: needing, wanting** Have a glorious capture and act accordingly The determination is auspicious It is favourable to wade across the big river			
Line 1	1 To follow its ring Wetting its tail No misfortune (possibly referring to bull)	**39 Jian: lame, trouble** Favourable: the southwest (kun) Not favourable: the northeast (gen) Favourable to be exposed to a considerably (large) cultivated one Auspicious determination			

All lines change in opposition		**64 Wei Ji: have not / did not cross a river / be of help** Smooth Small fox at the point of crossing the streamgets his tail wet Not at all favourable			

64 Wei Ji: have not / did not cross a river / be of help

Smooth
Small fox at the point of crossing the streamgets his tail wet
Not at all favourable

6 branches comparison:

	Zhoulinetext	Wen'guatext			
Line 6	Making prisoners of war while drinking liquor Not unfortunate for wetting one's head Making prisoners of war Losing sense of reality	**40 Jie: divide, seperate, untie, undo, explain, solve, comprehend, relieve oneself** Favourable: southwest No place to go to therefore turning back, auspicious Have a place to go to since long, auspicious			
Line 5	5 Auspicious determination The glory of the gentleman is without repenting Have prisoner of war Auspicious	**6 Song: arguing, lawsuit** Have a capture and they will be zhi-ti frightened Middle stage auspicious, end ominous Favourable to see the big cultivated one Not favourable to wade a big river.			

Line 4	4 Auspicious determination, troubles go Thunder used attack Just three years and there be reward to the big nation	**3 Zhun: birththrows** Smooth origin, benificial determination Do not use! Have a place to go to Favourable to establish an official	
Line 3	3 Not yet crossed the stream Ominous for going at long journey Favourable to go accross the big plain	**50 Ding: sacrificial vessel (Tripod)** Primary auspiciousness Smooth	
Line 2	2 To follow its ring Auspicious determination	**35 Jin: to enter, advance, promote** Lord of Kang (Health) uses giving of many (mated numbers) horses During light of day three joinings	
Line 1	1 Get its tail wet Distress	**38 Kui: (meditative) gazing** A small affair, Auspicious	
All lines change in opposition		**63 Ji Ji: already/now that cross a river/be of help** Smooth, little favourable determination Auspicious at the beginning, disorder at the end	

This concludes the translation and refelection on hexagrams and lines.

Add 1:
In addition some symbolic trigram associations

Tri-gram Figure	☰	☱	☲	☳	☴	☵	☶	☷
Binaryi Value	1	2	3	4	5	6	7	8
Wuxing	Yang metal	Yin metal ore	Yang	Yang wood	Yin wood leavage	water	Yin earth	Yang earth soil
Tri-gram name	乾 qián	兌 duì	離 lí	zhèn	巽 xùn	坎 kǎn	艮 gèn	坤 kūn
Dao	Will of heaven, strong	Opening pleasure	Radiance, light-giving, dependence	Shake, inciting movement	Ground, supporting penetrating	Gorge, dangerous	Bound, resting, stand-still	Field, devoted yielding
name	heaven, sky 天	lake 澤	fire 火	thunder 雷	wind 風	water 水	mountain 山	earth 地
direction	North-west, life door/ pillar, kunlun	West, moon rise	South face of the king, enlightenment, strongest yang	East, sun rise	South-east,	North, under-world	North-east, ghost door/ pillar	south-west
Family	father	third daughter	second daughter	first son	first daughter	second son	third son	mother
Body parts	head	mouth	eye	foot	thigh	ear	hand	belly
Behavioral Stage / State	Creative	tranquil, complete devotion	clinging, clarity, adaptable	Initiative	gentle entrance	in-motion	Completion	Receptive
Animal	馬 horse	羊 sheep, goat	雉 pheasant	龍 dragon	雞 fowl	豕 pig	狗 wolf, dog	牛 cow

Add 2:
Study of the classics: study of the Confucian text of great learning in combination with the Yi

"Things have their roots and branches, affairs have their end and beginning. When you know what comes first and what comes last, then you are near Dao."

Great Learning, chapter, book of rites

The yijing as a graphic image often is described as a tree of images. A tree, a pervasive living metaphor and mythical symbol throughout human cultures and icon of the branching, generation or lineage archetype, is employed as a teaching tool or hermeneutic device for explaining the relationship and operation of what East Asian Buddhism calls 'paired Essence-Function', where 'Essence' the deep underlying ineffable cause are the "roots", and the 'Function' are the discernible effects, the "branches". We can identify the metaphor of the "roots" and "branches" as an analogue of Essence-Function within the Great Learning, a main chapter in the Book of Rites. It states that: "Things have their roots and branches, affairs have their end and beginning. When you know what comes first and what comes last, then you are near Dao."

The will of heaven is the explanation of dao at work. In some ways we can say that Taiyi supreme god is the embodiment of the will of heaven.

Al Chinese classics deal with the study of the will of heaven. The yijing is no exeption to that point. For most westerners study of Dao and styudy of heaven seem to be two different things. But study of dao and study of heaven usually is seen as very closely relted in China's original mode of thinking. It seems obvious we study the daodejing for that purpose. And study of the daodejing certainly is important. But after the Daodejing many more texts were written about Dao as were many before. Confucian commentaries or the wings of the Yi are a prime example of that. For study of dao and yinyang people are usually referred to the yijing and daodejing. The study of the yi is often taken to the side, as if it a text that is a universe by itself. Ofcourse it is not. In fact many textbooks deal with the study of yidao 易道 [permutations of dao]. Famous is the work of Kongzi (Confucius), who was honoured with the title of Teacher or the Master. His followers were joked about as the weaklings, because they didn't emphasize martial prowess as the root of leadership and morality, but study of dao. One step further than these ru-weaklings went the daoists who created through Zhang Daoling's [张道灵] vision of heavenly order [tianli 天理] and bureaucracy a whole new way of learning about dao by placing a person not in society but in the complete realm of cosmological reality, trying to bypass and correct worldly coprruption. Han dynasty Confucianism gradually came to the understanding that spiritual attainment is as important for leadership as bodily cultivation. Through the successive steps in daoist development, at wudangshan [武当山] the circle became complete with the works of Zhang Sanfeng [张三丰] that emphasized that moral and spiritual cultivation cannot complete the official of dao or the commoner without developing martial prowes as if one is a king him or herself. One of the core ru-confucian texts is the Confucian ideology of self-cultivation in daxue [大学 big study/great learning/cultivation]

Learning and study go together like yin and yang. Together they represent taiji [太极] polarization and great unity [taiyi 太乙]. Both are aspects of movement. Movement is divided in Yin movement (contraction or coagulation) and Yang movement (expansion, change), relative rest and absolute movement. When we notice them we commonly see them in circling or spiraling relationships to each other.

In Daoism it is said that the primordial realm before everything is construed out of three realms for the accomplished immortals. Then there are 6 realms of becoming moving from the great expanse in ever more narrowly defined manifestations:

1. *taiyi (太乙 greater unity/change) realm is where Dao polarises without the presence of qi)*
2. *taixü (太虛 greater impoverishment) realm is the realm of clear limitless void).*
3. *taichi (太徵 greater substance-origin) realm where first phase of forming yuanqi [元炁 origin qi])*
4. *taishi (太师 greater start) realm of first shapes without substance)*
5. *taisu (太熟 greater substance start) realm of form but no being)*
6. *taizhi (太徵 greater unification) realm of first unified structure, shape and substance as existing before heaven and earth and the ten thousand things)*

At the Pre-daoist Lizi, which holds the first known representation of this ordering we find a shorter list. It states that:

'At the great origin there was no qi. The great origin was the beginning of qi [and thus dao]. At greater substance origin there was no form, the great substance origin is the beginning of form. At greater unification there was no matter, greater unification is the beginning of matter. When qi, form and matter were not yet separated this was called chaos'.

In both Daoism [daojiao 道教, teachings of dao] and Confucian Ruism [儒家 weakling family, Confucians] they claim that Dao is the guide of everything. They study the same truth. They also study how to clarify reality so that order comes about. They are learning in similar ways. They both think that taixü is achieved by reducing one's opulence, by impoverishing oneself and becoming weak. Through modesty and weakening of one's self and overbearings on society and nature the truth of reality can be perceived. Dao is not in the obvious, but in the subtle and hidden. Dao and qi are easily missed in one's perception of things. Dao's qi therefore only is a subtle something that has to be found in the smallest and tinyest core of the self and one's environment. It requires cultivation and has to be brought to great blooming. That blooming is called forth by cultivation of one's form and nature [xingqing 性情]. One's form and nature has to manifest one's 'weft of dao and de' [道德经]. When writing this weft [经] down, and it finds broad recognition for its importance it becomes a classic[经]. The daodejing [道德经] is a classic, and so is the great cultivation [大学]. Where the daodejing explains the nature and form of completion, the daxue explains how to achieve completion. The following summarizes the process of reaching completion on the basis of the text of great learning.

1) *First great unity [taiyi 太乙] principle [daoli 道理)*

The cultivation of one's character is at the core of all one's achievements

2) *The three-fold path of great cultivation (san qing)*

The first dao is developing one's inner luminosity as a tool of knowing oneself and developing moral character

The second dao is that of being a teacher in one's action to help people renew themselves. In Daoism that includes being a healer and let people return to the root of life and regain immortality

The third dao is that of being natural and unwavering in one's goodness and innocence as to not be seduced of the right path in life

3) The 8 aspected path of greater peace (tai ping) and its proceding reversal of faiths

The eight steps and their following reversal of faiths due to accumulation of substance through deepening within ones self shows Confucius applied yin yang theory and nothing more. Like the Laozi texts showed: from nothing comes the great one, from the great one the two divided and from the two divided the three purities. From the three purities follow the wuxing as an extrapolation of the 8 symbols, culminating from bagua into the 1wan [1.0000] thingnesses. Chen Tuan from Wudang shan daoist resort showed this explanation in his diagram at the end of the song dynasty and Zhang Sanfeng following Chen's admonitions to see the three teachings of Confucianism, Daoism and Buddhism following the same goal though differing ends and as fundamentally equal to each other. Mahayana Fijiao through its Daofication from its starting point that they later came to name as Nihayana Fojiao also prolongated this unity.

Wang [王 king] Wen (author of zhouyi, zhou's exchanges, explaining why shang dynasty kings lost the mandate of heaven and were no longer able to lead the people to renewal); Wang [王] Tang (author of admonitions to the greater family, and announcement to the lords of Kang that only heaven can judge one's mandate so one should always turn to heaven and not away from it zhuanshi[转世 ancestor] Yao (who's moral force guided all following generations) are examples of developed moral force and inner luminosity.

Wang Kang (Wen) and Tang said that renewal should be brought forth every day again so nobody can rely on previous achievement to take the right for a mandate. The weft of songs (to exemplify behaviors) underscores this by takeing the Zhou dynasty as an example. These examples proof that masters of noble character exercise their emotive and cognitive faculties to the utmost under all circumstances as part of their cultivation process.

Both the teacher Kong and Laozi the grandfather showed that Dao [道 track at the side of where we go]is the result of innate quality [De 德) of a thing or situation. One is the role one is appointed to by choice or circumstances, when one accomplishes that role to the best effort. From here we find deepest reverence, kindness, devotion, filial accomplishment and trustworthiness to ourselves and others. The weft of songs compares innate quality (virtue] to the river Qi, that is only itself in the landscape and nothing more, and because of that the prince standing next to it in all his glory becomes unforgettable. The landscape brought out the qualities of the prince of being cultivated, worked at the perfection of one's self, frightening to those of self-corruption, and radiant with authority. They became a match through their similar completion. This is the nature of elegance, moral force and consummate goodness. We know from this that everyone can be that prince at the side of the river Qi. It is that appearance even the immortal mountain men from wudang shan emulate.

In argument one should always imagine oneself in the place of that other to understand oneself in the argument. The understanding should cause the elimination of the litigation. This is understanding the core of moral cultivation, the fullest attainment of understanding.

Avoid one's self-deception as to achieve wholeness and ease with one's self. The person of mean character is guided by his or her self-deception, will scrutinize everyones behavior to find error and enter litigation.

Add 3:
Yijing and the human body

For those readers who did not study Chinese medicine or health techniques, here follow some particulars about the Chinese biology and its treatment of disease through developing health. Although there are many therapeutic techniques and approaches available to Chinese medicine its primary goal is not to cure diseases. It sees curing disease from a minimum impact approach, which means that if it can do less, it will do less.

Primarily Chinese medicine puts people in context of Heaven and Earth. It states that health is developed though adaption and adjustment. Chinese medicine gives people a special place among all the living beings due to its ability to develop deep morality, but it also says that people easily get distracted and due to distraction deviate from being human. Being human means among other things to be healthy in Chinese original view of biology, so being human is a state of being we aim for, or as tradition holds it: "We aim to retrieve our humanity". In Daoism that became: "Dao is in reversal". In Mahayana Buddhism, which is a typical East Asian phenomenon, deeply rooted in Daoist and Confucian values, it is described that in origin we are already enlightened but our Buddha-awareness is obscured with cloudy thoughts". In all these cases health is associated in being "magniminous/spacious like heaven and reactive/following like earth". Every time the yijing is a guiding form of reasoning to complete a set of thinking. It shows that halth is in relationship to the will of heaven and the malleable capacities from being like earth. Normally people should be healthy and there is no need to die. From here it can be deduced that chinese medicine in essence knows only one disease with 10.000 manifestations: Aging . Chinese medicine theory and practice are deeply intertwined with alchemical practice and thus Chinese medicine is a-priori an Anti-Aging practice.

Chinese medicine holds at its ethics that it is the moral djuty of each person to retrieve his or her dao, which means that one should retrieve its immortal nature/existence. It is therefore the task of every person not to be treated but to cukltivate him or herself away from needing treatment. Thee current medicalized world is sign for Chinese medicine practitioners of old that humanity is loosing its moral nature.

In experiencing the body by ourself people over time have developed the insight that aging is primarily caused by the advent of heat and fire inside oneself. The heat needs to be countereffected by water to keep the body fresh and functional. It is why the main school in Chinese medicine has been called the heat-school. This school holds to the idea that all deviations from health gradually turn into fire and heat. When we turn older we see a reversal from feeling warm at out lower body into feeling flushed into our upper body, this is casued by many factors, collected under the notion that lungqi and stomach qi weaken and cannot keep the warmth below. It is why in Indian yoga practice standing on one's head was recognized as of much value, because then heat can gradually return ton one's feet. Although the thought is a bit naïve mayube, it is an effective solution, but time consuming because you first have to come to a normalcy for the heart to pump the blood thuis far upwards.

From this idea we see that different ways of looking at the yijing become possible. When we see it as a reasoning tool and we see that all gua turn to heaven, all other gua gradually develop relationshiop between water and fire. When we look at the nuclear trigrams we see that the yi revolves around the emblems and emblems combined eventually show that the nature of a hexagram is either heaven-like (1), earth-like (2), helpful-like (63) and not helpful-like (64). Two emblems combined offer a trigram with or without moving lines, but however you combine them you always end up with heaven, earth, water or fire. Combined and recombined we find a variety of axis, like hexagram 11 and 12, or 29 and 30 that show symmetries with these four gua at the core of everything and how other hexagrams and trigrams are all extrapolations from these four. Health theory then follows the same reasoning:

1) We face heaven for guidance
2) We emulate earth to develop health
3) We balance water and fire to stay fresh
4) We resolve deviations

We do not go too deep into the subject as to avoid deviating too much from the subject. But below are some theoretical and practical considerations that will clarify more what is the connection between the yijing and health. First we start with theoretical assumptions in Chinese medicine:

1. Life aims to maintain itself through balancing of Yin and Yang

In order to achieve optimal health, the contractiong and expanding effects of Yin and Yang must be in balance. In treatment of disease and ailment the aims are to restore a relative dynamic equilibrium and remove pathogenic factors by dredging the channels (making them free from obstruction) therefore promoting the circulation of qi, ying, wei, jinye, yin, yang and blood. Other techniques aim to strengthen or weaken the substantiality of these contents.

The content of the channels is not necessary a plethora of different substances. The bounderies between those substances are often fuzzy and depending on location. The names merely represent different angles related to different purposes. Technically all substances hoover between being water or qi. The dragon moving through the lines of the first two hexagrams of the yijing describe the formation of qi from the body and water. You can imagine that hexagrams combining water and earth describe the process of life coming about from matter or of the dying process. We see for instance hexagram 7 and 8 which deal with education, discipline, smart choices and duration. They are described as surface streams and underground channels, myuch like our body form and our channels/collaterals, but also nr 4 and 39. Number 4 deals with the predictability of naivity and stupidity. It is water passing a mountain gradually eating away from the mountain. Nr 39 deals with difficulties due to malformation of reality. It can be described as the origin of water flow, That being a source or rain pooring down the mountain slopes. But hexagram 21 also shows in its nuclear trigrams the presence of hexagram 39. Here we see that dkifficulties can be overcome by regulating them, imprisoning them if you will by limiting their effect and freedom, in other words: discipline, hexagram 7. Hexagram 29 shows the interrelationship with the outer and inner trigrams, adding a layer to the complexities Chinese medicine theory wishes to address.

2. Life aims to maintain itself through regulating the internals by means of the Zang and Fu Organs

In Chinese medicine, the organs are divided into three categories:

- Zang organs, which do not come in contact with foodstuff and produce and store/memorize qi (heart, lung, spleen, liver and kidney). They are representative of the 5 xing, ways of consummation, and because they are more close to dao because more primary they are considered yin, fragile and spongelike.
- Fu organs, which receive, digest, transport and transform foodstuffs and substances (small and large intestine, stomach, gall bladder, bladder) are hollow vessels, and the channels are an extention of them. That is why the dantian as origin of the vessels is found in the intestinal region. If the intestines are foul the dantian cannot come about. Ironically the dirt often contributes to the strenghth of martial artists because of the heat and dampness lodging in the belly. It is not heat from the mingmen or heart that is the cause, but heat because of wrong diet, leading to constipation, diarrhea, bleeding interior, accumulation of slime and wind and so on. Because of the work being done in the changwei, stomach and intestines, they are often described as agricultural land, place of cultivation of nourishment and so on. They are yang in nature, active, expanding. They require the artificial while the yin organs require the natural. Likewise the channels need the quiet and the areas outside the channels need the wild, activity and vigorous exercise to develop health. Regulating the zhang and fu therefore is as continuous balancing of factors.
- Extraordinary Fu organs, which are a mix of Fu and Zang (brain, marrow, bones, vessels and uterus)

The aim is to regulate all organs, therefore inhibiting hyperactivity and stimulating underactive organs (called tonifying). These extraordinary organs are considered in relationship to fixed theory, because the ideas about them are mere after thoughts to the core theory. It is expected that through further discovery they eventually will find place in the whole. It is considered that a division such as that of heaven earth and humanity as exists in the yijing will be found. In that case the extra organs will be considered organs of purpose.

If eventually this is found to be true they will ofcourse become represented by the emblems at the heart of the hexagrams, of which the four emblems represent the outline division of the 84 hexagrams in 64 different wuxing combinations.

3. Life aims to maintain itself by means of constructive cooperation and communication through encouragement of flow within Channels and Collaterals.

The purpose of the channels is to circulate qi and blood, therefore nourish the body and stimulate the body resistance against decay, invasion, eating itself to increase protection against pathogens. The channels create surplus which is deposited in extraordinary vessels which number 8. Movement presses the surplus and unproductive behavior results into the minute collaterals where they eventually can become stagnant, fester and form the foundation of the 10.000 diseases. Therapeutic means therefore aim to undo the accumulation of substances in the micro collaterals and increase freel flow in the channels and collaterals. The individual linmes represent channel interactions, as do the internal trigrams.

It is easy to summarize the yijing and the visions of the human body. First of all the yijing bagua relates to certain body areas:

1) The eyes
2) The face
3) The palm of the hand
4) The belly around the navel
5) The body itself.

The areas show how the different functions of the body are represented by zheng, or sings.

These different models all are significant. They place the relationship of wuxing and yijyang into the context of the human body: the idea of mircopunctures such as ear acupuncture is based on treating the signs as to affect the roots.but primarily the bagua are tools to make proper diagnosis. From this we cand educe that:

* 8 diagrams as body regions,
** 64 heaxagrams as body process in relationship to health
***384 lines describe body relationships as yinyangwuxing settings that can change into each other.
**** 147.456 permutations of relationships of possible conditions for disease and health.

Each line has one to three parameters to define it depending how much it belongs to the human emblem at the core of a hexagram. Primary is the alchemical relationship between fire and water in the body: this is the interaction between kidney and heart, depicted as hexagram 63 and 64. They show the changability of the human body and the need to build a continuous alertness and discipline to deal with health. Healthjy behavior therefore includes everything that eradicates the influence of earlier unhealthy behavior, such as long sleeping, much eating, angry thoughts and so on. It shows that being a body and being a person is a practice, not a state of existence. This is confirmed in the first chapter of Huangdineijing, where continuous living, long life, is described the result of the a way of living, and not a given thing.

Likewise we see that fire and earth are a microcosmos within a macrocosmos comparable with the traditional statement we all have four parents: father, mother, heaven and earth:

This aspect is reflected in the relationship between all the involved hexagrams, such as 11,12, 63, 64 but also 5, 6, 13, 14 where the interactions of fire and earth and their transformations to and from heaven and earth are being discussed. We see here how alchemy, healthcare and medicine are one continuous whole, which nonetheless produces different outcomes. It is why from good doctors it is expected that they treat, teach and practice internalized alchemy. With any less than that it is not to be expected that they can grasp the full complexity of the human body. Ofcourse that trajectory is not easy, and for the sake of producing many therpists they left that alchemical and practice aspects to the individual and many schools dedicate themselves to the bookish learning of medicine.

In my own work I aim for completeness, so I have developed all these aspects as good as it goes. It shows that medicine is avery much an ad-hoc event and that not much of commonality can be assumed, as through statistical research.

All these notions we find implicated in the great commentary, the guiding textbook that accompanies the Yijing. The wings, as they are called represent the person, his body form, health and environment.

The chapter shuo gua states:

> "The numinous and bright made heaven three and earth two and so made the numbers the basis [of questioning the yijing]... as for the trigrams, these translate yin and yang into comparable images and so constitute embodiment of transformation and change."[186]

It further proofs that the yijing wants to extrapolate on the dao and heaven becadeue it shows that the gua themselves are aspects of heaven, and that trhough casting an oracle or calculating a hexagram we can come to understand the will of heaven. The person is like a vessel and its aim is or should be reflecting the will of heaven and the will of heaven simply wants people to live forever and be in harmony with all that happens. Therefore it is natural to associate the yijing with health and disease theory and practice.

When we examen the Great Commentaries we notice the dao-xiang-qi [道相脐 way-image-vessel] cosmology. This clearly represents an anaology between the body and heaven. Dao is not difficult to associate with yin and yang, after all 'one yin or one yang make dao', because Laozi says that dao is not the interaction of yin and yang alone, but even just yang or just yin already reflect dao at work. Whatever has dao is maybe

---

[186] Translation of the wangbi commentaries by Richard John Lynn 1994, Columbia university press.

almost unnoticed, but it certainly is iconic, because it will have qi. Qi is a character related to the intestines, as a tube shaped organ is is described as a vessel. All the jingluo are likewise described as vessels in this way, and that is why in daoyin practice people are expected to turn and twist their body, like in daoist wudang taijiquan to guide the movements of the body. In de daxue 'Dao-xiang-qi' stands for abstract principles, emergent manifestations, and concrete objects, respectively which leads to a possible analysis of the human body from the typical hierarchical but also holistic, process-oriented epistemology we cal chinese in medicine. Chinese medicine and its medicine view as such is different from western views because culturally it holds different views on the meaningfulness of the parts that constitute reality. The yijing is the epistemical tool to decript basically all of Chinese medicine and alchemical logical reasoning. Once you have received the key to do so it is not difficult:

1st you have to realize all movements of the person is directed towards heaven. Heaven is considered the best capable to grasp dao and inform us. The yijing is the reflecting the receptivity of earth extrapolating on the understanding of heaven. We are part of that extrapolation and so are our actions and our parts.

2nd all the actions fall in a combination of categories, such as being either yin or yang or changing from yin to yang or from yang to yin. Further we see that everything lives by means of consumption. Everything consumes something and consumes in its own typical way. That is where things can be categoriezed in wuxing. In our yijing we see the importance of this relationship described in a very simple graphical format. We see than that every line represents a placement to the middle two lines, rarifying closer to earth and heaven. This means that all comes closer to heaven or not, and all finds its origin in earth no matter what. In Chinese medicine it means that the body and its internal organization precede the reality that we exemplify in the outward directed lifestyles we live.

3rd we see that humanity is the densest of the three categories but is yin yang wise summarized in four emblems, which have 64 different images in relationship to wuxing.

4th all Chinese medicine theory takes a healthy person as its origin and endpoint. It does describe illness in terms of confusion, having lost its way, the maze of the body etc.

We see that both the interpretations of reality and being contained in the Yijing were developed by careful and detailled observation over time, and why they have deeply influenced China's philosophies and sciences, including medicine. The effect of the dao-xiang-qi doctrine on Chinese Medicine was essential for the formation of a unified and unifying Chinese medicine theory. It has its own typical epistemology that wants to investigate human health and illness by means of a focus on the nature of the living body. Therefore it does not so much look at its body parts and there workings, but to how the body parts work when alive, or how the body parts ideologically should perform if they would fit the yijing dao-xiang-qi approach.

Being less concerned with the physical details of body organs and tissues, Chinese classical medical investigations produced an analysis of how functions were related on many levels, from the vital and functional processes of the body to the emotions -to the natural and social environment of the person, and often also with therapeutic practice as a result. Parallel to this practice we see that alchemy of the internal body received its formal push towards systemic self cultivation towards immortality Neidan practice and disease treatment became coupled on the theoretical level, but also became opposite developmental trajectories. Chinese medical theories codified these relational qualities. They assumed principles of holism, embracing complexity, the connectedness and interaction of all things, and the non-separability of body, thinking and personhood. All were described as qualities of form and nature.

From this we see that the yijing and the body can only be understood from the perspective of complexity. We need to study the whole of the yijing and its implications to understand the body and our health because we also cannot understand the body with our method of thinking or our behavior as a person. As far as the Chinese classical sciences are considered, be it Mahayana Buddhism, Neoconfucianism, or Daoism, they all consider these issues too important to let their development free to random accidental development. As a social experiment ofcourse it is interesting, but it does not lead to co-operation or progress for humanity in a smooth way. It argues that therefore the development of the individual also cannot develop in a smooth way. A person this way can not stand on the shoulders of its predecessors. It also shows the importance of understanding Confucianism to even understand a bit of Daoism and Buddhism in China. Like learning Chinese medicine only partially, experimenting without a clear idea of how to reach a goal is considered immoral action and thus not advised to engender health and long life.

Following the yijing we need to look at ourselves as depending on our history, or how sometimes we have to break with history to affect change. Developing health and disease is the same. We can experiement with lifestyles and can be lucky, but in many cases experimenting is done without understanding but done to seek difference, neweness or excitement. They experiments are a sign of ignorance. Nedan is also an experiment with yourself, but wkithin the boundaries of accepted results and changes. It is clear where the goal is, and not a blind venturing in unknown space.

There are different versions of combining the bagua with the body. The most common is the following in that it follwos the yijing most punctually. It is the description of the inner body.

Gua	Name	Organ	Yinyangwuxing
Tian	Heaven	Large intestine	Yang metal
Kun	Earth	Stomach-spleen	Yang earth
Li	Sun	Mingmen	Yinyang fire
Kan	Moon/ water	Kidneys	Yinyang water
Dui	Cloud	Lungs	Yin metal
Xun	Wind	Liver	Yin wood
Zhen	Thunder	Gallbladder	Yangwood
Gen	Mountain	Urinary bladder	Yin earth

This second diagram shows the bagua in relationship to outward body geography:

It shows the layerdness of thinking in the epistemology of Chinese medicine logic. The hexagram in its layerness shows that the trigrams that form the hexagram are functional organs. The nuclear trigrams show the channels that are affected. Therapeutically things work theyir way up towards heaven.

To see it at work we just have to isolate one hexagram:

Line 6	6 Bitter node Ominous determination Troubles leave		
Line 5	5 Sweet node Auspicious Go and have a reward		
Line 4	4 Fixed node Smooth		
Line 3	3 Not like a node but like a sigh No misfortune		
Line 2	2 Not leaving from the fronyard gate Ominous		
Line 1	1 Not leaving from the frontyard No misfortune		

The upper trigram is kan, the diagram of the kidneys. The lower diagram is that of the clouds or the swamp/lake reflecting to the connection of the lungs with the kidneys and therefore also the qi. Because it is the lower trigram the swamp is more likely than the clouds. The upper nuclear trigram is that of mountain, the bladder channel. The lower nuclear trigram is that of wind, indicator of the liver but also vitality/blood.

The human emblem shows that the third line –which is a line of advancement is the qi, the bladder channel and the liver channel. It means that the problem will be located in the liver and bladder channels affecting the kidneys and the qi, possibly the breathing. The client might suffer a range of problems, such as asthma, short breath, superficial breath, cold feet and hands, incontinence, stiffness of the back or the legs and so on.

The therapeutic solution would be that the breathing has to be altered. The earth emblem shows that wind muddles yin metal, which might be lung yin. The solution will be found in how there is reach towards heaven. The method would be to affect the kidneys through the bladder channel and breathing practice as is aspect of for instance neidan alchemy.

The regulation of fire and water through breading affects the interaction between water and earth as to allow blending and thus making space for heaven and earth. The purpose of the circulation of water and heat makes the traces of heaven and earth more clearly visible and gives leads for application in for instance movement exercise. The blending of water and heat produces a gradual strengthening of yang, whioch stimulates the urge to move, increases therefore blood pressure and a need to relax deeper. It also shows that the yijing serves not to explain the body's energy but the workings of the body as a set of pressure valves and feedback loops. The primary cause of the body is in two yin and three yang. Two yin are the body matter originating in earth, and the water substance which is the foundation for life as well as its enemy. The earth matter might be needed to build a body, but water is required to be managed to get it to live. Three yang represented in Daoism as the three pure ones. One is movement, two is warmth and three is pressure. Yin is contracted substance and yang is expanding action.

Translations of Hetu and Luo Shu comments

1. introduction

These translations are to you an introduction to the content of the Yijing Ritual Counsellor Course. I have added them here as a bonus because they simply are not available outside this book anywhere in the west. This makes them unique.

It is ironic, because I spend several years on comprehending and translating the core body of text of the yijing. I focussed on the hexagram titles and texts, as well as the line texts. For study and use it is enough. But we are left with rather vague mythologizing stories about the origin and development of the Yijing, mostly because all modern translations go back to Richard Wilhelm (1924, 1950 by CF Baynes in English from German), and James Legge (1882). Both were products of their time, and most translations after are variations on their base text, while their root text to translate from were Qing dynasty products, and thus not actually representing its history.

In modern time there is more discussion about that translation work. In China I have met with people from the PRC translation guild, and anonymously they admitted there is a difference between whjat they read in the yijing and what their comissioners want to share with the world. They do not speak of censorship directly, but more of adaptation to current realities of understanding. In this they also look at Legge and Wilhelm, simply because we already know these. Famous for Chinese translators is the implementation as a form of binary hegelian dialectical system, the foundation of PRC scientific agendas. The Author of The book of Changes and Statistics (1993 IAP), Hou Wenxi, on the basis of that suggested that: "The yijing seems universable applicable in myriads of things with striking similarity or in conformaty with some modern scientific thought."

John Minford in 2014 published a study on translation of Yijing, found that in recent time translation have been more history based, changing also the translation from Yijing to classic of change to scripture of change, to suit that idea. Personally I see the meaning of Jing more as the result of weaving knowledge, a category of scriptures, dealing with the nature of reality. A comparable Indian translation is Sutra.

The translated texts show Pre-dynasty citations from the "zhouyi tushou zhonghui", illustrated zhouyi collection, a three part set of heavy bpooks each about 750 pages thick, illustrating the development of the Yijing through the ages. It is compiled by Lishen and Guohou, published in 1998, and in 2003 when I found it, it was already rare.

What you do find in the text are illustrations of remarks from a variety of documents about the origin and meaning of the Yijing or where the yijing is mentioned before the Qin Empire was established by Qin Huang.

In the Citations we find many images and cultural references that are part of the Yijing worldview. Major is that the argument is that the yijing is to help you focus on the will of heaven as to correct your behavior. The use of the Yijing as an oracle or predictive instrument was always seen as a corruption of the text, propagated by some fangshi, travelling soothsayers. We als see references to the mandate of heaven to rule, we see references to the directions, gods, stories etc, but also to the founders of the yijing tradition of science or reality.

Moreover, we see a worldview where none of the concepts used to translate nowadays play a role.

There are concepts in the text that require additional commentary, so where required I added them as subtext between { } -accolades. More and more chapters you will find in our Yijing counsellor course. You will find there 45 variations on the known Hetu and Luoshu, illustrated, as well as the translations of theories up to the Qing Dynasty, starting with these subjects and then about the hexagrams, complex diagams etc. We use them to illustrate the complexities of developmental models, incorporating thought about fengshui-geomantics, Mingshu-astrology, leadership, biology, medicine, Neidan-alchemy, etcetera.

1. "Book of Shang: Gu Ming":

In the fourth month, the Hun {heavens envoy in the embryo to help a person become intelligent and creative} was born, and the king was not surprised.
On the first day of the first month, the king went to the Tao River.
The prime minister wore a crown and sat on a jade table.
He summoned Taibao Shuang, Rui Bo, Tong Bo, Bi Gong, Wei Hou, Mao Gong, Shi Shi, Hu Chen, Bai Yin, and Yu Shi.
The king said, "Alas! My illness is getting worse. I am dying, and I am afraid that I will not be able to succeed you as promised.
I will now teach you carefully.

In the past, King Wen and King Wu { first interpretors of the Yijing diagrams, writing the names and line texts} spread glory and laid down the teachings. If you follow them {the teachings} without violating them, you will be able to achieve the Great Destiny. You who are in the future should respectfully welcome the Majesty of Heaven and inherit the Great Teachings of Wen and Wu. You dare not go beyond the rules.

Today, I have been sick, and I am afraid that you will not wake up to realize it. You should follow my words, respectfully protect Yuan Zizhao, help people in difficult times, be gentle to those far away and able to be close to you, and persuade the common people, of big and small cultivation {The small people are people who talk from their feelings, while the big people are the ones who have civilized themselves through self cultivation. The discerment is often made in the Yijing, showing what kind of results you can expect from behaving small or big.}. Madam Si has disturbed her dignity, so you should not use Zhao to pay tribute to Fei Ji!"

After receiving the order, I returned and went out to the courtyard to sew my clothes. On the day of Yichou in Yueyi, the king died {using branch and stem time markers here}.

The Grand Protector ordered Zhong Huan and Nangong Mao to send the Marquis of Qi, Lü Ji, with two spearmen and a hundred tiger soldiers {Tigers and Dragons are often used as symbols in the Yijing, medicine, Taijigongfu, and Neidan self cultivation as postural or behavioral aspects}, to the south gate to arrest the rebellious Zi Zhao. He invited him { Lü Ji} into the wing room and comforted the family. On Dingmao {time markeer}, he ordered the preparation of the imperial edict. Seven days later, on Guiyou {time marker}, the Prime Minister ordered the scholars to find talents.

Di set up Fuliang and Xiuyi.
The window room faces south, with heavy bamboo mats, Fuchun, Huayu, and a table.
The west room faces east, with heavy mats, Xiuchun, and a table with patterns.
The east room faces west, with heavy mats, painted, and carved jade.
The west room faces south, with heavy bamboo mats, Xuanfen, and lacquered.
Yue jade five layers, Chen treasure, red knife, Daxun, Hongbi, Wansuo, in the west room;
Dayu, Yi jade, celestial ball, river map {Hetu}, in the east room.
Yin's dance clothes, Dabei, and drums are in the west room;
Dui's spear, He's bow, and Chui's bamboo arrows are in the east room.

The big carriage is in front of the guest steps,
the decorated carriage is in front of the east steps,
the first carriage is in front of the left school, and
the second carriage is in front of the right school.

Two people wearing quebian, holding hui [kind of ax], stood inside the closed gate.

Four people wearing qibian, holding spears with blades, stood between the two steps.
One person wearing a crown (mian), holding a liu-battle ax, stood in the east hall;
one person wearing a crown, holding yue-battle ax, stood in the west hall.
One person wearing a crown, holding gui-lance stood in the east chui-border;
One person wearing a crown, holding qu-shurikan, stood in the west chui-border.
One person wearing a crown, holding a sharp jian-sword, he stood on the side steps.

The king wore a hemp crown and a red robe, and ascended the throne from the ornamented steps.
The ministers and the princes of the states wore hemp crowns and red robes, and ascended the throne.
The Grand Protector, the Grand Historian, and the Grand Emperor all wore hemp crowns and red robes.
The Grand Protector carried the jade tablet, and the Grand Emperor both carried the same likewise, and ascended the throne from the north steps. The Grand Historian held the book, and ascended the ornamented steps, and passed the king's decree. The words were: "The Queen stood on the jade table, and spread-out the last will, and ordered You to inherit the teachings, to rule the country, to lead the people, to harmonize the world, and to spread the glorious teachings of the civil and military officials." The king bowed again, stood up, and replied: "I am a young boy, how can I cause chaos in the four directions, and also respect the Majesty of Heaven?"

Then he received Tong (allegiance) and Mao (politeness), and the king stayed for three nights, offered sacrifices three times, and sang three times. The emperor said to the ancestor: "Enjoy!" The Taibao received Tong, surrendered, and made an alliance. He held the scepter and made wine with it. He gave Tong-connection to the clan members and bowed. The king bowed in return. The Taibao (great treasure) received Tong, offered sacrifices, and sang a house {I assume this means projecting a house during the ritual}. He gave Tong to the clan members and bowed. The king bowed in return. The Taibao surrendered and collected. The princes went out of the temple gate and waited.

Today, Sufu is a king who likes to attack, and he also embellishes his words, saying that he is not a disciple.

Mozi said: "I think it is unjust to attack, and it is not a gain. In the past, Yu conquered the seedlings, Tang attacked Jie, and King Wu attacked Zhou. Why are they all established as sage kings?"

Mozi said: "You didn't understand what I said, and you didn't understand the reason why I was attacked.

If the sun comes out at night, then there is rain and blood for three dynasties.

If Dragons are born in the temples, and dogs cry in the market, the sky is full of ice, the ground is full of springs, and the grains are changing. The people are in great spirits, and there were seedlings. Four lightning currents were used to lure them, and there was a god with a human face and a bird's body. Ruo Jin was there to serve him, and the arrows showed the auspiciousness of the seedlings. The Miao army was in chaos, and then there was a lot of chaos.

Since Yu had conquered the three seedlings, they were able to turn them into mountains and rivers. There were objects above and below, and the rural system was great. However, the gods and the people did not violate it, and the world was peaceful. This is why Yu wanted to conquer the seedlings. It was built to the hand of King Jie of Xia, and there was a Decree from Heaven.

The sun and the moon were not coming at all times, the cold and heat were coming, the grains were scorched to death, ghosts were calling the country, and cranes were singing for more than ten nights. Tian Nai ordered Tang to go to Jian Palace to receive Xia's great order: "Xia De is in great chaos. Now that he is dead, his fate is up to Heaven. If Heaven goes to punish him, you will be embarrassed." Tang Yan dared to lead his people, so the village had The realm of summer. The emperor sent Yin to violently destroy the city of Youxia. A little god {demon} came and said: "Xia De is in great chaos. Go and attack it. I will definitely make you miserable." Since I have been ordered by Heaven, the Heavenly Mandate merges with the fire in the northwest corner of the city of Xia.

"The Soup served Jie to conquer the Xia Dynasty, which belonged to the princes. He recommended the Decree of Heaven and spread it to all directions, but no prince in the world dared to disobey him. This is why the soup was used to kill Jie. As fast as the Shang King's sword, God could not preface its virtues, the sacrifices are out of time, and for ten days at night, the rain and soil are thin, the nine tripods (Ding) are moved, the female demons come out at night, there are ghosts (Gui/unmouths) singing at night, there are women who are men, the sky rains meat, thorns grow on the national road, the king's brother himself assemble's too. Chi Wu held a Gui (turtle) in his hand {turtle shells were originally used to practice burnscarring and crack the shell as a means to predict events. The dots on the map and book might be signatures of this practice} and descended to Qishe of Zhou, saying: "It is destiny for King Wen of Zhou to attack Yin Youguo. Taiyan is a guest, the river is green and the earth is yellow.

When King Wu was practicing his martial arts, he dreamed of three gods who said to him: "Since I have imbued Zhou with the virtue of wine, if you go to attack him, I will definitely make you miserable." King Wu is attacking the crazy man and rebelling against the Zhou Dynasty of Shang. God gave King Wu the yellow bird flag. Now that the king has conquered his stock, he becomes an emperor, divides the gods, worships the ancestors of Zhou, and connects all the barbarians in the world, and everyone in the world is a guest, so how can he follow the trend of Tang? This is why King Wu executed Zhou. If we look at it from the perspective of the three holy kings, it is not called attacking, but it is called killing."

Yi is consistent with Heaven and Earth, so it can master the Dao of Heaven and Earth. Looking up to observe the astronomy, looking down to observe the geography, this is why we know the dim light; the original is the end, so we know the theory of death and life; jing-coherence is the thing, and the wandering Hun {heavenly envoy} is the change, so we know the mood of ghosts and gods (guishen); it is similar to heaven and earth, so it does not violate. Know all things around and help the world, so there is nothing left; go aside without wandering, be happy with Heaven and know Fate, so don't worry; be at peace with the Earth and be benevolent, so you can love; the range of Heaven and Earth can be transformed without passing by, the music can be made into all things without leaving behind, and it can be connected day and night. We know the way, so Shen has no method and easily has no body.

Confucius said: "What is the meaning of "Yi"? "Yi" is to create things and accomplish things, to follow the way of the world, and that's all. "That's why the sage opens things and accomplishes tasks to understand that the will of the world is to determine the world's business and to resolve the world's doubts. Therefore, the virtue of goodness is round and divine, the virtue of the hexagram is square and knowledgeable, and the meaning of the six lines is easy to contribute. The sage cleanses his heart with this, retreats and hides in secret, and shares good and bad with the people; the gods know the coming, and the knowledge hides the past. Who can compare with this! The ancients were knowledgeable and wise, and the gods were powerful but did not kill! Therefore, they understand the dao of heaven and observe the people's reasons. This is to promote the shen and things before the people use them. The sage uses this to warn and use the gods to make their virtues clear! Therefore:

closing the door is called Kun,
opening the door is called Qian,
opening and closing a door is called change,
    endless coming and going is called communication;
seeing is called image,
taking shape is called instrument,
making it into use is called method,
using it to make it come and go, and the people use it is called divine.
    Therefore,
Yi has Taiji, which gives birth to Liangyi,
Liangyi gives birth to Sixiang,
Sixiang gives birth to Bagua,
Bagua determines good and bad, and good and bad give birth to great
    cause.
    Therefore,
the greatest law is the heaven and earth,
the greatest change is the four seasons,
the greatest brightness is the sun and the moon,
the greatest sublimity is wealth and honor;
the greatest preparation of things for use, the establishment of tools for
    the benefit of the world, is the sage;
the greatest exploration of the hidden, the hook deep and far, to determine
    the good and bad of the world, to make the world in order, is the
    tortoise shell.

Therefore,
when the gods are created by heaven, the sage follows them;
when the heaven and earth change, the sage imitates them;
when the sky shows signs, good and bad luck, the sage imitates them;
when the map appears in the He River and the book appears in the Luo
River, the sage follows them.
The Book of Changes has four images, so as to show; the words are
attached to it, so as to tell; and the determination of good and bad
luck is so as to judge.

As for the image, the sage has a way to see the ups and downs of the
world and imitate their appearance and the appropriateness of things, so
it is called an image. The sage has a way to see the movement of the world
and observe its convergence to carry out its rituals, and to attach words
to it to judge its good or bad fortune, so it is called a line. The one who is
concerned about the world is in the hexagram, the one who is inciting the
world to move is in the words, the one who transforms and cuts it is in the
change, the one who pushes and carries it out is in the communication,
the one who is divine and clear is in the person, and it is accomplished
silently and is believed without words, which is in virtue.

2. "The Book of Changes: Xici II":

In ancient times, when Baoxishi ruled the world, he looked up at the sky to
observe the patterns, and looked down at the earth to observe the laws,
the patterns of birds and beasts and the suitability of the land, and took
things from his body and things from far away. Then he created the Eight
Trigrams, in order to understand the virtue of the gods and to classify the
feelings of all things. He made knotted ropes to make nets for farming and
fishing, which was probably inspired by Li. After Baoxishi died, Shennong
came to power. He made a hoe from a piece of wood: He rubbed a piece
of wood to make a hoe. He taught the world the benefits of hoeing,
which was probably inspired by Yi. He set up a market at noon, attracted
people from all over the world, gathered goods from all over the world,
traded and left, and everyone got what they wanted. This was probably
inspired by Shi Ke. After Shennong died, Huangdi, Yao, and Shun came to
power. They understood the changes and made the people tireless. They
transformed the people with their Hun (heavenly envoys) and made the

people adapt to the changes. When Yi is exhausted, it changes. When it changes, it is smooth. When it is smooth, it lasts. Therefore, "God blesses it, and there is no harm." Huangdi, Yao, and Shun put on clothes and the world was in order. This was probably inspired by Qian and Kun. When wood is lined up to make a boat, then wood is used as an oar. The benefits of boats and oars are to help people overcome obstacles and to reach far distances, thus benefiting the world. This is probably derived from Huan. Harnessing oxen and riding horses to pull heavy loads and reach far distances is beneficial to the world. This is probably derived from Sui. The doors are closed and drums are beaten to keep out the invaders. This is probably derived from Yu. Cut wood to make a pestle and dig the ground to make a white one. The benefits of the white pestle are used by the people to help them. This is probably derived from Xiaoguo. String wood is used to make bows and sharp wood is used to make arrows. The benefits of bows and arrows are used to intimidate the world. This is probably derived from Yao. In ancient times, people lived in caves and lived in the wild. Later, sages changed this to palaces with roofs above and eaves below to withstand wind and rain. This is probably derived from Dazhuang. In ancient times, people buried their dead with thick clothes and firewood. They buried their dead in the wild without burying them in the ground or planting trees. The mourning period was countless. Later, sages changed this to coffins. This is probably derived from Daguo. In ancient times, people ruled by knotting ropes. Later, sages changed this to written contracts, which were used by officials to govern and by the people to observe. This is probably derived from Fu.

Therefore, Yi means image; image means imaging. Imagined means material; Yao means the movement of the world. Therefore, good and bad things happen and regrets are expressed separately.

3. The History of Emperor Mu:

On the day of Wuyin, the emperor went north to attack and cut off the Zhang River. On the day of Gengchen, he reached Kou and held-up the emperor on a rock. The emperor played Guangyue. He stood there without stopping until he reached the foot of Qianshan. On the day of Guiwei, it snowed and the emperor went hunting in the west of Yanshan.

He then captured the troops that had cut off Qianshan. He marched northward in order to capture them.

On the yang day. On the yiyou day, the emperor ascended to the north at the kou-mouth, and the emperor went north to attack the quanrong. The quanrong kouhunao attacked the emperor on the yang side of the dangshui river, and the emperor then gave the seven cuisines to fight. On the gengyin day, there was wind and rain and snow in the north, and the emperor ordered the kings to rest because of the cold. On the jiawu day, the emperor went west to attack, and he broke off the yuguanlong. On the yihai day, he arrived at the yuzhiping of yan. On the xinchou day, the emperor went west to attack, and he arrived at the na people. The descendants of the hezong, nabaixu, rebelled against the emperor at the zhizhi □, and first gave the emperor ten leopard skins and twenty-six good horses. The emperor sent jingli to receive them. On the guiyou day, the emperor stayed at the qize, and then went fishing in the river to the west to observe the zhizhi □. On the jiachen day, the emperor hunted in the shenze, and then he got a white fox and a black roe, and offered it to the hezong. On the bingwu day, the emperor drank at the ah of the river, and the emperor ordered the six divisions to the south of nabang, on the shenze. On the day of Wuyin, the emperor went westwards, and he reached the Yangyou Mountain. The Hebo Wuyi people lived there, and that was the Hezong clan. Hezong Baitian went against the emperor to the Yanran Mountain, and used a bundle of silk and a jade disc. The emperor first sent Nafu to receive it.

On the day of Guichou, the emperor held a grand meeting at the Yan (swallow) Mountain, at the riverside, and ordered Jingli and Lianggu to lead the six divisions. The emperor ordered an auspicious day of Wuwu, and the emperor wore the imperial robes: a crown, a broken belt, a carriage, and a belt. He held the jade and stood facing south under the cold, and Zeng Zhu assisted him. The officials laid out five animals. The emperor gave the jade to He Zong, who received it from the sky, facing west and sank it into the river, bowing twice and kowtowed. He sank cattle, horses and sheep in prayer/offering. Zong gave the order to the emperor, and He Bo called him: "The emperor said: "Mu Man, you should be the water and do good things." He bowed twice to the south, and He Zong called him again: "The emperor said: "Mu Man, show you the beauty of the spring mountain, and order you to Kunlun to give up the four flat springs for seventy.

Go to Kunlun Hill to see the beauty of the spring mountain. Give you the words of the dark." The emperor accepted the order and bowed twice to the south. On the day of Jiwei, the emperor held a grand meeting at the Huang (yellow) Mountain. (He was about to go to the River) He opened the map and looked at the rituals, and used them to look at the emperor's jade and utensils (the ritual map that the river looked at), and said: "The emperor's treasures: (said to be the "River Map") jade fruits, pearls, candle silver, and gold paste. The emperor's jade is worth ten thousand gold, the jade is worth a hundred gold, the class of the scholar is fifty gold, and the jade of the deer is worth ten gold. The emperor's bow for shooting people, the foot sword, the cattle and horses, and the rhinoceros mouth are worth a thousand gold. The emperor's horse can run a thousand miles and defeat people and beasts. The emperor's dog can run a hundred miles and catch tigers and leopards." Bai Tian said: "The expeditionary birds use wings, the sun mouth black chicken, the crane chicken flies eight hundred miles, the famous beasts use the foot mouth to run a thousand miles, the wild horse of the lion mouth can run five hundred miles, the Qiongqiong Juxu can run a hundred miles, and the deer mouth can run twenty miles." Sun Baiyao all brought the River Map. (The map means ritual. From then on, all the above things were recorded in the "River Map". He Bo regarded it as a ritual, and the ritual was given to Mu King.) He rode on the chariot of Qu Huang and preceded the emperor to the far west.

4. "Engaging the Crown Prince and Spending Ten Thousand Years":

The phoenix is the bird of fire, the jing-essence of Yang; the unicorn is the beast of the dark sky, the jing-essence of Yin. The people are the jing-essence of De-[inherent]virtue. If [inherent]virtue can achieve it, its jing-coherence will be fully realized. ....Therefore, its [inherent]virtue reaches the highest heaven, reaches the highest peace, and reaches all Hun in the world. When the blue dew falls, the white cinnabar blooms, the sweet spring emerges, the red grass grows, and all auspicious signs are present. (Lu Dian's explanation: It is said that the king harmonizes yin and yang, and the qi of rest is filled and full, and auspicious signs are all present, and De-virtue comes. When thus virtue reaches the sky, the Big Dipper is bright, the sun and the moon are shining, and sweet dew falls; when virtue reaches the earth, good crops grow, pods stand up, and wine comes out. When thus virtue reaches cultural writing, the stars are visible and the five latitudes follow the track; when virtue reaches plants and trees, red grass grows and trees interweave; when virtue reaches birds and beasts, phoenixes fly, phoenixes dance, unicorns are pearls, white tigers arrive, white pheasants descend, white deer are seen, and white crows descend; when virtue reaches mountains and tombs, auspicious clouds appear, and chrysanthemums grow abundantly. In the tombs, rare cinnabar appears, in the hills, cages appear, in the mountains, vehicles appear, and in the marshes, divine tripods appear; when virtue reaches the deep springs, the yellow dragon appears, sweet springs gush out, dragon maps appear in the river, tortoise books appear in the Luo River, large shells appear in the river, and bright pearls appear in the sea. When virtue reaches the eight directions, auspicious winds arrive, good qi comes, bells and rhythms are tuned, music is spread, the four barbarian peoples become civilized, and the Yuechang pay tribute.)

5. *"Lüshi Chunqiu·Shijunlan·Guanbiao"*:

It is not just the horse that is like this, people also have their own signs, and all things and countries have their own signs. The sage knows that the past is a thousand years old, and the future is a thousand years old. This is not because of his intention, but because he has his own words. The green picture banner is thin, and I will be born from now on.

Chen Qiyou's "Lüshi Chunqiu Jiaoshi" notes that Gao's note says that "a flag is also thin, and it is made of forged iron, so it means thin and thin. Bi Yuan said that the words are not detailed, and it should come from the Wei book. The note is also unclear. The word "thin" may refer to a flag. Liang Zhongzi said that "Huainanzi, Yizhenxun" has "'Luo' came out of the red book, 'He' came out of the river, a "Green map". Liang Yusheng said, green is probably the same as net, and flag is probably written as scatter. Thin is curtain. "Huainanzi, Lanming" Mi Sheng Wang Ruiying said: "Maison Luotu, yellow cloud net."

[Notes the map is listed as the order of mat. One said, the map is on the mat on the cart (later said it was). Net is the hanging net of the cart. The yellow cloud's air nets the cart. This means that the Ruitu is tied to the thin flag. Gao's note is wrong. Sun Porang said, this note is difficult to understand. Thin should be called Bo Lingbo. It means to use gold and iron as a hammer to hit the thin. "Erya·Shiqi" said: "Talking about gold is called rice. "薄-bao (slight)" means something like a gold plate. Tan Or said before, "Selected Works of Literature: Eastern Capital Fu (talisman)" "Emperor Gaozu received the map", so this green character is a homophone of someone. According to "Huainanzi, Human World", "The Emperor of Qin took the map of Lai, and saw that the legend said "the one who will destroy Qin is Hu", so he sent out 500,000 soldiers, and ordered Zi Gong and Yang Zizi to build the Great Wall", Xu Shen's note said: "Fu means to spread. Qin sent Doctor Lu Sheng to the sea, and returned to compile books to the First Emperor. "According to this, the scene is quite similar to the Wuwei book of the Han Dynasty. In the late Warring States period, as the Yin-Yang school Nan Gong said, "Although there are only three households in Chu, it will be Chu that will destroy Qin", it belongs to this category. Therefore, the above text says, "The saint is like a thousand years old, and the people below know that he is a thousand years old. This is not intentional, but he said it himself." The meaning of "banner" is difficult to be sure, and it is suspected to be something like green map. It is also suspected that "banner" may be the same as the "banner" in "Mencius" "Fanran Gairi", and Zhao's note is "reverse". Bo may be read as Xu's note "pu". "Guangya": "Pu means to display. "Then the Green Picture Banner is just a book that predicts the misfortunes and blessings of the world, such as "The Hu who will destroy Qin" in the Qin Dynasty and "The Red Fu Fu" in the early Eastern Han Dynasty. Gao's comment is incomprehensible. In the case of Qiyou, Tan said that the Green Picture is a scene map, which is quite similar to the prophecy book of the Han Dynasty. Yang said that "The Green Picture Banner is just a book that predicts the misfortunes and blessings of the world, such as "The Hu who will destroy Qin" and "The Red Fu Fu". All of them are true. But Tan said that "The Green Picture Banner is just a book that predicts the misfortunes and blessings of the world, such as "The Hu who will destroy Qin" and "The Red Fu Fu". No. Seal, map, banner and paper are four things. "Mozi, Fei Gong Xia" says: "A red bird holds a jade tablet in its mouth and descends to the Zhou shrine, saying "Heaven has appointed Zhou Wen to attack the country of Guyou". A green map appears in the river and a yellow map appears on the ground." "Beitang

Shuchao, Di Bu" quotes "Sui Chaozi" as saying "When the Ji family rises, a green map appears in the river." "Yiwei·Qian Zaodu" says "Chang received the mandate from Xibo, changed the calendar, announced the title of king to the world, and received Lai Yinghe map." And judging from the texts of "Huainan", "Ni Zhen" and "Renjian", the green map is the seal map, which is undoubtedly a book of prophecy. "Qian Zaodu" and "Dongjing Fu" talk about tea and map separately, which clearly indicate that they are two things. "Shuowen": "Lai means ability; Lu means high basket. "Then the prophecy written in a high bamboo basket is called "tea". Jing is made of bamboo, while Bo is made of cloth (details to be given later), and Bo is also made of bamboo (details to be given later), so Gao's note "pretend to be iron" should refer to "pictures", so the book showing good and bad luck destroyed in the iron object is called "pictures" (pictures do not have to be graphics, and can also have text. "Han Feizi·Shoudao" says "pictures do not include the prime minister, and do not mention the six ministers", and "General" says "heroes are not famous in books", all of which can be used as evidence. Generally speaking, the so-called "pictures" have both graphics and text). Looking at the books cited above, I and the pictures all came from the water (the "green picture" carried by the King of Qin was played by Lu Sheng when he returned from the sea, so it also came from the water). It can be inferred that the reason why Lai made it into a high basket and the reason why the picture was forged into iron objects was that it was easy to preserve and pass it on to the person. If it was cloth or bamboo slips, it would be small and not easy to be discovered by people. Now, it is also easily washed away by water.]

6. Bamboo Annals:

"Dragon Picture" comes out of the river.

7. "Guan Zi·Xiao Kuang":

In the past, people who received the mandate of heaven had dragons and tortoises, maps from the Yellow River, books from the Luo River, and a yellow horse from the Earth. Today, no one has seen these three things. (Fang Xuanling's note: The three auspicious things refer to the tortoise and dragon, the books, and the yellow horse.)

8. "Book of Rites: Li Yun":

The sky does not love its way, the earth does not love its treasure, and people do not love their emotions. Therefore, the sky sends down the oil and dew, the earth produces sweet springs, the mountains produce vehicles, the rivers produce horses, the phoenix and the unicorn are all in the suburbs, the tortoise and the dragon are in the palace, and the eggs and fetuses of other birds and beasts can all be seen from above. This is for no reason. The ancient kings were able to cultivate rituals to achieve righteousness and practice trust to achieve obedience, so this is the reality of obedience.

9. "Historical Records: The Family of Confucius":

In the spring of the fourteenth year of Duke Ai of Lu, he went hunting in the wilderness. The driver of the Shusun family caught an animal while hoeing the river. He thought it was a bad omen. Zhongni looked at it and said, "It is a unicorn." He took it. He said, "If the Yellow River does not produce a map, and the Luo River does not produce a book, I am done."

10. "Huainanzi·Chuzhenxun":

In ancient times, when virtue reigned supreme, merchants enjoyed their business, farmers enjoyed their work, officials were content with their duties, and hermits cultivated their ways. At this time, wind and rain did not destroy or break plants, the nine tripods were rich in flavor, pearls and jade were moist, red books appeared in Luo River, and green maps appeared in He River.

11. "Huainanzi·Ben Jingxun":

At the beginning of Taiqing, it is harmonious and quiet, genuine and simple, quiet and not agitated, pushing without reason. Inwardly it conforms to the Dao, outwardly it is in harmony with righteousness. ....At this time, the mysterious arrives at Dang and shines, the phoenix and unicorn arrive, the good tortoise shells take omens, the sweet dew falls, the bamboo is full of fruits, the yellow water comes out and the red grass grows.

"*Zhou Li: Di Guan Situ*": appendix

Only the king can establish a country, clarify the direction, understand the country and the countryside, set up officials and assign duties, and serve as the people. Then he establishes a local official, Situ, to be in charge of the state education, to help the king to pacify the state.

The duty of the Grand Tutor is to manage the maps of the lands of the states and the number of their people, so as to assist the king in pacifying the states. With the maps of the lands of the world, he can know the number of cities and wide circles in the nine provinces, and distinguish the names of mountains, forests, rivers, lakes, hills, tombs, and plains. He can also distinguish the number of states and capitals, and set up their borders and ditches and seals them, set up their altars and grains, and plant trees for the landowners, and name their altars and fields according to the trees that are suitable for their fields.

2. "*Zhou Li·Xia Guan Sima·Zhi Fang Shi*":

The Zhifang clan was in charge of the map of the world and the land of the world. He could distinguish the people of the states, capitals and borderlands, the four barbarians, the eight wild men, the seven kingdoms, the nine tribes, the five Rong peoples and the six Di peoples, as well as the key points of their financial resources, the nine grains and the six livestocks, and was fully aware of their benefits and disadvantages.

3. "*Huainanzi·Spiritual Training*":

If he were asked to hold the world map in his left hand and dig his throat with his right hand, a fool would not do it. From this point of view, Sheng is respected by the world.

4. "Historical Records: The Family of Prime Minister Xiao":

When Emperor Gaozu rose to be the Duke of Pei, He Chang was the chancellor and in charge of the affairs. When Duke of Pei arrived in Xianyang, all the generals rushed to the palace to divide the gold and treasures, but He alone collected the Qin chancellor's censor's laws and books and kept them. When Duke of Pei became the King of Han, he appointed He as the chancellor. King Xiang and the princes burned and slaughtered people in Xianyang and left. The reason why the King of Han knew the courts and fortresses of the whole country, the number of households, the strengths and weaknesses, and the sufferings of the people was because He had obtained the Tai books.

5. "Records of the Grand Historian: Biographies of Assassins":

(Jing Ke) then arrived at Qin...The King of Qin said to Ke: "Take the map held by Wuyang." After Ke took the map and presented it to the King of Qin, the King of Qin unfolded the map, and when the map was unfolded, the dagger appeared.

6. "Book of the Later Han Dynasty: Biography of Ma Rong":

In the second year of Yongchu, the general Deng Ma heard of Rong's name and summoned him to be his attendant, but he did not like it, so he did not accept the appointment. He was a guest in the border of Wudu and Hanyang in Liangzhou. At that time, the Qiang barbarians rose up, the border areas were in turmoil, and the price of rice and grain soared. From the west of the pass, there was famine on the road. Rong was hungry and exhausted, so he regretted and sighed, and said to his friend: "The ancients said: "With the left hand, you can hold the map of the world, and with the right hand, you can cut your throat. A fool would not do it. The reason is that life is more precious than the world." Now, for the shame of the vulgar, you destroy your body without money. It is not what Laozi and Zhuangzi said. "So I went to respond to the call of Lu.

7. Hu Ai's "Zhouyi Kouyi":

According to this, the River Map is a sign of good fortune from Heaven. If a sage is in power, his supreme virtue will move Heaven and Earth, and the people of the world will be harmonious, then the harmony will fill the space between Heaven and Earth. Then the River Map and the Luo Book will appear, which will be a sign of good fortune. Therefore, the reason why sages make laws is that they act according to the time, so it is said that "the sages follow the way". However, according to the view of various Confucian scholars, the River Map and the Luo Book appeared in the world, and Fuxi drew the Eight Trigrams because he got them, which was a sign of good fortune from Heaven. Moreover, in the ancient times, there were no laws and regulations, and Fuxi, with the talent and virtue of a sage, took the position, so he managed Heaven and Earth and drew the Eight Trigrams as a rule for all ages. If the River Map and the Luo Book had not appeared, Fuxi should have drawn the Eight Trigrams as a rule for future generations. Moreover, the River Map and the Luo Book are great signs of good fortune from Heaven. If the River Map and the Luo Book already have the Eight Trigrams, then the Eight Trigrams should not be said to be drawn by Fuxi. According to the Luoshu, which was given to Yu, the Eight Trigrams were drawn by a sage. According to the Xiaxi, when Fuxi ruled the world in ancient times, he looked up at the sky to observe the patterns, looked down at the earth to observe the patterns, observed the patterns of birds and beasts, took things from his body and things from far away, and then he created the Eight Trigrams to understand the virtues of the gods and to classify the feelings of all things. The Eight Trigrams were created by Fuxi observing the heaven and earth and taking things from them. How can we say that Fuxi drew the Eight Trigrams inspired by the Hetu and Luoshu? If the Hetu and Luoshu already existed, Confucius should not have said that Fuxi created the Eight Trigrams by looking up and looking down. For example, Confucius said, "If the phoenix does not come and the river does not produce the map, I am done." This means that Confucius created the book because of the phoenix. He also said, "The turtle and the dragon are in the suburbs." The map appeared in the river and the book appeared in Luo, which is also because of the turtle and the unicorn. This is because Confucius said that the unicorn and the wind were auspicious things in the sky that are difficult to see. If a sage is in power, bestowing the five blessings on the people, governing the country with good policies, and filling the heaven and earth with harmony, then the River Chart, the Luoshu, the tortoise and the unicorn, the dragon and the wind will appear as auspicious signs. The sage will follow the times and do things accordingly, so it is said that "the sage follows it."

Yijing, bagua and xiantian daoism

This chapter is based on my translation of chapters from the book "Wudang early civilization" by editor in chief Zhang Huapeng and Zhang Fuqin that I bought in 2007 just after it came out.

The book is exploring archeology of the Wudang Mountain, the heart of Xiantian daoism, and as you will see later on also the root of the 8 diagrams as used in the Yijing, the bagua.

As a whole the chapter is almost integrally used but with additions or adaptations for comfort in explanation to westerners. After all the book is written for Chinese people, often even referring to we Chinese, and other nationalist idioms.

The reason why I added is because most Yijing books remain distant and abstract, disconnected from their culture. Having a perspective to its history creates a clearer perspective on its content, where it comes from, especially the textual parts, of which we mostly just follow what popular chinese ideas reach us, and not so much the nitty gritty research, like in this chapter.

What is important is that the chapter investigates aspects of Bagua and Luoshu and Hetu diagrams.

We know that in the premodern era, also called a theocracy era, "superstition" was often regarded as truth, and scientific truth was obstructed and persecuted. In my own school I follow the idea of anthropology that every culture in essence is a worldview, and that every worldview is primarily scientific with the tools it develops within that culture. Some of these are material or observational tools, some are more spiritual or even demonic. You can go to different cultures and non can be seen as not having a worldview. That means that one can understand the world of that worldview only through its scientific model. Cultural science is therefore the correct description, in stead of theocratic, religious or supersitious thought. Modern science in east and west sees itself as the tip of cultural evolution, therefore discriminating the past and dehumanizing the complex thoughts people had over time. They call it even the law of human social evolution - from stupidity to intelligence, from crude tools to modern tools, and from theocracy era to the scientific era.

An issue historians found is that Wudang was in the past called Taihe mountian. Taihe meaning bigger harmony mountian. But nobody could tell when that name was changed. Nowadays though there is an idea, and that idea links Wudang mountian closely with the Yijing, but for this we need to delve into the world of neolithic times. The historians nowadays consider that "changing the name of Taihe to Wudang" was correct and already existed in the human mind 4 thousand years ago. It was part of a repression of a passed that shamed people, as well as helped create the cultural identity we nowadays call Chinese, or the culture of the Han, as the Chinese see themselves as a mixed tribe or nation.

The authors suggest that it is reasonable for today's scholars to be skeptical, but we should not be blinded by a leaf and fail to recognize the true face of Mount Taihe. The name "Wudang Mountain" still exists today and is well-known at home and abroad for its Taijiquan development primarily, and as a tourist center for study of Daoism as resurrected after the cultural revolution in the second degree. The reason for its historical fame is inseparable from the Xuanwu God. The Xuanwu god is the god of the northern sky dome, and is comprised from a turtle with a snake encapsulating it, but also as a Black Warrior, later to be called Zhenwu. "Wu" in both names means warrior, or discipline, hence the name Wudang means Warrior Service. Wudang Mountain is named after Xuanwu. This is an indisputable fact today. It is said that King Yu change the name of Wudang Mountain? Was it simply because "If it is not Xuanwu, who can enjoy it?" Please see the following text.

Jiuqiu Jingwei Tiandi Li is the title of a Daoist book, and the book itself is only partial interesting for this chapter. There are many myths in Daoist books, these stories might not all be true, but it cannot be said that Daoist book stories are all myths. There are still historical facts as their basis. This can be seen from the activities of Yu, the founding emperor of the Xia Dynasty, in pre-literate times. In addition, the time when King Yu changed the name to Wudang is the same as the Shanhaijing (classic of mountians and sea) era studied by many scholars. At present, Shanhaijing is mostly believed to be a collection of stock cultural legends. But some of it in fact is more in line with historical events. The problem is very clear. According to the previous article "Jiuqiu Jingwei Tiandi Li", King Yu named the mountain "Wudang" after Dahe Taihe mountain. First, it means that it was called Taihe Mountain before the Xia Dynasty and it was already very famous. Second, the name of the mountain must have had a deep meaning when the dynasty changed. The author believes that the name "Wudang Mountain" is a triple intention by King Yu, which contains the meaning of "only Xuanwu can handle it" and "block it with force". Although King Yu was very smart, he could not get rid of the theocratic priesthood at that time as guardians of cultural science. "Yi Guan" states in the Zhou dynasty: "Observe the Dao of gods in the world, and the four seasons are not wrong. The saints set up teachings with gods, and the world is [to be] convinced. "As a king, how could Yu not know the principle of ruling the people joined with gods - using gods to fool the people makes it easier to rule. The gods are synonimous to the Zhou dynasty principle of Heaven, The qian hexagram in the yijing and the tian diagram in the 8 diagrams or Bagua. Therefore, Yu would vigorously promote "If it is not Xuanwu, who can enjoy it?" Later, scholars evolved it into the saying "If it is not Xuanwu, the being (god) is not enough to be in charge of it." Furthermore, Xuanwu itself has the meaning of using force, it means Dark Warrior, or Occult Warrior. The above mentioned book's chapter "Supplementary Notes" says: "It is said that turtles and snakes "have scales on their bodies, so they are called martial". The first battle between Yao, Shun, Yu and the ancient Miao was at Danshui on the northeastern border of Junling. "Lüshi Chunqiu Zhaolei" says: "Yao fought at Danshuipu and subdued the southern barbarians. "The

"Southern Barbarians" here refer to the ancient Miao. According to legend, the Miao Nationality has originated from a tribe called Jiuli that lived in the lower reaches of the Yellow River more than 5,000 years ago, so when we mention Miao we mean their ancestors. Later this tribe migrated to areas in the middle and lower reaches of the Yangtze River to form the Sanmiao Tribe.

The "Continuation of Junzhou Records" also says that in the ancient Junzhou territory, "it started from the conquest of the Miao and Guifang." The "Yu Di Ji Sheng" says: "The King of Barbarians' home is 200 steps south of Wudang County." There was a war of conquering the ancient Miao that lasted for more than a hundred years. This is the second meaning of Yu's renaming of Wudang Mountain. In the era of so called theocracy, King Yu could not say it clearly, but could only show his intention. This is why I admire the scholars who first proposed the theory that Wudang "originated from the use of force to block external forces". The word "Wudang" is real when used here. The "North" in "divide the North Three Miao" is the "policy" of keeping the good and sending the bad, so we know that a large number of Miao people stayed here. After Yu destroyed the Miao, it was a time of regime change. There were still a large number of Miao people who did not resist Yu's regime. "Later, they followed the rule of the gods", which also meant to keep them. Yu did not kill the Miao people who did not resist, and respected their belief in the Xuanwu God. He did not completely follow the name of "Taihe Mountain". Yu "changed the name of Taihe to Wudang", which symbolized the right and reasonable move and facilitated the rule. This is Yu's true intention and his wisdom. The Xuanwu God still retains the cultural characteristics of the embryonic form of the "Sanmiao" nation, and eventually gradually merged into the Huaxia people, becoming a part of the Han nationality, and the Xuanwu God culture also became Han culture. The Xuanwu totem worshipped by the ancient Miao evolved into the Holy Father (divine king of the east), the Holy Mother (divine Queen of the west) and the Prince of Jingle Kingdom (Zhenwu). The modern term is "Sinicization". This has been confirmed by many experts and scholars who study the "Sanmiao" culture, so there is no need to elaborate. Because of Yu's emphasis on the Xuanwu God of Mount Wudang, the Xuanwu God of Mount Wudang was able to exist and develop rapidly over the thousand years of the Xia, Shang and Zhou dynasties. By the

Spring and Autumn Period and the Warring States Period, it had become "different from other mountains". After Daoism was founded in the Eastern Han Dynasty, Wudang Daoism became an important sect of Daoism in China. Since King Yu changed the name and developed it to the present day, it has a civilization history of more than 4,000 years. To have established this puts a first light on the original meanings of the bagua trigrams.

The River Map and the Luo book

In the book "Daoyi Centering" The Yijing is described and discussed as a system. It is written by Hu Zi and published in 2009, all the different aspects of Yijing systematics and history are being discussed, similarly as in the Online Yijing Counsellor Course. I have absorbed the translations of this book into the course together with other textbooks.

I usually explain Daoist cultural science as related to yijing, Taiji gongfu, neidandao meditation and medicine as a collection of 13 theories, where modern western sources only discuss westernized interpretations of yinyang and wuxing. An important part are many other theories. The theories of Hetu and Luoshu are part of that. They are at the root of yinyang theory, seem to relate to both astrology and fengshui, and graphically they seem to link to scapulamancy, the prediction of the future by means of burning holes in turtle shells.

According to Zheng Xuan's note, there are two words "Luoshu" and "Hetu". According to his remarks, the records of Hetu and Luoshu have existed as early as the Zhou Dynasty in "Book of Documents". They were mainly used as treasures for emperors to pass on their thrones and govern the country. "Guanzi Chapter Xiaoqu" said that "Hetu came out of a river, Luo came out a river, and Chenghuang came out of the earth", which was a sign of a ruler receiving a mandate in the past. "Yi Zhuan" in the Warring States Period said: "Hetu came out, Luo came out, and the saints followed it." The "Xici" chapter of Yijing 10 wings began to connect Hetu and Luoshu with "Zhouyi". The "Emperor's Chronicle" also said: "The Yellow River produced a dragon map, and the Luo River produced a tortoise book." Some people even interpreted the mythology as the dragon map being the map carried by the dragon horse of the Yellow River, and the tortoise book being the book on the back of the Luo River god tortoise. This turns it into the theory of the dragon map and the tortoise book. In fact, the more reasonable and correct explanation of "the dragon map comes out of the Yellow River, and the Luo River produces a tortoise book" may be that a jade map with the number of elephants (that went extinct in ancient times, therefore dragons or horses were used to replace the word elephant to express, and dragons and horses can also represent yang) appeared in the Yellow River (or the Milky Way, or the round river in the sky), and a book on the back of a tortoise appeared in Luoyang City (or the Luo River area) (it should be an oracle bone diagram written on the back of a tortoise, which can represent yin); or the round map of the Milky Way and the square map of the Luo River changed into the River Map and the Luo River Book: Therefore, there is the theory that the River Map and the Luo River Book express the round sky and square earth. If we interpret the words of the River and the Luo River, they all come out from the water in the north, and the image can be round and square.

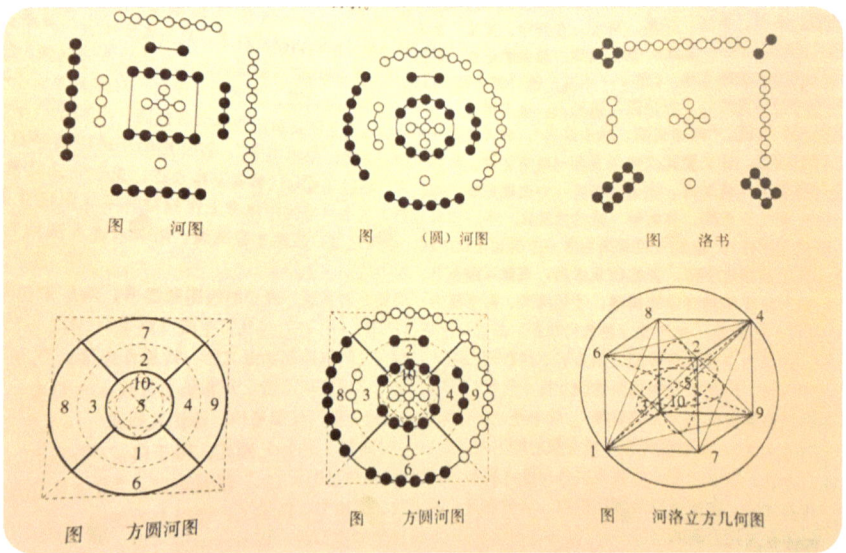

It was not until the end of the Western Han Dynasty that the philosopher Yang Xiong regarded the River Chart and the Luoshu as the source of the Zhouyi. The current River Chart and Luoshu are both the diagrams of the Dragon Chart of Yi by Chen Chi in the early Song Dynasty, and the diagrams of the Five Xing generating the River Chart (see above and below) and the Nine Palaces generating the Luoshu (see above and below) in Liu Mu's Yishu Gouwen Diagram. The diagram used white dots to represent odd-numbered Yang and black dots to represent even-numbered Yin, and the fixed dots were connected by lines like knotted ropes and characters, thus establishing the book theory of the River and Luo. However, Ruan Yi of the same period in the Northern Song Dynasty objected to this, saying that Liu Mu had reversed the River and Luo chart and made it wrong, and that it was not the real diagram of ancient times. He also replaced its network diagram and forged the book Guanlang Yichuan. With the support of Song Yi, Cai Yuanding of the Southern Song Dynasty compiled the diagram of Guanlang Yichuan into Yixue Qimeng. In my translation of the chapters on Luosu and Hetu in Li Shenguo's "Zhouyi Illustrated Collection" in 3 parts of together 2500 pages (about) many variations of the diagrams are offered and explained. In the Yijing counsellor course the chapters discussing the Xia to the Ming are offered for comprehension and academic study. The Original Meaning of Zhouyi, which have been handed down to this day as the current diagrams of the River Chart (see below) and the Luoshu (see below). Na Zi said: "The circle is the number of the River Chart, and the square is the text of the Luoshu. Therefore, the text was used to create the Book of (ex)Changes, and then the biography was used to create the Fan." Cai Yuanding said: "The biographies of ancient and modern times have been passed down since Kong An Guo, Liu Xiang and his son, and Ban Gu all believed that the River Chart was given to Cheng and the Luoshu was given to Yu, the same king as discussed above. Guan Ziming and Shao Kangjie (i.e., Bu Zi) both believed that the number ten (even/yin) was the River Chart and number nine (uneven/yang) was the Luoshu. "It is said that there was a detailed explanation in the "Book of Jie" (see "Weishu Jicheng") before the Han Dynasty, which also included "Yi", "Li" and "Chunqiu", "Book of History", "Book of Songs", "Book of Music", "Analects of Confucius", "Book of Filial Piety" and other seminal texts. According to the research of ancient books, it is said that the River Chart mostly refers to the emperor's rule. It is considered that the Hetu map of the country is a map of the Yellow River with Kunlun Mountain as the center. Luoshu refers to the image and number documents of the customs and people of Luoshui in the nine states. In fact, no one has ever seen what the "map" and "book" look like, and there is therefore no clear discussion of these original maps, but its influence is far-reaching enough to have formed the "Heluo civilization" of the Heluo River Basin in China. Around Heluo Town 130 km west of Zhengzhou, Henan Province, where the Yi and Luo Rivers meet and join into the Yellow River, archeologists have found a large-scale central settlement of an ancient state ca. 5,300 years ago. The site displays what a city was like at the origin of Chinese civilization. Due to its location in Heluo town and its importance as a landmark in Chinese archaeological history, experts have proposed naming the culture "Heluo Civilization."

There are many different diagrams and discussions of Hetu and language books from ancient times to the present, and Figures below are generally the main figures.

The "Xi Ci" says: "Heaven is one, earth is two, heaven is three, earth is four, heaven is five, earth is six, heaven is seven, earth is eight, heaven is nine, earth is ten, the number of heaven is five, the number of earth is five, the five positions are in harmony, the number of heaven is twenty-five, the number of earth is thirty, the total number of heaven and earth is fifty-five, this is why changes are formed and ghosts and gods are moving." Where did the theory of the number of heaven and earth come from? The debate throughout history has not reached a conclusion. It is believed that it is closely related to the astronomy and numerology of ancient times. This can be inferred from the points and lines of the ancient star map. For example, in the diagram of "Shi's Star Classic" by Shi Zhong, a Chinese astronomer in the Warring States Period about 2600 years ago, we can see the use of points and numbers in the classics. It is also because of this record that the "Book of Changes" has a close relationship with the Hetu and Luoshu in terms of the doctrine of the image. Therefore, in the past, those who talked about the Eight Trigrams must also talk about the River Map and Luoshu, and those who talked about the River Map and Luoshu also inevitably mentioned the theory of the Eight Trigrams in the "Book of (ex)Changes". The origin of the trirgram or Bagua symbols is a long and complicated issue. Now people have found that some carvings on pottery fragments dating back about 10,000 years ago seem to reveal a connection telling that weaving (经-jing) is like painting. This might be the origin of the Jing in Yijing, which is interpreted as classic but also means weft, in this case the weft of yin and yang in the natural tapestry of reality. The Book of (ex)Changes 易经 Yijing was written 700 to 800 years earlier than the Book of Yizhuang 易传 (Changing Passes). It is undeniable that the Eight Trigrams were not based on the River Chart and the Luoshu, but their correlation must exist. The Yi Zhuan is an ancient philosophical and ethical work, a classic work that interprets the Yi Jing , and a collection of essays that explained and elaborated the Yi Jing during the Warring States Period. The formation of the thought of rigidity and flexibility in Yi Zhuan and the shift in the paradigm of Yijing science interpretation. The Yi Zhuan states that the first line (first line), third line, and fifth line of the Yi Gua/trigrams are all yang positions, because their line positions are odd numbers, and odd numbers are yang numbers, so their line positions are yang positions. The Yi Zhuan states that the second line, fourth line, and sixth line (upper line) of the Yi Gua are all yin positions, because their line positions are even numbers, and even numbers are yin numbers, so their line positions are yin positions.

In terms of the ideological system of Yi Zhuan , its naturalistic view of the Dao of Heaven, its holistic thinking mode of inferring human affairs from the Dao of Heaven, and its thinking on the development and change of things are all consistent with the Yin-Yang School.

Many scholars originally believed that the current Hetu Luoshu had records in ancient times, but the graphics were drawn by people in the Song Dynasty. The Yidao explains that it was not until 1977 that a large and two-nine-meter-long figure was unearthed from the tomb of a marquis in Shuanggutui, Yuanyang County, which was buried during the Western Han Dynasty, that it was confirmed that language books appeared in ancient times. This also proves that the graphics drawn by people in the Song Dynasty have a basis, and it cannot be said that they were created by people in the Song Dynasty, so, they can only be said to be interpreted and displayed by them. The author of the mentioned research believes that both the Hetu and Luoshu can be used as square and solid diagrams, and that the Hetu should mostly represent the sky, while the Luoshu should mostly represent the earth. In fact, the Hetu should mostly be a three-dimensional or spherical diagram, so when looking at the diagram, we should add more time and space concepts of front and back (or inside and outside) on the circular Hetu. I think this is also what Steve Moore in his 1989 book "the trigrams of Han" discussed when discussing the devil vally diagram from at least a few centuries after the Han dynasty, anmd possible the Song dynasty. The Devel Valley diagram is supposed to link heaven and earth where the hetu and luosu represent heaven and earth. He saw in this the link between Fengshui and Mingshui, wind-water and name-water. In all cases, 5 can be used to represent the time and space position of the starting quantity black road in front and the center of the circle, while 10 is the back or the center of the circle. The "Hetu" that we generally refer to now is composed of five groups of white circles (total 25) and black dots (total 30). The white diagram symbolizes the positive, called the number of heaven, which refers to the odd numbers 1, 3, 5, 7, and 9. The black dots symbolize the negative, called the number of earth, which refers to the even numbers 2, 4, 6, 8, and 10. Heaven and earth each have five numbers (i.e. five groups of image numbers), and the total number of circles and dots of heaven and earth is 55 (note: 55-1+3+5+7+9+2+1+6+8+10). It is a typical combination of images and numbers. The Hetu follows the order of up, down, left, right, and center, combined with the order of heaven and earth turning counterclockwise (1, 3, 7.9 odd and 2, 4, 6, 8 each form a double spiral, with 5 and 10 in the middle), divides the numbers into young, old, yin, and yang numbers, and combines the black dots and white circles to form a time and space image number diagram. The ten complete numbers of the Hetu are the natural images given by the natural qi of heaven and earth. Please refer to the figure for the River Chart below.

The layout characteristics of the Yin-Yang and Five Xing of the River Chart are as follows:

"Heaven One produces water in the north,

Earth Two produces fire in the south,

Heaven Three produces wood in the east,

Earth Four produces gold in the west,

Heaven Five produces earth in the middle...

Six becomes water in the north, together with Heaven One:

Heaven Seven becomes fire in the south, together with Earth Two,

Earth Eight becomes earth in the east, in the well of Heaven Three:

Heaven Nine becomes gold in the west, together with Earth One,

Earth Ten becomes earth in the middle, in the well of Heaven Five."

Another vivid description is as Zhang Jiebin of the Ming Dynasty said in "Leijing Tuyi":

"The birth number is the main one and thinks about the inside, the completion number is the matching number and is outside, and this is the fixed number of the period chart. ... (with) Yin and Yang Qingchang (rise and fall) matching each other, such as the position of Lao Yin (old yin) is one and the number of Lao Yin is six, Shaoyin (few yin) is in position two and is paired with Shaoyang (few yang), number seven; Shaoyang is in position three and is paired with Shaoyin, number eight; Laoyin is in position four and is paired with Laoyang, number nine. This is the wonder of the mutual concealment of yin and yang."

What we generally call "Luoshu" is similar to Hetu, which uses numbers from one to nine to divide the sky into Yang and the earth into Yin, with white dots as Yang numbers and black dots as Yin numbers. They are arranged in the squares of the Nine Palaces. The Luoshu is actually the Nine Palaces Mountain. The total number of Yin and Yang of heaven and earth in the Luoshu is 45 (Note: 45-1+9+3+7+2+8+4+6+5). The number of the River Chart is ten, which is the body number, and the number of the Luoshu is nine, which is the use number.

The nine numbers in Luoshu are also called the nine numbers. They are the number that gives birth to Taiyi and becomes the number of polarized nine. They are the result of the time-space distortion of the transposition of 2 and 4, 7 and 9 in the River Chart and the reverse rotation to form a square. Wei Zhen said in The Original Meaning of Zhouyi: "Diagrams and Explanations" that "Luoshu is like a tortoise, so the number is nine on the top and one on the bottom, three on the left and seven on the right, two and four are shoulders, six and eight are feet (note: there is also the phrase "five in the center")." I think it is also the diagrammic foundation for the bagua map of 4 directions and 4 pillars, which also is foundational for mandala thinking.in China. He also said that Luoshu has fifteen vertically and horizontally to show the principle of the center of the river map. The four sides are called the eight poles, and the five are in the center, and the nine palaces are completed, so-called "getting the center of the ring to respond to the infinite." The image of the one in the center is motionless, which is the principle of Taiji, so-called "the movement of the world is centered on one." Lai Zhide said, "A magical tortoise came out of Luoyang. The tortoise's body shell has forty-five numbers, nine on the head and one on the feet.

洛书传说

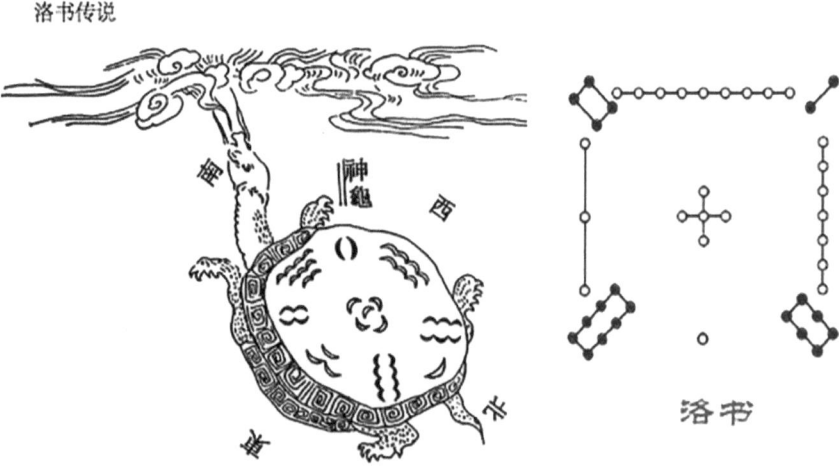

洛书

Three on the left and seven on the right, two and four are shoulders, six and eight are right, and five is in the middle. The sage drew the patterns on the tortoise's body as Luoshu. However, each dot is straight like a character, so it is also drawn based on its image, so it is called "book". If the dots are also circles, it is not a book! This book is different from the books handed down in the world, so it is called "ancient Luoshu." Luoshu is shown in Figure. The nine-square grid is a 3×3 square matrix. Lai Zhide's ancient Luoshu is shown in Figure. The mathematical feature of Luoshu is that the sum of the vertical and horizontal numbers surrounds 5, which is 15.

Mount Wudang in the Shanhaijing Era

There are many experts and scholars who have studied the naming of Wudang Mountain. Above we have already concluded that Xiantian Daoism links directly to the Wudang mountain, but also to the neolithic Miao people. In this chapter we discuss the geographic nature of the wudang area in regard to its history and the links to bagua. Above we already showed that Gen trigram likely represents Wudang mountain and Xuanwu mountain.

Volume 43 of Taiping Yulan records: "The Classic of Mountains and Seas (Shanhaijing) says that the source of the Ji River in Wudang Mountain flows underground for more than 300 Li-miles. Dai Sheng, the general of the palace left by Emperor Wu of the Han Dynasty, went to this mountain to collect elixirs and attained enlightenment and never returned." The Classic of Mountains and Seas is an ancient book that records ancient things, which shows that the ancient Wudang Mountain had become a sacred mountain a long time before. In the book "Chinese Daoism", the two scholars Wang Jiayou and Sha Mingshou said in "Study on the Naming of Wudang Mountain": "The Daoist "Kaishan Jing" says: Doushan (Bean mountain) has five caves, connecting Kunlun, Longshan, Wudang, Qingcheng, and Chang'an... Therefore, we know that "Wudang" originated from "Wuzai" of the Ba people of Taihao", and in "Shanhai Jing" "The Xuandan Mountain in "Dahuang Xijing" is the Wudang Mountain", and "Guangyun has Zaiguo, and Zai is pronounced differently. Wu is written as 武-Wu and Zai is written as 当-Dang", and "Wudang Mountain was originally the eastern mountain of Wangmo, the capital of Kunlun in Daoism. It can be explored from the migration history and routes of the Ba people (Bao) who were divided into Taihao (Nuwa Fuxi Longhu Division)." The Ba people used to live in eastern Sichuan and were conquered and assimilated in the Qin empire. Ba is a character in the past meaning "seem to eat snakes", and nowadays is an expression of desire for something. As for the origin of the word "Wu Zai", the author has found three places in the "Classic of Mountains and Seas": "Overseas Southern Classic" says: "The San Miao country is east of the Chishui River, and its people are The country of Zai is located in the east of the Wudang Mountains. Its people are yellow and can shoot snakes with bows. It is said that the country of Zai is located in the east of the Wudang Mountains. The Wudang Mountains are the place where the ancient Sanmiao people lived. This "Sanmiao" must be related to Wudang. "The Great Wilderness Southern Classic" says: "There is a country called Daimin. Emperor Shun was born without prostitution. He descended to the place where Zai was born. They are called Wuzaimin. Wuzaimin is named Pan." "The Classic of Western Mountains": "Three hundred and twenty miles west, it is called Fanjia Mountain. The Han River originates from it and flows southeast to the Mian River... Three hundred and fifty miles west, it is called Tiandi Mountain." This "Tiandi Mountain" on the bank of the Han River has special significance in the Classic of Mountains and Seas and should be explored. This record is consistent with the current situation of the Han River flowing from Fanjia Mountain to Wudang Mountain. So is this "Tiandi Mountain" the Wudang Mountain? It remains to be verified. According to this, the problem still needs to be discussed from the perspective of the Ba people, their settlements, their migration, the Sanmiao, the Zai State, and Wu Zai in order to be true and reliable. The author has learned that Professor Zhang Lianggao, an architectural expert at Huazhong University of Science and Technology, is compiling his research results, "A Different View of Ba History", which includes research on such issues. It can be easily solved. Professor Zhang said: Wudang Mountain is also known as "Xie Luo Mountain" because "Wu Xie and Wu Luo" were active here in the "Classic of Mountains and Seas" era. The research of scholars such as Wang, Sha, and Zhang traced the naming of Wudang Mountain back to the ancient times of Taihao (Fuxi), which is already a great achievement. From the above, there is a consensus that many scholars traced the naming of Wudang Mountain back to the prehistoric medieval period. This is a blessing for Wudang Mountain. Is it a conclusion? No. With the in-depth study of Wudang culture, there will definitely be deeper discoveries. What does make sense in the way the 8 trigrams developed paralel to the neolithich culture situated around the mount Wudang. In ritual that means that the mountian trigram corner in the northeast is directed to the worship of Xuanwu, opposite to the Heaven in the North west, where the heaven tilts downward.

Natural Numbers the human body and nature

The same Daoyi book we discussed before also explains the relationship of the trigrams with the reality of nature as a whole, where people live between heaven and earth, as discussed above in a map that is often called a magic square, based on the luoshu, and often described as the postnatal order of the trigrams, and which in modern sources explains the link beteen luoshu and the trigrams. In this heading we will discuss the realization of the trigrams and the natural world, and the human body.

The Daoyi explains that natural images and their mathematical principles are reflected by various things, whether animals, plants, or the human body, etc., all show or hide holographic evidence of the spiral aura that exists in the universe, which is the symbol of all things. Spiralling is also seen as natural in taiji thinking. Taiji boxing is making use of the spiral movement in the body and the way how it applies force in behaviour and martial arts.

Nature belongs to the spiral shape of Dao Teaching, and Daoism includes ideas of holography, spiral rising shape, circle shape, round-trip shape, etc. In the shapes of plants and animals, many of them leave the "S" shape (or "卐" shape, which is called Yin-Yang Gate Dao) of the cosmic spiral aura. This "S" shape is the beautiful natural shape that brings us to enjoy the beauty of nature.

In art the s curve is seen as a sign of feminity, as shown in Maria statues in the Catholic faith, but also in fashion photography and movies. The claim here is that the esthetics of humans goes back to the inherent appreciation of forms in nature, where the feminine than represents the natural.

For example, there are leaves that are "S" shaped, grape tendrils that are spiral-shaped, and gourd-shaped melons. Among medicinal plants, the human-shaped Polygonum multiflorum is a miracle. It is not only human-shaped, but also can be divided into male and female shapes. Ginseng is also human-shaped. The parrot snail, which is known as a living fossil, as well as snails, snails and other shell animals, mostly present clockwise left-handed patterns. Among shells, the abalone, its shell pattern is a simultaneous trajectory of the interweaving of the positive and negative cyclones.

Therefore, from animals and plants, we can deduce that there are three main natural aura spirals: one is the clockwise left-handed positive spiral; the other is the counterclockwise right-handed negative rotation, and the third is the left-right rotating yin-yang combined rotation.

It is said that the solution to the spell is also related to the spiral spiral worm shape, which is related to the holographic nature of the energy information such as the aura (i.e. physiognomy) and the simulated correspondence. These are also our ancient holographic concepts of "correspondence between heaven and man". In nature, whether it is animals or plants, they also present the yin and yang mathematics of heaven and earth in various forms to a greater or lesser extent.

The ancients said that "most flowers of plants have five petals, and snowflakes have six petals." That is to say, the flowers grown by general plants are mainly five-petaled, and the hexagonal snowflakes that are crystallized when water meets freezing are actually mostly five-shaped. The flowers among plants are also divided into yin and yang. This is because the flowers of plants are from Yangming (Yangbright) and are the middle yang number five, while the snowflakes are from Jueyin and are the middle yin number six. These are all reflections of the connection or holography of the Qi between heaven and earth.

In the human body, for example, people have four limbs, hands and feet with yin and yang, and the hands are divided into left and right hands, and the left and right hands contain yin and yang. Each hand has five fingers, and the thumb is the main one, which is thick and short, and the other four fingers are auxiliary and long, and the middle finger is the longest. There are ten fingers in total on both hands. The number 10 in the ten fingers of these hands is the natural number of solar time counting heavenly stems that we are most familiar with, that is, the full natural number of the yang number 10, and the five senses, five internal organs, and six bowels of the human body, and the twelve main jingluo-channels running through the body muscle channels, etc. The saying that the human body has "seven holes bleeding" should refer to the two eyes, two ears, two nostrils and the mouth, which is related to the seven-star number. If the whole body is taken into account, plus the neglected genitals and excretory holes, then men should have nine holes (that is, seven holes plus the penis urethra and anus), and women should have ten holes (that is, seven holes plus the vulva urethra, vaginal opening and anus). This can be said that the number nine is exactly the positive number, and the number ten (or the regressive number zero) is exactly the negative number. Therefore, relatively speaking, oviparous animals have a very high number of positive holes, and the number ten (or the regressive number zero) is exactly the negative number.

Among animals, such as insects, there are six-legged ants, eight-legged spiders, centipedes, etc., which are also the numbers of heavenly stems and earthly branches.

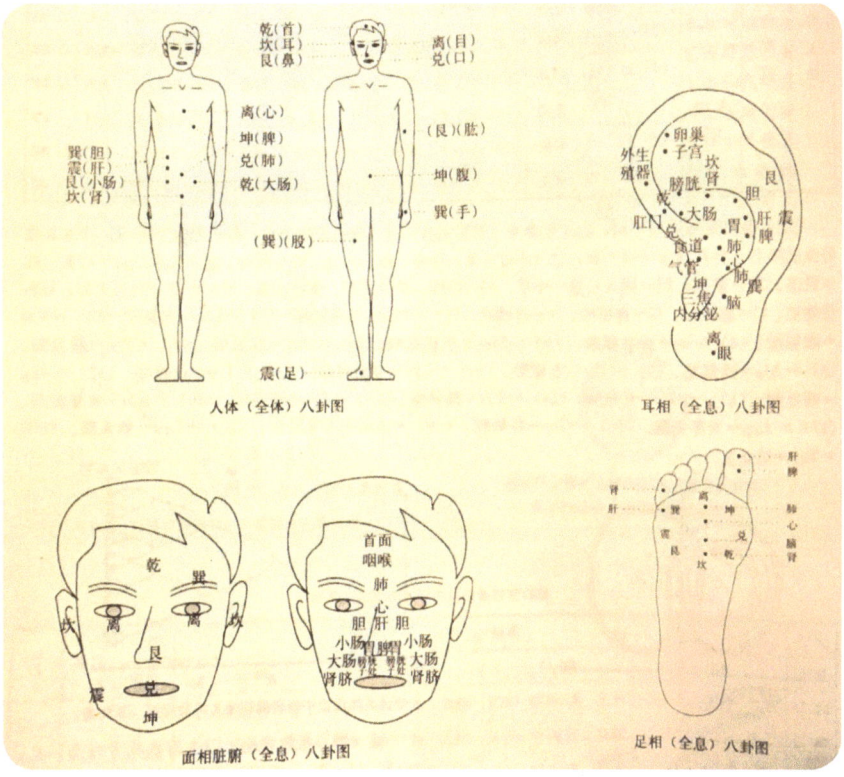

All this we call the phenomenon of the natural numerical manifestation of the yin and yang of numbers. As mentioned above, the number of heavenly stems is a positive number, that is, the whole number of 10, which is open-minded; the number of earthly branches is a negative number, that is, the whole number of 12, which is closed. The number 2 is a left-right symmetrical number of yin and yang, which often appears on the left and right sides of animals as yin and yang correspondence. The number of heavenly stems 5 is often based on half of 10 as the base number for yin and yang, which often appears in the number of petals of plants or the numbers of animals and human limbs, and the number of earthly stems 12 is often based on half of 6 or 3. It is manifested in the numbers of mineral crystals or insect caputpods, etc. Yijing numerology takes some time to get aquined with, but it roots back to the connection between fengshui directionology, the luoshu and the bagua trigrams. For spiders with eight legs, it can imply the number of the Eight Trigrams. If two antennae are added, it becomes the number of Heaven and Earth. For common flying insects, they all have six legs and four wings, which add up to the number of Heaven and Earth. If two antennae are added, it becomes the number of Earth and Earth. These are all holographic reflections of the numbers of common natural objects.

For human fingerprints, they are also a reflection of the lateral cyclone. Fingerprints are divided into three categories: bucket (radish bucket) shape, dustpan shape, and arch shape. Among them, the bucket shape can be divided into eight types: ring, spiral, and capsule shape; the dustpan shape pattern can be divided into positive dustpan shape and reverse dustpan shape; the arch shape pattern can be divided into tent shape and arch shape. The fingerprints we are familiar with are actually the reflection of different vortexes of the universe in the human body. Although everyone's fingerprints are different, they are actually the same in essence, just like the infinite decimals between 1 and 0.

From the natural opening and spiraling images of animals, plants, and humans, and the yin and yang numbers of heaven and earth, it is a reflection of the holographic image numbers of the natural universe in the individual. These shapes and patterns inform the bagua, and with that the movements of yin and yang in the yijing.

In the issue of human race, most people say that humans are divided into four major races based on skin color, which are white, black, yellow, and brown. These four colors can be said to be the four directional symbols, which can also be the five xing of gold, wood, water, and fire. The fifth xing of earth can be said to be generated by all directions. It can be seen as a mixed race.

Besides the clearly visible there also are holographic biological heritage codes in the bodies of animals and plants. In the cells of organic life, protein is the form of life. Protein is composed of a series of amino acids and has a spiral structure like a chain.

The two types of "secondary structures" of proteins are generally "a" helix and "b" fold or line, among which there are single helix, double helix, triple helix, etc. For example, the entire peptide chain of keratin in hair is an "a" helix structure. Collagen is the most abundant protein in the human body and the main component of connective tissue. Its structure is very similar to a hemp rope made of three strands. If the collagen molecule is broken, it loses its helical configuration and becomes a straight line. Modern hair like the current genetic code, DNA, is a double helix structure.

Therefore, we can see that the cyclonic movement of macroscopic celestial galaxies mostly presents the yin-yang structure cyclonic movement of "square in circle, circle in square". And for the microscopic life information system structure, it mostly presents the yin-yang structure cyclonic movement of "straight in curve, curve in straight". However, these various chain rotations all belong to the category of rotation circle. No matter what phenomena are in the macroscopic or microscopic world, they are all amazingly similar to the Taiji Yin Yang (Yi Hu) diagram.

This Yidao appendix also provides holographic diagrams of some major TCM human body parts corresponding to the Five Xing and Eight Diagrams for reference.

Note that in the diagram of the human body, the "Shuo Gua" says that Gen-mountain corresponds to the hand, while Chen Tuan says that Xun-wind corresponds to the hand. This is specially explained. Chen Tuan explained in "Zheng Yi Xin Fa Zhu": "The "Zhuo" says "The nose is the Gen-mountain on the face." It also says "The wind can inspire all things, and the hands dance." Qian-heaven is the head, Kun-earth/field/soil is the abdomen, and the heaven and earth are well positioned. Kan-river/rain is the ears, Li-Sun is the eyes, and water and fire meet. Gen is the nose, Dui-cloud/lake/marsh is the mouth, and the mountain and the marsh are connected. Xuniwind/life is the hand, Zhen is the foot, and thunder and wind are close to each other." Although the number of the Gen symbol can be five fingers, the symbolic meaning of stopping can also be feet, and the back can also be the back. If the hexagram symbol is combined, Xun is the hand, so what Chen Tuan said is very reasonable. In the figure below, Gen corresponds to the hand and Xun is the thigh. Li is the eye and the liver governs the eye, which is the difference between the pre-heaven and post-heaven hexagrams. If the acquired internal Zhen liver corresponds to the external eyes, then Li corresponds to the tongue.

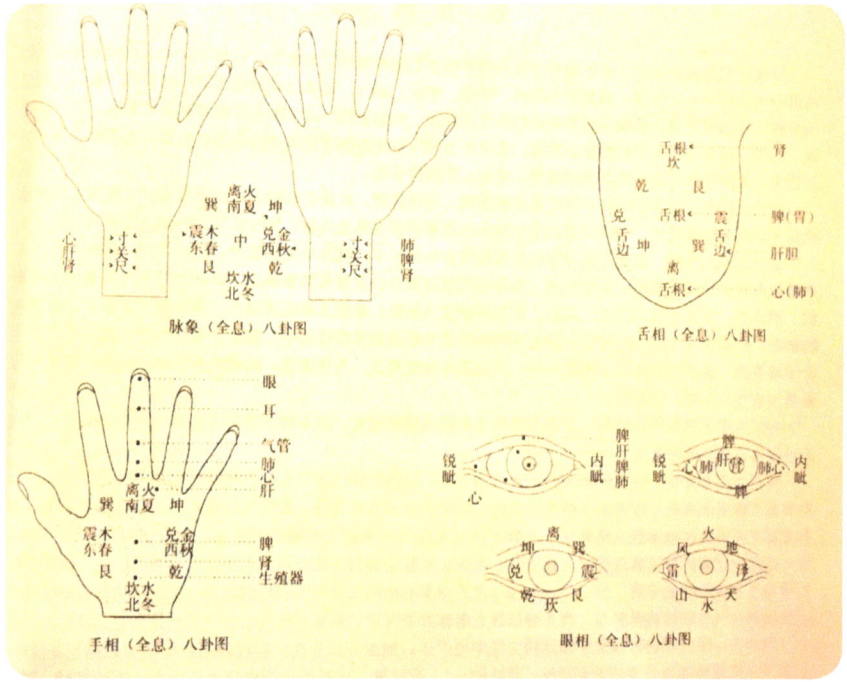

Shao Zi said: "The mouth and eyes are horizontal and the nose and ears are vertical. Why is that? The body must be connected." This is what I mean by the opposite of body and function. The mouth and eyes are horizontal and the nose and ears are vertical, which are external functions.

Its inner body is also round. Qu Shengjie, a disciple of Xinhui, said in his book "Hetu Luoshu Shuo": Is there anything about the human face that can be compared with the Hetu? The one that does not move in the middle is the nose, which is the middle of the fifty. The pillar (note: the bridge of the nose) is one, which is the odd number of five, and the two holes are the even number of ten (note: one inside is five and twenty outside, ten is the face of a person, the inside is the middle of the five).

The lower one is water, and the mouth responds to it. The yang of one is inside, and the yin of six is outside. Therefore, it can inhale. Therefore, it does not move upward but moves downward. This is the trend of moistening downward (Note: one mouth can taste the six flavors of the earth). The upper two is fire, and the eyes respond to it. The yin of two is inside, and the yang of seven is outside. Therefore, it can see upward. Therefore, it does not move downward but moves upward. This is the trend of burning upward (Note: two eyes can see the seven colors of the sky). As for the wood of three and eight, and the metal of four and nine, they are arranged on the left and right, and the two ears represent them (Note: the two ears of wood and metal can hear the nine sounds from all directions). Wood can remove obstructions, which is why the ears are open; metal can make sounds, which is why the ears hear. Water and fire are often active, and the mouth and eyes are moving in accordance with them. Wood and metal are always quiet, and the two ears are also quiet in accordance with them. Or it is like the Luoshu.

The middle five is yang but does not move, and its image is the nose. If one is at the bottom, it is the position of old yin, and nine is at the top, it is the number of old yang. Old yang can move and change, and the movement of the mouth and eyes is due to it; three is at the left, it is the position of lesser yang, and seven is at the right, it is the number of lesser yang. Lesser yang does not move or change, and the movement of the two ears is due to it. Then the two and four at the top corners are the two eyebrows. The two fires have the tendency to burn upwards, but if they are happy, they will gather in fear and relax in joy. There is also the meaning of four golds following change. Then six and eight at the lower corners are the beard and mustache. Six waters have the tendency to moisten downwards, but the beard overflows to the sides and the mustache hangs straight down. There is also the recognition of eight woods being straight and crooked. (Note: The numbers in Luoshu, the upper nine corresponds to seven colors plus two eyes' black and white colors. The lower one still dominates the lower straightness, so one and nine are still yang movement; left and right three and seven should be the ears rotating three times and listening to seven sounds, changing the number to listen to movement and the body being still; two four, eight six, all assist with the circle and square, the difference is two, so the eyes have two eyebrows and lips and four eyelashes, the head, face and teeth should correspond to eight sides and six circles combined).

This concludes these set of commented translations on the relationship between daoism, luoshu and hetu, the human body, yijing and fengshui, taiji gongfu and even neidan practice. I did not give a verbatim translation of these chapters but interspeced them with my own thought to not make the work too dry and clinical. My main aim here is to show what my educational programs reveal, and how much still is unknown, and what an enormous mass of knowledge needs to be studied, that will force us to revise our ideas on yijing, yijing translation etc. It is clear that the yijing as a product of hermetic thought represents a holist perspective on life. I read somewhere the idea that the Yiji g is like an old style Chat GPT, but that is not true. The yijing is more like a mirror. What you put in will come out. So your limits in knowledge and worldview will also limit the understandings of the yijing suggestions. The yijing does not provide understanding or knowledge. It only shows the weft of yin and yang in everything, and it shows that the appearant layering of reality is not just hierarchical, but that the layering gives opportunity to personal growth and learning, to the development of morality and devotion to life and natuire. After all, the Mission of the yijing is to help you see that we emulate earth to comprehend heaven, and eventually unify with Dao, as for instance Laozi suggested. In medicine the yijing shows not so much relationships between organs and tissues, but relationships and how to use them to come to a healthy life. The yijing shows how the only way to live is to adapt to Nature and Dao, become a Homo Universalis of sorts to help us become more wise, and thus that enlightenment is relative, becasue we could always become more wise than we are today by doing more and studying more.

A thank you by way of conclusion

Please be aware that self development is a life long endeavour. It is not easy to obtain real results. It is easy to have experiences, but in self development and health care there is no such thing as a final result or a lasting result. So having an experience in itself doesnot mean anything. Actual results often take years to obtain due to the slow capacity for change our bodies and minds are subjected to. We always have to ask ourselves if we truly are the genius we hold ourselves to ben and are the exeptional one in a few million or are we plain arrogant or delusional? Daoism doesn't want to elevate you to a metaphysical glamour world of immortals but wants you to follow the track of modesty and taking the backseat in events (leave no traces) and that what precedes reality as a means to improvement.

If you feel inspired to become a yijing adept or counsellor, this is the link towards the 2 year coubnsellor course which also contains many other translated resources from the books mentioned in this book:

https://daoland.samcart.com/products/the-yijing-ritual-course

My excuses for missed grammatical- and spelling errors. In a next version we hope to have all your comments incorporated.

游理欧

Wishing you well

René Goris, PhD transcultural healthcare/comparative medicine Daoist name: 崔理欧, 15th generation disciple of enlightened master Zhangsanfeng, European representative, student of daoshi 游玄德 since 1999, wudangshan, 2013, may 22, Amsterdam, public presentation text results july 2016, Amazon publication dec 2019

Page Index

Used referencials (booklist)

- Allen, Sarah: the shape of the turtle. State university of new York 1991

- Bary and Lufrano: sources of Chinese tradition. Columbia university press, 2nd edition 1999

- Berglund, Lars: The secret of Luo Shu. Instituten for konstvetenskap Lunds, 1990

- Campany, RF: to live as long as heaven and earth. University of california press, 2002

- Chan, AKL: two visions of the way. State university of New York press 1991

- Chu, MK/Sherrill WA (editor): the astrology of yijing. Routledge 1976

- Hansen, Chad: a daoist theory of Chinese thought. Oxford university press 1992

- Hendrischke, Barbara: The scripture on great peace. Unioversity of California Press 2006

- Huang, Jane: the primordial brerath I. 1987, the primordial breath 2. 1990 Original Books inc.

- Huang, Chunchieh/Zurcher, Erik: Time and Space in Chinese culture. Brill 1995

- Jay, Martin: Cultural semantics. University of massechusets press 1998

- Karcher, Stephen: Ta Chuang. St Martins press 2000

- Karlgren, Bernhard: Gramatica Serica Recensa. SMC publishing 1996

- Knoblock and Riegel: the annals of Lu Buwei. Stanford University press, 2000

- Kohn, Livia:

- Laughing at the Tao. Princeton university opress 1995

- god of the dao. University of Michigan 1998

- Kunst, Richard Alan: The Original Yijing: A Text, Phonetic Transcription, Translation, and Indexes, with Sample Glosses 1998

- Lafargue, Michael: the tao of taoteching. State university of newyork press 1992

- Lagerwey, John (editor) Religion and Chinese society volume 1. University of Hongkong 2004

- Lambek, Michael (editor): a reader in anthropology of religion. Blackwell Publishing/ Boston University 2002

- Lewis, Edward: the construction of space in early China. SUNY 2006

- Loewe, Michael: Divination, mythology and monarchy in Han China

- Lopez jr, DS (editor): religions of China in practice. Princeton university press 1996

- Lynn, Richard John:

- I Ching as interpreted by Wang Bi. Columbia UP 1994

- Taote Ching, De Laozi as interpreted by Wang Bi. Columbia UP 1999

- Machle, EJ: Nature and heaven in the Xunzi. SUNY 1993

- Magala, Slawomir: cross cultuiral competence. Routledge 2005

- Major, John S: the huinanzi by Liu An: Columbia univrsity press 2010

- Meyer, JAM de/ Engelfriet, PM: Linked faiths. Brill 2000

- Michael, Thomas: the pristine dao. SUNY 2005

- Needham, Joseph: science and civilisation of China II, III, V-5. Universityb of Cambridge press

- Nylan, Michael: the canon of supreme mystery by Yang Hsiung. State university of new York 1993

- Owen, Stephen: the end of the Chinese middle ages. Stanford University press, 1996

- Peereboom, RP: Law and Morality in Ancient China. SUNY 1993

- Poo, Muchou: in search of personal welfare. State university press of New York 1998

- Reiter, FC (editor): foundations of daoist ritual. Harrasowitz Verlag 2009

- Rickett, WA: Guanzi vol I, II. Princeton university press 1998

- Robinet, Isabelle: Taoist Meditation, SUNY 1993

- Saily, Jay: the master who embraces simplicity. Chinese materials center. 1978

- Saso, Michael: The gold pavilion. Charles E Tuttle 1995

- Shaughnessy, Edward:

- Before Confucius , SUNY 1997

- I Ching. Ballentine books 1996

- Siu, RGH: A legacy of the I ching. MIT, 1968

- Smith, Kidder, Bol, Adler, Wyatt: Sung dynasty uses of I Ching. Princeton University press1990

- Smith, Richard: fathoming the cosmos and ordering the world. University of Virginia Press 2008

- Sivin, Nathan: Chinese alchemy, preliminary studies. Harvard University press 1968

- Unschuld, Paul: Huangdineijing suwen and Lingshu. Universty of california press 2011

- Wagner, RG:

– the craft of a Chinese commentator. University of newyork press 2000

– a Chinese reading of the daodejing. SUNY 2003

- Yoke, Hopeng: Explorations in Daoism. Routledge 2007

- xie rixin: Yidao Zhonghu, guangdong Publishing group/huacheng press, 2009 (CN)

- Xu Gan, Balanced discourses. Yale University press/Forreign language press beijing, transl John Makeham 2004

- You Xuande: Wudang Taiji Neidan shi . Hubei Commercial press 2012 (CN)

- Zhang Huapeng and Zhang Fuqin: Wudang early civilization, East China Normal University Press, 2007. (CN)

- Zhouyi Tushou Zhonghui 周易图说总汇: 上中下 (CN)

(Note: I am sorry, other titles are boxed, so I am not able to complete it. Also, I used the texts to confirm of criticise things daoist told me about the yijing, reffering her specifically to what my teacher Liu Dongan introduced me to. If the book is succesful, I wish to make a 2nd edition where I mirror all the materials of these books on the original texts. Many of these books provide context, if not illustration or alternatives. I like to remind that I started the yijing translation as part of a hobby but found it quickly essential for my Master and PhD studies in comparative medicine that are the foundation for the IOC Daoland study program and my ideas about transculturalism as the way forward for studies in cultural sciences and even modern science as a cultural science.

www.ingramcontent.com/pod-product-compliance
Lightning Source LLC
Chambersburg PA
CBHW040843120626
46547CB00001B/4

RICH
B$TCH

MONEY GOALS

Published in Canada, for Global Distribution by fEMPOWER Publications
www.fempower.pub | For more information email: media@fempower.pub

ISBN trade paperback: 978-1-998721-03-0
eBook: 978-1-998721-04-7
Audio: 978-1-998721-05-4

To order additional copies of this book: media@fempower.pub

KYERA KACEY

RICH

B$TCH

MONEY GOALS

BECOMING THE ENERGETIC
MATCH TO WEALTH

TABLE OF CONTENTS